M000159672

THIS MAGIC MOMENT

My Journey of Faith, Friends, and the Father's Love

WILLIAM H. MORRIS

Fitting Words

THIS MAGIC MOMENT

Copyright © 2019 by William H. Morris

Fitting Words

All rights reserved. No part of this publication may be reproduced, stored in a retrieval system, or transmitted in any form or by any means—electronic, mechanical, photocopying, recording, or otherwise—without the prior written permission of the publisher.

Although the author has attempted to be as factually accurate as possible, this book is not a documentary. Rather, it is a chronicle of one man's experiences and recollections as shared by four singers of another era.

Much of this book involves the history of one member of the original Drifters, Bill Pinkney. Over the years of our friendship, Bill told me his story—both the good and the bad—spanning his fifty-plus-year musical journey, in which he experienced much disappointment, litigation, and anguish over who had the right to use the name "The Drifters." For a detailed chronological account of their history, I refer you to Ahmet Ertegun's book, *"What'd I Say?": The Atlantic Story, 50 Years of Music*. This rich resource is interwoven with slices of life from a plethora of stars featured in this magnificent era of music.

With apologies to literary literalists and English teachers, the author has taken some liberties regarding sentence structure in this book. Sentence fragments and incomplete sentences are occasionally used when such construction is believed to heighten the effect.

Cover: "This Magic Moment" by John Carroll Doyle, © 1997

www.johncdoyle.com

Cover: John Langston

Interior Design: Brian Kannard

Publishing Services: Fitting Words www.fittingwords.net

Publicity and Marketing: Morgan Canclini-Mitchell and Kristen Carver Smith

two|pr – Nashville, Tennessee

Library of Congress Cataloging-in-Publication Data

Hardcover: 978-1-7322391-6-6

Audio ISBN: 978-1-7331023-2-2

Printed in the United States of America

For the blessing of my wife, Camille,
who loves and nurtures me

Contents

ACKNOWLEDGMENTS

For dear friends who inspired and encouraged me to write—Willie Morris, Dan Singletary, Guff Abbott, Bob Morris, Nancy Chamblee, and members of The William Morris Group.

For fine writers whose published works motivated me to learn their vocabulary and their means of expression—Margaret Walker Alexander, Fitzsimmons Allison, Stephen Ambrose, William Barclay, Thad Barnum, Patti Carr Black, Rick Bragg, Minor Buchanan, William F. Buckley, Hank Burdine, Will Campbell, Oswald Chambers, Bennett Chotard, Rick Cleveland, Nadine Cohodas, Pat Conroy, Ellen Douglas, Bill Dunlap, Ainsley Earhardt, Margaret Eby, John Faulkner, William Faulkner, Beth Ann Fennelly, Bill Ferris, Richard Ford, Tom Franklin, Robert Gordon, Richard Grant, John Grisham, Winston Groom, Barry Hannah, Sam Haskell, Beth Henley, Zora Neale Hurston, Greg Iles, Peter Jenkins, Harnett Kane, Tim Keller, Harper Lee, C.S. Lewis, Suzanne Marrs, Willie Morris, Darden North, Henri Nouwen, Walker Percy, William Alexander Percy, Ron Rash, Julia Reed, Ferrell Sams, David Sansing, Michael Shaara, Elizabeth Spencer, Kathryn Stockett, Donna Tartt, Mildred Topp, Dean Faulkner Wells, Eudora Welty, Neil White, Curtis Wilkie, Richard Wright, and the many others I am thankful to have read.

For the privilege of being born into a family from whom I received love and creative gifts, allowing me to write so as to bless others. I am thankful that both sides of my family loved the Lord, thus giving me fertile soil in which to develop spiritually—pure grace—nothing I could have done.

For people of "music" who, by their efforts and gifts, have assisted in preserving the mystical joy of what has been given to us—Terry Stewart-CEO R&R Hall of Fame Museum, Bennett Chotard, Robert Johnson, Eli Goodman, Richie Burnette, David Hervey, Raphael Semmes, Harry Turner, DJs Cousin Brucie/Cool Bobby B., Tommy Couch, Wolf Stephenson, Michael Frascogna, Bob Davidson, William Griffin, Bill Harvey, T. J. Lubinski of the PBS doo-wop and R&B specials, and the many DJs of WLAC, Nashville; WOKJ, Jackson; and WDIA, Memphis.

For my daughters, Camille and Kathryn, who tolerated me at times when I might have embarrassed them with my singing. Later, they embraced it!

For my teachers and professors who had the faith that lifted me to desire to give back in the written word.

For my dear editor, Anne Severance, for whom I had prayed for many years—not knowing who it would be, just searching.

For Dan Wright, publisher of Fitting Words, my deepest appreciation for bringing to the table your energy, experience, and creativity. Your insights and knowledge of the current industry are priceless!

For John Langston, my gifted friend who designed this book and my prior coffee table book, *Ole Miss at Oxford.*

For publisher Neil White and his invaluable courses, taught on the campus of the University of Mississippi.

For my friend, coach, and Director of Communications Nancy White Perkins.

For LaVerne Washington, who assisted me with photo credentials.

For my dedicated staff, who helped immensely: Leila Manning, Sarah Morgan, Krysten Jernigan, and Gwenyth McDonough.

For the fine photographers who helped to preserve the memories visually: Tom Roster, Gib Ford, Will Jacks, Karla Pound, Sissy Scanlon, Chris Walters, and the numerous others to whom I handed my camera when I was in the photo.

For the singers, writers, and musicians who created the music that formed the foundation of memories enveloped by the mystery of it all—and thus, the feelings born of the music, which brings joy to our hearts and tears to our eyes. Most especially for four of the closest friends of my life—Prentiss Barnes and Harvey Fuqua of The Moonglows, Bill Pinkney of The Drifters, and Rufus McKay of The Red Tops and Ink Spots.

For Chris Walters, my business partner, who cared about my singer friend, Prentiss, as deeply as I.

For the blessing of the Father, who orchestrated all of this.

Introduction

My deep and abiding bond with music—when did it all begin? Was it before I was born, hearing the rhythmic beating of my mother's heart when she was carrying me in her womb? Could I hear the sounds of the early 1940s at that time? Probably so. But the first cognitive recognition began when I was about three and a half while living on Council Circle in the Fondren area of Jackson, Mississippi. Other than my four years away at college and two years as an officer in the U.S. Army, Jackson has always been home.

Sitting at my father's feet, I remember listening to seventy-eight records—songs like "Brazil" and "Ah, Sweet Mystery of Life," along with more serious works such as "The Warsaw Concerto"—played on the Victrola for most of that day. He was no longer away in the army, and I was grateful just to have him near me. In this secure setting, I learned to love all kinds of music—classical, big band, and pop. Music helped me recall the times, melding the memories that were becoming part of my very DNA. To this day, whenever I hear a recording of Glenn Miller and his orchestra playing "Moonlight Serenade," I feel moved in a most comforting way. Maybe, for some, music was an escape from the realities and horrors of World War II, although I don't remember much about the war except for snippets of conversations overheard between adults.

Shielded from the latest news of the front, the remnants of the Great Depression era, and any hint of racial tension—of which we children were completely unaware—we were carefree and content. As a little boy, I enjoyed outings to The Farm, a magical spot out in the country. The antebellum home and property had originally belonged to a Colonel Porter. In 1945, my grandmother, Mrs. Webster Millsaps Buie, purchased the place, along with some wooded acreage. Here she, my mother, her siblings, and the twelve cousins spent leisurely days during the long summers. The old homestead became the weekend retreat for our family. Summertime, and the livin' was easy. . .

On the trip out, my dad would stop at Mr. Brown's Log Cabin Country Store on Old Raymond Road and load up the trunk of the car with cases of Grapette, Lymette, Orange Crush, and other soda pops. For the adults, it was Cokes, Budweiser, and Miller High Life. On the farm, we savored the flavor of fish—bream and bass—fresh-caught in the nearby eight-acre lake and cooked in a clay pot. I can still taste that first bite—my teeth crunching into the crispy fried batter, then sinking into the tender, sweet meat beneath.

After a full day of play, the cars were loaded and packed, and we exhausted children would pile into the various vehicles for the eighteen-mile trip back to Jackson. As night fell, my mother and father would turn on the car radio, and we would listen to Guy Lombardo and his Royal Canadian Orchestra. Lulled by these soothing melodies, by the time we arrived at our home on Arlington Street, four sleepy little bodies would often have to be carried into the house and tucked into our beds.

On my sixth birthday, I was given a Roy Rogers cowboy outfit and a number of Tex Ritter records. I put on my outfit and played those records all day long on our front porch. By then, I had begun to associate country music with cowboys, and Roy Rogers was my hero. I began to listen to the radio stations in hopes of getting to hear a bit more of the "cowboy" sound.

On Saturdays, my friends Bill Barksdale, Randy Harding, Wes Godwin, and Guff Abbott and I would stand in the long line at the Pix Theatre, waiting to see the latest Roy Rogers movie at the matinee. I could almost picture us—like Roy and his singing buddies, the Sons of the Pioneers—riding off into the sunset. Sadly, all of these friends, with the exception of my lifelong, closest friend, Guff, have taken that last long ride Home.

Naturally, being raised in a Christian family, we went to church and learned to sing the beautiful old hymns that comfort me and continue to provide sustenance for my soul. Even at a very young age, I knew God had a purpose for my life.

At age ten, the transition began from boyhood to young manhood. My mother scheduled me for dancing lessons at Arthur Murray Studios located in a large Victorian home on North State Street. There must have been about twenty of my sixth-grade classmates there. I still recall watching a pretty girl across the room while the instructor taught us how to do the fox-trot to the song "Blue Moon." I learned to waltz too . . . barely. Then along came the jitterbug—the predecessor to the bop—the "in" thing with the big band crowd. Those lessons at the Arthur Murray Studio were my first introduction to girls and dancing. Until then, I had not connected the two.

The summer of 1953 brought the moment of truth—a transition during puerile days. It began with a party at the home of a classmate—on her back deck. Forty-five rpm records were now coming into vogue. There, for the first time, this callow boy heard the enchanting sounds of a new wave of music known as rock 'n' roll and doo-wop, sung by The Moonglows, The Heartbeats, The Platters, The Drifters, and, of course, Elvis Presley.

Many of our high school dances featured The Red Tops, an orchestra from Vicksburg, comprised of twelve African-American professional musicians. The group took its name from the red coats they wore with black tuxedo pants, a shiny satin stripe down the side. Most of them had other jobs, but on the weekends, they were a hit in towns all over the state of Mississippi, primarily in the Delta. Their lead singer was Rufus McKay, who had one of the most mellow tenor voices I've ever heard. People would literally travel a hundred miles each way to hear him sing "Danny Boy." Often, couples would stand still, the boys wrapping their arms around their dates and listening as Rufus crooned that great tune. By the end of the song, there would be tears in many eyes.

In those days, it was not all play and no work. In our family, we were expected to help carry the load. But there were not many employment opportunities for high school kids. A few worked at soda fountains or sacked groceries. Still, I lucked out and landed a job at the Pine-sol plant, where I was the only white boy working with a crew of black guys. Side by side, we loaded and stacked fifty-pound boxes all day. Along with developing some pretty impressive muscles, I picked up the lingo of my new colleagues and thoroughly enjoyed their company. To help pass the time, we listened to their distinctive style of music—a style I was fast adopting as my own. It was their radio stations I wanted, their music I craved.

★   ★   ★

The years seemed to fly by, and before I knew it, I was preparing to leave home and enter college at the University of Mississippi, affectionately known as Ole Miss. In his wisdom, my father wanted me to pay for half my college expenses. His idea of having "skin in the game" was an excellent one, as I look back on it.

To defray those expenses, I was going to need something more than my Pine-sol job. I remember walking into the National Guard Armory on Northwest Street in Jackson to a late spring dance. It was a public venue, so anyone could come. The sponsor, Bill Dotson, was at the front door, drinking a beer as he collected money. Cash was sticking out of all of his pockets, giving a not-so-subtle hint of the financial success he was enjoying along with his beer. I paid my two-dollar entry fee then made my way to the bandstand to get a closer look at Huey "Piano" Smith and the Clowns. Dressed in all-white tuxedos, they were singing "Dearest Darling," a song that was soon to become one of my all-time favorites.

That experience gave me an idea. I became an entrepreneur overnight and threw my first dance down at Speed's Lodge. The lodge no longer exists, but the memories do. I had lined up King Mose and his Royal Rockers, featuring Sammy Myers, for seventy-five dollars and a fifth of whiskey (to be delivered at intermission). They came to play what would become the music of people who are Blues icons in the music world: Howlin' Wolf, Muddy Waters, B. B. King, and Little Junior Parker. I made a little money that night and learned a lot. My confidence grew.

I threw fifteen dances over the next several years to pay for college. Selecting the right time, the place, the band, and designing all the advertising—radio, posters, etc.—were all a part of my duties. And securing a good venue for a dance on the night of the Mississippi High School All-Star football game virtually guaranteed a full house. The game was always played in early August—usually on the first Saturday night of that exceptionally hot month in the Deep South. People would come from all over the state to see their favorite football all-star player perform. Naturally, they wanted somewhere to go afterwards, and I had just the ticket!

The dance at the King Edward Hotel Crown room was a mob scene, with people pouring through the doors. We collected cash as fast as we could. All the while, the bands blared out the unforgettable sounds of that era. I'm so thankful I was able to help others create wonderful memories while helping to pay for my college education. People still talk about those dances.

The last dance I held was after graduating from college. At the time, I was serving as an army officer living in Fort Rucker, Alabama, 328 miles from Jackson. Determined to pay off my remaining college debt, I enlisted a fraternity brother, David Hervey, to help me with the details of the most prodigious dance I would ever sponsor. At the Heidelberg Hotel, we rented the Olympic ballroom and the adjoining Victory room. The Olympic room alone would hold over 2,000 people, and the Victory room, another thousand, with a band in each room. The people lined up for hours, and we collected money at two doors as fast as we could make change! The memory was phenomenal, and we made enough for me to pay off my college loan with my half.

Music was a big part of my life, and I even considered making it my career—as a promoter. I decided, instead, to make insurance my life's work . . . and I have not regretted that decision.

My intent in writing this book was never to promote myself. Rather, it is to celebrate the lives of several African-Americans who left an indelible impression on my soul. Despite our differing backgrounds, we were drawn together by the universal language of music, woven into the fabric of creation.

All nature sings. It is the very rhythm of life. It is the accompaniment to my story—that of a white businessman from Mississippi who, in a pivotal moment—a "magic moment"—became fast friends with three legendary black Rock & Roll Hall of Famers . . . and one more.

This book is a love story of deep friendship, given from above. It was these men I am blessed to have known.

★   ★   ★

After this book was completed, I sat for a while, pondering the years. By my mid- to late thirties, I had already achieved a significant part of my life's dreams and fondest wishes. There was nothing I lacked in business, and God had given me a wife and two beautiful young daughters. I was profoundly grateful.

Amid all of this joy came a heartbreaking incident. My father-in-law, whom I loved dearly, died after a tragic accident resulting from a mishap while attending to his family homestead acreage. At that time, my knowledge of the Lord was superficial at best. I was not able to comfort my wife as she cried herself to sleep night after night for well over a year. This was when I was rescued by our heavenly Father and discovered the Source of the deepest joy imaginable. I was now able to pray meaningful prayers with Camille, as I would with others from that point forward. My life's journey took on new meaning as I became acutely aware that everything I am or ever will be—everything I have or ever will own—comes from His merciful hand.

At age forty-one, I yearned to express my newfound understanding and appreciation to the Giver of Life. On November 1, 1983, I began spiritual journaling—my love letter to the Lord. Now, seventeen volumes later, there was a total of 2,700 legal pages of handwritten notes, compiled over a thirty-five-year period.

Then, about five years after my journey with my singer friends began, during a Thanksgiving visit to Natchez, Camille's hometown, I was awakened at four o'clock in the morning by a strong, silent, solitary word:

WRITE. I knew that Voice, and I eased out of bed and into the den where I had left my briefcase.

Retrieving my dictation device, I slipped out the back door and settled into a swing under an oak tree. The words began to flow, and I wrote the initial fifteen pages of this book before the first rosy streaks in the sky emerged as the sun began its slow ascent on the horizon. Once again came the confirmation of a deep purpose for my life … and for the message of this book to be shared with you, my readers.

Their sound represented a genre that was haunting and unique, never to be duplicated, but a gift for us for all time—a truly wondrous art form. Thus, it is our sacred obligation to preserve it, teach about it, and disseminate it.

~Eli Goodman, MD & DJ

~ 1 ~

MOONGLOW

Washington, D.C., 1980. The wheels turning in my head kept pace with the traffic as the taxi wound its way through the busy streets back toward the hotel. I had been replaying the events of the evening over and over, deluged with a flood of memories and emotion. Now I had to share it with someone, and since I couldn't wait any longer, the cab driver was my captive audience.

Having flown in from Jackson, Mississippi, for an insurance conference a few days earlier, I had checked into the Hilton. My wife, Camille, was busy with our two young daughters and could not attend this convention with me. I picked up a copy of *Where* magazine from the lobby and began to turn through its pages to see what was going on in the capital city. Skimming through the advertisements, I was ineluctably drawn to an ad for Hogate's Restaurant & Lounge, a popular dining venue overlooking the canal next to the Potomac. This was no frat house or smoky dive. This upscale establishment was known for bringing in quality musical entertainment.

Appearing that Saturday night were The Clovers, famous for the song "Devil or Angel." Unwilling to pass up this tremendous opportunity, I went to hear them croon the tunes that took me back to my teenage years. Harold Lucus, one of the early members of the group, was still singing with them, and I was thrilled to talk with him during one of the breaks. I thought that nothing this week could surpass that moment.

The Moonglows, led by their original virtuoso singer, Bobby Lester, were also going to be performing at Hogate's that week. Bobby and a former member, Harvey Fuqua, had tutored many other legendary celebrated groups such as The Dells and The Spinners. Bobby was now joined by Billy McPhatter, the son of Clyde McPhatter, one of the founding members of The Drifters. Clyde had one of the top tenor voices in all of rock 'n' roll. Gary Rogers, Bobby's nephew, and Robert Ford rounded out that group. The Moonglows were known for such songs as "Sincerely," "The Ten Commandments of Love," and "When I'm with You." Their tunes, perhaps just short of a hundred in total, were among the most popular hits of the day. No way would I miss the opportunity of hearing them while I was in the vicinity.

★   ★   ★

With me on Monday night was a friend from high school and college, Troy Mashburn, who was working out of D.C. at the time. An accomplished pilot, he had been selected to fly such dignitaries as Ronald Reagan, J.W. Marriott, and others. Over dinner, Troy and I reminisced about old times at Murrah High School in Jackson, and later at Ole Miss, our alma mater, in Oxford.

At my persuasion, we stepped over to Hogate's Lounge, which was conveniently located next door. I couldn't believe it when I witnessed The Moonglows singing the very songs I loved so dearly. Their voices, harmonizing flawlessly, sounded almost exactly like their earlier recordings when I had first discovered them. The audience was electrified by their performance, with spontaneous applause and shouts of encouragement erupting throughout their act.

At intermission, I could not resist—I *had* to meet these people. Troy waited for me while I asked the manager where I might find them. He pointed up the stairs. I could hear my heart pounding by the time I reached the top. The door was locked. I pressed the button.

"Who is it?" called a voice from within.

"It's Bill Morris from Jackson, Mississippi."

Then I heard a buzzing sound, which released the lock, and the great Bobby Lester himself allowed me to enter. The fellows inside were probably thinking, *Who in the world is this guy?*

But I was the first to speak: "I can't tell you how much I've loved your music since I was a boy. Always takes me back to those early days. So you have no idea how thrilled I am to meet you guys tonight!"

Then I addressed Billy McPhatter, who was standing a few feet away. "Billy, do you remember when your dad and The Drifters sang 'Whatcha Gonna Do'?"

I began to sing the song that Clyde McPhatter had helped to make famous. As Billy sang along with me, the other three were listening to a cassette tape on a boom box, playing the original version of The Moonglows' songs.

"Guys, don't ever let the sound of The Moonglows die," I overheard Bobby Lester say with a sense of urgency. I knew that Bobby was the only one of the original Moonglows singing in the group that night. The others had gone their separate ways. "Don't let this sound die," he repeated, intent on driving his point home. I wondered what was up. I noted, too, that he was instructing them in how to hold a particular note and do whatever singers do when they're learning close harmony. But other than that brief observation, I was tuned in to Billy and having a ball singing with him.

Billy and I were still singing together when I started into "Daddy's Home," a number made famous by Shep and the Limelights. The rest of the group suddenly stopped and circled around me to join in. We sang a cappella right there in the dressing room. When the song ended, Bobby Lester exclaimed, "Come on, baby! You gotta do this one with us in the second show! You take the lead and we'll back you up!" I'm not sure what it was, but they must have heard something in my voice.

"No, man," I protested. "I've never sung in any group before nor ever had a mic in my hands. I'm very honored that you would ask me, but this is your show, and I'm not going to mess it up." They kept insisting that I join them, but I was just as insistent I shouldn't.

With intermission nearly over, Troy came up to the dressing room to let me know he had to work early the next day, so a late evening was not in the cards for him. My old friend and I parted, and I went back downstairs and took a seat off center stage. The master of ceremonies joined me at the table.

The Moonglows returned for the second half of their act and did about three more numbers before Bobby Lester made an announcement. "And now . . . The Moonglows would like to introduce a very special guest from Jackson, Mississippi—Mr. Bill Morris."

I was astounded and stood up to wave at the crowd, thinking I would sit right back down. But the band had something else in mind. They had already started the lead in to "Daddy's Home." The four Moonglows gathered around three of the microphones, leaving one mic free, and beckoned me to the stage. All I could think in that moment was, *Well, by gosh, this is my chance. I'll do it!*

Never having attempted anything of this kind, I cannot imagine what possessed me to get up there. We did the number, though, which seemed to come off well. We did some high fives and received a tremendous round of applause. I didn't know it at the time, but there were other groups in the audience.

To my surprise, singers and fans alike began coming up to my table, asking my name and the name of my group. I stayed until the end of the second performance, not wanting the evening to end. As a matter of fact, it did not.

Dream When the Day Is Through

Heading back to the Hilton, there was no doubt that something very special had happened that night. But as yet, I had no idea what. It was a surreal experience. As I looked out of the cab window, a full moon was aglow, and I said under my breath, "Lord, did I really sing with The Moonglows tonight?"

Then, again, in a very strong, but inaudible voice, I heard the response: *I did this for My glory, Bill, and I will reveal to you in due time what I mean.* The message was so clear I was certain that something was going to happen.

Having shared something of my stellar evening with the cab driver, I leaned back against the cushioned headrest and let the feelings of euphoria wash over me. Had I really sung onstage with this group I had loved so dearly as a teenager? Back then, I would have given anything just to hear them in person, let alone meet them. Now, at almost thirty-eight, to be asked to sing with them was beyond my wildest dreams!

Funny how music can transport one to another time and place. Certain songs always evoke an inexplicable sense of joy in me. There was a mystique to those ballads that said all the things we felt as teenagers but could not articulate. The music, still playing in my head, took me back to the days of junior high and my first dance parties.

Over in the corner of Nancy Lynn's or Sylvia Bradley's carport would be a record player with a stack of ten or fifteen 45s on the spindle. Entranced by this powerful, new wave of music, people were dancing to The Moonglows singing "Sincerely" or maybe The Penguins' "Earth Angel." Bob Johnston was there, the letter "B"—for Bailey Junior High Panthers—emblazoned on his leather football jacket. He was slow dancing with his girlfriend, Susan Barry, to Johnny & Joe's "Over the Mountain and Across the Sea." And I can still see Tommy Cato and Peggy Ray. Boy, was she gorgeous with her flippy ponytail and sparkling green eyes! I was envious of both of those guys.

It didn't matter that the records were scratchy—in a way, that added to the nostalgia. This was especially true if we were riding in a car, trying to pull in some distant radio station. The less accessible, the more it seemed to draw us.

We all listened to AM radio—there was no FM in those days. At night, for most of us in the South, it was WLAC in Nashville, Tennessee, which would broadcast until the wee hours of the morning. We would hear the captivating voices of disc jockeys—Hoss Allen, John R. (John Richardson), Gene Nobles, Herman Grizzard, and others—promoting "Randy's Record Shop" or "Ernie's Record Shop." In some cases, they would be pushing a hundred baby chickens for the ridiculously low price of $10.95 plus shipping, no cockerels included. Other sponsors were White Rose's petroleum jelly and Royal Crown pomade products. They would put together packages of various recordings of six different songs for $5.95 plus shipping. This would include a variety of the songs that were popular at that time, from the up tempo type blues of Lazy Lester's "Sugar-Coated Love" on the Excello record label to The Platters' ethereal "Heaven on Earth" on Mercury.

We became attached to the sound of the DJs' voices. They introduced us to legions of songs that will forever be a part of us. I can still remember exactly where I was when I first discovered hits such as the all-time greatest slow-dance number, "In the Still of the Night" by Fred Parris and The Five Satins. That particular song came over the airwaves after a Red Tops dance at about 1:00 a.m. in Yazoo City, Mississippi. Little did I know that someday I was to meet, photograph, and fraternize with this phenomenal group.

There was also the Shamrock Drive-In, located on North State Street just outside the Jackson city limits. Like so many others springing up around the country, the Shamrock featured a menu of burgers and other items, with carhops coming out to take your order at curbside. People would congregate at Pete Costas's place to enjoy the delicious food and to connect with friends. A highlight of this experience was the music. I can see it now—some of us in convertibles with the tops down, listening to the tantalizing sounds coming from the various car radios as the memories were melded into our beings, becoming a part of us.

There was something mysterious and alluring about this new form of music. Some of the songs were absolutely mesmerizing, and I listened to them over and over, wanting to immerse myself in these beautiful strands of harmony coming to us over the air.

Throughout the South, the DJs of WLAC had a way of making us all feel such a part of it. I would hear them saying, "This next number is for the Phi Delts (or maybe the Dekes at Chapel Hill or the SAEs down in Athens, Georgia). They're having a big soiree down there tonight, and Jim wants me to dedicate this song to his girl, Caroline." The sounds would flow, and my imagination would take me there. These enchanting ballads live with me to this day.

★   ★   ★

Reaching the hotel, I was still fired up. Obviously, my wife, Camille, was the first person I wanted to call, so I woke her to share my fabulous news. She wasn't quite sure what to think about it, but she was happy for me. The second was a friend of mine, Dr. Dan Cox, who probably had the best doo-wop group harmony record collection of anyone I've ever known. He couldn't wait to tell some of his friends. Needless to say, the rest of the insurance convention seemed pallid in comparison with my experience on that Monday night.

Now, back at work in Mississippi, I was constantly thinking about my newfound friends and wondering when I would get to see them again. Three weeks later, on my thirty-eighth birthday—June 9, 1980—I received a package addressed to Bill "Daddy's Home" Morris. Inside was an eight- by ten-inch glossy photograph of all The Moonglows with each singer's signature and a special inscription. They went to the trouble and expense of mailing this package to me—without any request from me! It seems to me that night must have meant something special to them too.

I was soon to find out the deeper purpose behind those magic moments—a little less than a year later.

~ 2 ~

HEARTBREAK HOTEL

It was May of the following year when I walked to the end of the driveway to pick up the morning paper. I was stunned to see that almost three-quarters of the front page was a story about Prentiss Barnes, the original bass singer of The Moonglows. Prentiss was considered to have one of the broadest and most mellow bass voices of anyone in rock 'n' roll. This particular article was about his success . . . and his decline. What I couldn't believe was that Prentiss was now living right here in Jackson! Once again there was an overwhelming sense of the Father's voice—inaudible, yes, but with power—speaking to me: Do you know now why you sang with The Moonglows? Now go take care of him!

After reading the article, I called the *Clarion-Ledger*, the local statewide newspaper, and talked with Peggy Elam, who had written the story. She told me how to get in touch with Prentiss. I dialed the number immediately.

"Hal...lo . . ." The voice on the other end of the line held none of the vibrancy of his youth. It was dull, dead, bereft of all joy—forlorn.

"Prentiss?" I asked, not sure I had the right number.

"Ye . . . ahh." There was bitterness here, too, layers of pain buried deep somewhere in his soul.

"It's Bill Morris. I just read your story in the paper."

"Ye . . . ahh." This man seemed to be broken in every way a man could be broken. I could tell he did not want to talk to me.

I pressed on. "I sang with The Moonglows last year in Washington. . ."

"Yeah?" For the first time, there was a hint of interest. His now lighter tone shifted from suspicion to surprise.

As I began to relate my experience with The Moonglows, he choked up. "Man, you 'bout to make me cry."

"Oh, Prentiss, I don't mean to do that."

I inquired about his record albums, and his response was startling. "Don't have none," he said. "The kids—my nephews prob'ly—carried 'em off."

Could it be true that he had *none* of the recordings his group had pressed into vinyl? They had actually recorded somewhere in excess of seventy-five songs—or maybe a hundred, I don't know. In 1981, before it became customary for music to be re-released on CDs, cassette tapes, or new albums, many of them were extremely rare and difficult to find.

"Prentiss," I said, broken-hearted at this discovery, "I know someone who has virtually all of your music. I'll come pick you up and take you to his house so we can record them for you. We'll make a tape."

He agreed, and I assured him that I would get back with him very soon.

From the article, I had learned that Prentiss's circumstances had taken a tragic turn when he left The Moonglows to seek stardom on his own. In 1968, he was heading to the West Coast via San Antonio, Texas, in his Chrysler Imperial. Stopping at a railroad intersection, he waited for the locomotive to go by, not realizing that another train was following close behind on a parallel track. In the dark of night, Prentiss thought the way was clear and drove his car up onto the tracks. In the resulting collision, he was severely injured and lucky to be alive. Two years and ten operations later, Prentiss had lost his left forearm and suffered a crushed hip, causing him to walk with a pronounced limp.

Although Prentiss could still sing, his appearance had suffered with the pain and limitations of his injury. In addition, modern times were more demanding of performers, who were expected to be able to accomplish a few dance moves as well as sing. No longer young and agile, he had looked for work outside of the music field, but his lack of education kept him from the kind of jobs that did not require physical exertion. Although he had a few friends and some family, they all had their own problems and concerns. Most of them were also struggling to make ends meet. Alone and unappreciated, Prentiss was a man without anything or anybody in the world who was able to help him. He told me later he really didn't want anyone to know who he was. He was so ashamed.

Down Lonely Street

Depressed and partially disabled, Prentiss began to drink heavily and eventually wound up in a chemical dependency unit (CDU) on more than one occasion. During this low point in his life, I would visit him from time to time. Once, I took my two young daughters, Camille and Kathryn, with me. This meant so much to him, and he would mention it many times in the years to come.

Another epiphany he experienced was a spiritual awakening. This is when he joined the choir at the Morning Star Baptist Church in Jackson. Even so, a lot of bitterness still haunted him between visits to the CDU. But the insidious disease of alcoholism had taken its toll on him and was not to let go easily, fueling his resentment about all the achievements he could and should have attained. Although Prentiss said he wrote several of the more popular Moonglows songs, when the records were released, his name did not appear in the list of credits. With perhaps one word changed, others claimed authorship. This kind of thing was prevalent throughout the industry. Consequently, some were never compensated.

Even when The Moonglows had the top hits in the nation and were performing in such prestigious venues as Carnegie Hall and the Apollo Theater in New York City, sometimes they barely had enough funds to pay for their hotel room. It was such a shame that much of this talent was essentially unrewarded financially. Most of the promoters, agents, recording studios, disc jockeys, and sometimes even other members of the groups seemed to take the lion's share, leaving the others little or nothing except the memory of the applause from the night before. Because of this kind of rivalry and greed, the seeds of bitterness were planted and began to germinate. Therefore, very few of the original recording groups remained intact.

A couple of weeks after I talked to Prentiss, I lined up the meeting at the home of Dr. Dan Cox, my friend with the great music collection. We spent an entire Saturday listening to the music of The Moonglows. Some of their songs were even pirated overseas from original unedited tapes. In the background, you could hear Prentiss and the other members of the group talking and joking between takes and the engineer behind the glass partition, saying, "Come on, fellas! Cut out the ***! Let's get it right this time." In those days, without modern technology, it took much longer to perfect the numbers. It was really hard work.

That afternoon, we recorded all of the music Prentiss wanted on a couple of tapes. It was the beginning of a beautiful friendship.

Eager to share the news of my newfound friend with Bobby Lester and the other Moonglows, I wrote Bobby a letter and included a copy of the article about Prentiss.

Several weeks after I mailed the letter, I received a phone call from a man whose deep voice I didn't recognize, probably someone from Bobby's family. "Understand you're tryin' to get in touch with Bobby Lester," he said.

"Yes, I am."

"He dead."

"He's dead?"

"Yeah, died last October. Lung cancer."

So . . . I was too late. Less than five months after I had sung with the group, life had taken some pretty fast turns. That's when it dawned on me that I had overheard some of Bobby Lester's last words to his singers in their dressing room that night: "Don't ever let the sound of The Moonglows die!" He didn't tell them of his illness until near the end. So none of them knew of his impending death. And, of course, neither did I.

Another member who sang in Washington was also dead within the year. Robert Ford, who was exceptionally talented and played classical music, including the oboe, was killed in an automobile accident.

Unfortunately, Bobby Lester's and Robert Ford's early deaths are not the exception to the rule. Life seems to run short for many musicians and vocalists. So often they lead a precarious lifestyle. They are on the road constantly and many times exist for days on only a few hours of sleep. Going from venue to venue—many smoke-filled—and then usually eating less than a nutritious diet—grabbing a quick hot dog or burger—it is no wonder their health is compromised. To those of us who only observe their performances and hear the rousing ovations, we think how wonderful it would be to be able to entertain like that.

Far from being a life of ease and gratification, however, the entertainment field is fraught with dangers of many types, not the least of which is financial. I had heard Prentiss's story. Now, apparently, God expected me to do something about it.

"If You've Got the Money . . ."

Learning more of Prentiss's plight, I found he received a Social Security check of approximately $350 per month for his disability. In fact, there was a quirk in the law that did not allow him to have a Medicaid card for the medication he needed because he received twenty-five dollars too much from his disability payment. He had even inquired if he could forfeit that much in Social Security in order to qualify, but the system wouldn't allow it. I began to fight for him by going to our congressman and writing people in authority to see what could be done. No luck. With all the bureaucratic red tape, Prentiss and so many like him were shut out. I was able to get him some occasional

Advertisement for the first dance Bill Morris sponsored in 1959

BOBBY LESTER
and The Magnificent Moonglows

This unsolicited photo arrived at my home three weeks after singing with the legendary Bobby Lester & The Moonglows, 1980

Prentiss Barnes of The Moonglows on the left, Bill Morris at his home early in their friendship singing together.

Harvey Fuqua—R&B 1995 Pioneer Awards LA

The Moonglows performance at The Pioneer Awards Ceremony

Junior Walker receiving a Pioneer Award 1995 LA

Lloyd Price and Little Richard—1995 Pioneer Awards LA

Lloyd Price—1995 Pioneer Awards LA

Darlene Love and Billy Vera—1995 Pioneer Awards LA

Booker T and the MG's receiving Pioneer Awards in LA 1995

The MCs of The Pioneer Awards in LA—Jerry Butler and Martha Reeves of the Vandellas

Floyd Dixon, Fats Domino, Bill Morris—Pioneer Awards in LA

Whitney Houston singing a tribute to her mother, Cissy Houston, at the R&B Pioneer Awards in LA

Inez Foxx & Charlie Foxx ("Mockingbird")—Pioneer Awards LA 1995

Bill Morris and Charles "Please Come Home for Christmas" Brown

Fred Schneider (B52), Frances Preston (CEO and President of BMI (1986–2004), and Ray Benson (Asleep at the Wheel)

relief through our church, and I tried to help him out personally all I could, though he never asked me for money or help of any kind.

From time to time, Prentiss would lapse into the old drinking habit that had caused him such distress and pain. I suspect this may have even been the root cause of the tragic accident in San Antonio. So the church and I had to apply tough love: "Prentiss, there will be no more payments coming to you as long as you continue drinking." This was our way of trying to force him back into the CDU to get assistance. That treatment did help some, but now underlying his condition was the bitterness of seeing his picture on the cover of a new album or CD as his music was again being released. By the mid to late 1980s, the large music companies were making big money on him. Still there was no compensation for Prentiss. He was a deeply sad and troubled man. He couldn't understand it. *I* couldn't understand it. What in the world had happened to the wheels of justice in our society? These talented people who had given so much were still left out.

As my friendship with Prentiss deepened, and his trust in me grew, he began bringing me all correspondence addressed to him, seeking my advice as to whether that particular offer/deal would be in his best interest. When a letter arrived from Chuck Rubin of the Artists Rights Enforcement Corporation in New York, Prentiss brought it to me right away. Apparently, this office pursued the moguls of the music industry to help obtain settlements for people like Prentiss. Being more than a little skeptical, I took the letter to good friends—Mike Frascogna, an entertainment lawyer, and Guff Abbott, a professor of law at Ole Miss. They looked it over. The consensus was: "Well, Bill, what has he got to lose?"

With that, I convinced Prentiss to sign the forms, and we sent them off to Chuck Rubin. Finally, some relief was obtained and Prentiss did receive a settlement. It was not a lot of money by most people's standards, but it was a fortune to him because he had never had money in the bank before.

Knowing that Prentiss did not have much experience in managing money, I encouraged him to be extremely cautious about how he handled this newfound resource. After withdrawing some cash, he put the rest in a safe deposit box. Feeling like a rich man, he immediately bought himself a new couch, a TV, and some other items. These new additions did not go unnoticed by friends and family who dropped by for a rare visit. When the word got out about Prentiss's windfall, other needy folks were soon at his door with their hands out. And he gave generously. Too generously. For a short while, he could hold up his head again, but that money was soon gone.

As Time Goes By

Over the years, I enjoyed many special moments with Prentiss and, directly or indirectly through him, I was also placed with various singers of other doo-wop groups. In February 1985, we had a huge ice storm in Jackson. The city was virtually immobilized, and most all the residents stayed indoors, not daring to drive on the treacherous roads.

But Camille and I had our hearts set on attending a charity ball that month—a fundraiser for the Diabetes Association. It was a Saturday event to be held at the Hilton Hotel on County Line Road, and ice or no ice, we decided to take a chance. After all, The Drifters would be appearing, or at least a reasonable facsimile thereof. I couldn't believe that the original group would brave this kind of weather!

Upon walking into the Grand Ballroom, I was not expecting to find the actual Bill Pinkney and his Original Drifters. But to my amazement, the moment I heard their harmony, I knew they were the real deal, and Camille and I headed to the dance floor to enjoy the music.

After a few songs, Vernon Young, the lead singer, decided to engage the audience with a number made famous by The Impressions, "I'm So Proud." Walking offstage and onto the dance floor, Vernon strolled among those who had come to enjoy the entertainment and sang one line, then reached out and positioned the mic in front of someone in the audience to sing the next.

I saw him approaching us, and the next thing I knew, he was standing in front of me and singing: "Compliments to you from all the people we meet. . ."

When he extended the mic, I didn't miss a beat. I knew that song too: "And I'm so proud, I'm so proud to be loved by you."

People later told me they thought we had been rehearsing together. I knew the answer to that. Having loved that music for so long, the lyrics to many songs are always on my mind. The pitch and the key have long since been recorded in my memory. My memory conveys them to my heart, and my heart connects with my lungs and my lips.

Shortly after that "duet" and wanting to visit with Bill Pinkney, I made my way over to him during intermission. I had not seen Bill since 1963 when his group performed for a sorority formal at Ole Miss during my college days. I recalled heading back to the dressing room at the break. There he was, changing from his white tuxedo into his red one. He was hopping around on one leg, trying to get into his trousers, but he greeted me cordially.

As I reminded him of this, he engaged me in conversation, intent on telling me about his history with The Drifters. I then told him about my association with Prentiss.

He looked up from adjusting his bowtie. "You know Prentiss Barnes?" he exclaimed.

"He's a good friend of mine."

"Where is he? I want to see him."

We arranged to meet the next day at the Ramada Inn Coliseum, where Bill and his group were staying. When big, burly Bill Pinkney saw Prentiss, no doubt shocked at his old friend's appearance, he just reached out with his huge arms and hugged him. "Awww, Prentiss, brother, I've missed you so much." I could tell it was all Bill could do to hold back the tears. It was a touching moment for me, too—one I will never forget.

We spent three hours together in Bill's room as I listened to the two men reminisce about old times. I remember hearing them tell of their experience at New York City's Apollo Theater, where James Brown, a virtual unknown at the time, was a fill-in act.

Although not physically disabled, Bill had been abused legally and financially. He implored me to get in touch with Dick Clark of American

Bandstand to request that Dick get these early vocal groups together for a reunion to recognize those who had truly started the 1950s group harmony music. Bill was so earnest about this that while Prentiss and I were there, he wrote down on the back of an envelope the names of eighteen vocal groups who were still around, where they were located, and how we could get in touch with them. He wanted Dick Clark involved because he had the resources. Bill wanted Americans to remember and appreciate those who had made such a significant contribution to our musical history.

It was not to be. I wrote a letter to Dick Clark. Registered mail...personal and confidential. It was sent to him in New York City, but three weeks later, he corresponded with me from Los Angeles. Even though Dick Clark did give a very thoughtful response to my letter, he stated that he had already set the stage for his program, "The History of Rock 'n' Roll," which aired in October 1985. This program focused more on those who came right after the earliest groups. So, as it was, the real pioneers were left out . . . once again. Yet, there was a reason for this meeting—a blessing to come.

★   ★   ★

In May, almost exactly eleven years after my joyful experience in Washington, D.C., Gladys Knight and the Pips were performing at the City Auditorium to headline Jackson's Jubilee Jam. The jam was a three-day event, with stages set up all over downtown Jackson. One could walk from one outstanding musical act to another, all within a few blocks of each other.

Camille and I had obtained front-row seats for the opening event at Thalia Mara Hall on Thursday night. We had asked Prentiss to be our guest. It was a dressy affair with many in formal attire. Prentiss looked as distinguished as anyone there in his dark suit, red bow tie and cummerbund, set off by his ebony skin and short, white curly hair. He flashed a huge smile during the entire evening.

We delighted in listening to Gladys Knight as she, the Pips, and the band entertained us. The mayor, the governor, and other dignitaries who were sitting down front came over to introduce themselves. People were beginning to take notice of Prentiss, thank goodness. Again and again, as we continued to enjoy time together, God was building our friendship.

Happy Birthday!

Upon celebrating my fiftieth birthday, one of the executive assistants in my office said that she had never seen anyone so happy to have reached the half-century mark. "I have every reason to be happy," I told her. "I've had such a wonderful life, and I look forward to the years ahead with joy." The source of my elation I knew. It was an eternal gift from above.

Since this is a milestone for any of us, we felt it should be celebrated. Camille was determined to do it right. We thought about getting a band, but I knew it would be very difficult for any local band to duplicate the doo-wop kind of music that I could now play from my CDs. We would now be able to listen to the original sounds from my favorite vocal groups of the 1950s and 1960s.

Wanting Prentiss to be a part of this beautiful experience, I had tried for several days to reach him, but without success. Finally, I called a neighbor of his the day before the party and asked him to leave Prentiss a note, just in case he came back before the party.

On the night of the event, our home was full of our friends, and the party was soon in full swing. In this celebratory atmosphere, I was experiencing life to the fullest. Outside speakers had been installed specifically for this type of entertainment, and the music went on well into the wee hours of the morning.

A number of my friends couldn't be there, particularly those from out of town. I missed them all—especially Prentiss. It was a frustration that I had not been able to get in touch with him so that he could share this momentous occasion with me.

Late in the evening, a guest approached to tell me I had a telephone call. I went inside to the den. On the other end of the line was the mellow voice I longed to hear. "Well, hello there," Prentiss said.

"Prentiss, brother, can you come over right now?"

Tired from a trip to attend the funeral of a relative in South Mississippi, he tried to decline gracefully. Nonetheless, hearing the merriment in the background, he couldn't resist and agreed to come.

What a pleasure it was to introduce my friend Prentiss to so many of the other people I love. As the night wore on, Prentiss and I laughed and talked and even sang a few of the old songs he had helped to make famous.

Our friendship was a blessing that had begun in Washington with his fellow singers, The Moonglows—many years earlier.

"The Same Kind of Different as Me"

Prentiss and I were very different. I am a white businessman—from one of the early pioneer families of Jackson. Through God's grace, I have achieved success as the world measures it. Prentiss, on the other hand, grew up in a small home in the woods outside of Magnolia, Mississippi, with very little of this world's goods. Although he, too, enjoyed success for a season, he had found himself again with little.

In spite of our differences, Prentiss and I enjoyed a deep common bond that had brought us together—our faith and our mutual love of music, especially black vocal group harmony. These wonderfully inspired singers like Prentiss gave so much to us in the 1950s when people of his ethnic background were having to battle racial, economic, and legal issues, which we still do not fully comprehend. My parents had taught me to respect the dignity of every human being, but I did grow up in a segregated society, which remained so in the Deep South until the mid-1960s.

To communicate to Prentiss how I felt about him and our friendship, I put part of our story on a cassette tape. Having bought Prentiss a portable cassette player, I had him come to my office one Friday before he was due to leave for a special trip up East to receive an award given by the Vocal Group in Harmony

Association. Sitting in our conference room, he listened to the tape. About thirty minutes later, I walked in to see how he had enjoyed the story.

He looked at me and, with tears running down his cheeks, said, "Brother Morris, you have meant more to me than many of my own people."

What Prentiss did not fully understand was that he had enriched my life immeasurably. There was no way I could adequately repay him. I told him so.

~ 3 ~

OH, WHAT A NIGHT!

Something significant was unfolding in Prentiss's life. Something far beyond any concoction of his wildest imagination. Something big!

Various organizations were beginning to recognize his true worth, along with the other members of The Moonglows. In November 1994, the group was invited to be among the honorees at the Sixth Annual Pioneer Awards of the Rhythm & Blues Foundation to be held March 2, 1995, at the Hollywood Palladium in Los Angeles, California. Prentiss brought the official invitation, along with other correspondence from this foundation, to my office. One of the benefits was permission for The Moonglows to invite three other people to join them at their table that evening. I was one of them. I submitted it to the Father, "Lord, if this is only about me being with famous people, take it away from me." Ultimately, I accepted, feeling I should go, yet not knowing how I would manage being out of the office for even a couple of days. Timewise I was slammed.

I made my flight plans anyway. Knowing that Prentiss had to be in Los Angeles on Tuesday, February 28, for two days of rehearsals before the big evening, the best I could do was to leave on the morning of the evening event—Thursday, March 2—and return on Friday, March 3, in order to take a flight to Washington, D.C., for an insurance conference on Saturday.

Exceptionally excited about my trip, I arrived at the Jackson airport on Thursday morning, unaware that anything was amiss. I strolled down to the gate, rolling my carry-on luggage behind me. When I got there, it did seem strange that no one was in the gate area except for one of the cleanup crew, pushing a broom.

"I think that flight has been cancelled," he replied when I inquired.

"Cancelled??" I raced back to the American Airlines counter to find a well-dressed gentleman ahead of me, pleading with the agent behind the desk.

"Sir, there is nothing I can do," I heard her say. "I told you the flight has been cancelled due to ice in Dallas." She made a few more clicks on her computer keyboard. "However, I can send you through Nashville and get you to Los Angeles at about 7:00 p.m."

With no other options available, he gave up. Finally, disgusted, he shoved his hands into his pockets and strode away, shaking his head.

"Sir, may I help you?" the ticket agent asked me.

"Well, I need to get to L.A. too."

When she laid out the same scenario I had overheard, I interjected, "That really won't work, I'm afraid. You see, I would miss the very reason for the trip. My friend—a black man—is receiving an award tonight, and it would break his heart—and mine, too—if I were not there. . ." I paused. "Would you mind if I took a moment to pray about it before I give you an answer?"

I turned my back to collect myself, feeling the moisture welling up in my eyes. It would be such a shame to have to abort this trip.

Silently, I talked with the Lord. *I thought You wanted me to be there for Prentiss, but if You don't, it will be all right and I will accept it.*

I wasn't paying much attention to the agent, except to be vaguely aware of rapid keyboard clicking. Within less than a minute, I heard her voice behind me and turned.

"Mr. Morris . . ." She was leaning forward over the counter, speaking in a near whisper. "Don't tell anyone, but I am going to get you out there on time.

I've checked with Continental Airlines, and they have a flight via Houston that will get you in to LAX by 4:06—will that be OK?"

My home state was in transition from its past racial issues. The agent must have felt compassion for Prentiss. Not so much for me, but for him. She had already turned me down, along with the gentleman ahead of me.

I've had a lot of prayers answered in my lifetime. But this must have been the most immediate response I can recall. It is my understanding that it is quite rare, when one uses frequent flyer miles, for any airline to send a passenger to another carrier. The cost—around $1,300 for a last-minute ticket—would be almost prohibitive. American was under no obligation to do so.

The atmosphere around the counter was suddenly electric! At that moment, I had no further doubt that I was destined to make the trip, that this journey was about far more than myself . . . or even Prentiss. Before I hurried off to the other gate, I told the agent how deeply I appreciated this courtesy and that I was going to write a letter of commendation on her behalf to American Airlines. I did.

★   ★   ★

En route to LAX, with the clock ticking, I managed to change into my tux in the tiny airplane lavatory. When I emerged, I received many a curious glance. I suppose none of the passengers had ever seen a man traveling in formal attire. Now they have.

While still in flight, using the phone on the back of the passenger's headrest in front of me, I was able to call to line up a private town car to take me across L.A. as quickly as possible. Waiting at the gate was a driver with my name written on a placard. He grabbed my carry-on, and we literally ran through the terminal doors to a car pulled curbside. On the way to the venue, we battled rain as well as rush hour traffic. But my driver knew the side streets and didn't mind taking them.

I called Prentiss from the car and explained the delay. That's when he told me he had a surprise for me.

"What's that?" I asked.

"Bill Pinkney has come out to L.A. to be with us."

Now in a state of euphoria, I told Prentiss that if he didn't mind waiting for me, I would like to ride over with him and the other Moonglows.

In the Spotlight

Since the event was scheduled to get underway by 5:15 at the Hollywood Palladium, I was nervous on our hour-long drive. It was 5:30 when we arrived at the Universal City Hilton. There, waiting, were Harvey Fuqua, his lovely wife, Carolyne, Pete Graves, Doc Williams (Doc sang with Pete's group of Moonglows), and Prentiss. I rushed inside and left my baggage at the check-in desk, asking them to have someone deliver it to my room.

"Oh, Mr. Morris, we are so glad you're here!" the clerk gushed. "We have upgraded you to a double suite, sir."

No doubt they thought I was the William Morris of the William Morris Talent Agency. It was not the first time. But I couldn't spare a moment to correct the impression. Actually, it was a good thing I had already changed into my tuxedo, for a stretch limo pulled up at that moment to take us to the event.

Just as we left the hotel entrance, Harvey said, "William Morris . . . I have been hearing a lot about you. How about singing that song 'Daddy's Home'?"

Having just met these guys, except for Prentiss, and a little out of breath from our hectic pace, this was not ideal timing. I sang anyway. They all joined in the song, and we had fun knocking it out in the limo.

When we arrived at the Palladium, it was dark, and spotlights swept the sky. With cameras flashing and TV equipment recording the mounting excitement, journalists and fans milled about. It was a scene straight out of a Hollywood premiere. I felt like a real celebrity, but more than that, I was so happy for Prentiss.

True to my expectations, the place was aglow with a galaxy of stars—the movers and shakers of the music industry. Stepping out of the limo, I looked to my left. Beside me were singers Bonnie Raitt and Jackson Browne, and

Ed Bradley of *60 Minutes*. I talked to Bonnie for a minute and was able to pass on greetings from Dick Waterman, her former agent, who now lives in Oxford, Mississippi. As Bonnie and I ran into each other several times that evening, I had a chance to visit with her and thank her for all she had done for these deserving singers in her role as vice chairman of the Rhythm & Blues Foundation.

Who's Who of Rock 'n' Roll

A few minutes after Prentiss and I began to sample some of the fancy hors d'oeuvres they lavished upon us, we bumped into Bill Pinkney. He was so happy to see us! A bit later, we were ushered into a room where many of the honorees were also enjoying the food and catching up.

Many of them had not seen each other in fifteen or twenty years, when they had been on the road together, playing in venues across the country and living on only a few dollars a day. Others had written, produced, or engineered the very first records in this genre, establishing a sound that would rock the world. Interesting, that many of these artists were writing and performing in their singular style, creating an atmosphere of love, romance, and joy, at a time when racial tension was high. Yet people of all races and ethnic backgrounds danced to their tunes. And this white boy from Mississippi was one of their biggest fans!

After many hugs and much back-slapping given and received by old friends, we were led to the main ballroom where the induction ceremony was about to take place. Here, circular tables for eight had been set up throughout the room, with a huge stage at one end. Prentiss's table was on the front row, slightly to the right of center stage—the perfect spot from which to take photographs of the evening's proceedings! I had come prepared—with my professional camera and gear.

When I have a camera in my hands, I am compelled to capture the moment, a flash in time that can never be relived. With major moguls in the music and entertainment industry and musicians all around me, it was a dream come true! (What I did not know until later was that professional photographers at the event were required to pay a hefty fee and were cordoned off from most of the crowd. Believe me, ignorance *is* bliss!)

It was literally a Who's Who of industry greats! I did not know the names of most of the people in the room, but that soon changed as I made my way from table to table, saying, "Mind if I get a photo of this fine group?"

I was able to photograph Junior Walker and his son, Whitney Houston's mother, Cissy, who later sang a gospel song introduced by Whitney. Charles Brown ("Please Come Home for Christmas") allowed me to get a shot of him with his former wife and current honoree, Mabel Scott ("Elevator Boogie"). We also met The Marvelettes ("Please Mr. Postman") and Martha Reeves of The Vandellas ("Dancing in the Street" and "Heat Wave"). This went on until around 8:30—hours that seemed like mere minutes. It was time for the show to begin.

Honored that night were The Moonglows, The Marvelettes, Inez and Charlie Foxx ("Mockingbird"), Darlene Love (originally with The Blossoms), and Darlene with The Crystals ("He's a Rebel") and later recorded under her own name, "Today I Met the Boy I'm Going to Marry." She also played a role in the movie *Lethal Weapon.* The Moonglows, introduced by Curtis Mayfield, brought the house down with their performance of "Sincerely" and "The Ten Commandments of Love." It was thrilling to hear Prentiss's gravelly bass voice coming through.

Other performing honorees were Lloyd Price ("Lawdy, Miss Clawdy"), Junior Walker ("Shotgun" and "What Does It Take to Win Your Love?"), Booker T. and the M.G.s ("Green Onions") and Justine "Baby" Washington ("That's How Heartaches Are Made"). In addition, there were these artists: Illinois Jacquet, Arthur Prysock, and Fats Domino. Individual artists were awarded a cash gift of $15,000, and groups, $20,000. Consequently, as part of a group, each of The Moonglows received $5,000. This was a lot of money to Prentiss.

Our seating arrangement also afforded me the opportunity to mingle with the stars and their entourage. Little Richard was sitting at a table right behind me, and I was able to meet and converse with one of the congenial hosts for the evening, Jerry Butler, when he broke for intermission.

"Jerry," I began, after introducing myself, "I understand that you're from my home state—Mississippi. As I recall, when you wrote your signature song for an English class—"For Your Precious Love"—the teacher gave you an 'A.'"

Jerry, who was then a city councilman in Chicago, whipped out his wallet and handed me his card. "Next time you're in the Windy City, please give me a call." I did, a couple of years later.

During the evening, quite a few people approached, thinking they knew me. While I was chatting with Mary Wilson of The Supremes, who is also from Mississippi, I remember asking her, "Do you know what 'The Dells' would have to say about this?"

"No . . . what?"

With that, I belted out, "Oh, What a Night!"

Overhearing me, an agent who represents many of the artists asked for my business card. He wanted to see about booking me! I gave him my card, but I didn't tell him that I was not in the music business.

When that many musicians (many all but forgotten) get together to create music, there is an ineffable synergy that defies explanation—all those wonderfully gifted people, reliving the long-ago in an explosion of memories.

"Do you remember that time when . . ."

"I'll never forget . . ."

Good times. Hard times. Times of tension and tears. Times of laughter and downright hilarity. All of it culminating in a crescendo of unforgettable sounds on this marvelous evening! And there I was in the midst of it, clicking away from every angle, recording the moments with my camera. Creating a different kind of symphony.

Rock Around the Clock

On the way back to the hotel in the limo, Pete Graves was trying to teach me how to sing The Moonglows' songs. Demonstrating their distinctive nuances of interpretation—called "blow harmony"—he held certain notes for a prolonged period of time. At the hotel, we visited in the lounge area until the wee hours of the morning.

Around 2:00 a.m., I was sitting with Fats Domino, reminiscing about my teenage years. One dance, in particular, stands out. Fats was playing in Jackson the year his song "Blueberry Hill," was released. I remember so well seeing him sitting at the piano up on the stage, smiling and playing, as we teenagers danced to the hit tunes of our era.

In those days, the interaction between entertainer and audience was close. There was no need for "security," as we know it today. Oh, to return to those kinder, gentler times.

I could have rocked around the clock! I really hated to cut our visit short, but I was going to have to be up at 5:00 to catch an early flight home. It was time to say goodnight.

What if I had not made the effort to come? So many people would have given anything to have had my experience. All I could do was feel a deep sense of humility and gratitude, for I could not have orchestrated this at any price. It was, indeed, a gift, and I knew the Giver. There was no doubt in my mind that His plan was unfolding.

On the flight home, I had some time to reflect. A change had taken place in Prentiss Barnes during our stay in L.A. The melancholia had lifted, and his countenance was radiant. To be honest, I actually forgot about his physical limitations. Caught up in the glory of the festivities, I think he forgot about them too.

Friends Forever

A couple of years went by, and Prentiss and I grew closer and closer. He was now trusting me as a close advisor. At least once or twice a week and every weekend, I would check in with Prentiss to see how things were going. There were ups and downs, particularly financial ones, but he seemed to be gaining positive momentum.

Somewhere along the way, a gifted freelance writer by the name of Linda Temple called to ask if she could write an article about Prentiss, highlighting our friendship. We agreed. I recall the excitement that sizzled through my home the entire three hours she was interviewing Prentiss and me. She was so inspired by our story, she almost forgot that guests were scheduled to arrive at her home at 5:00 p.m.. At 4:45, she tore out of there, assuring us that she would be calling for further details.

Her article, published in the *Clarion-Ledger* a few weeks later, was an exhilarating exposition of two people who lived in parallel universes. While I was in Jackson, Mississippi, listening to the music of the 1950s and 1960s and throwing dances to pay my way through college, Prentiss was performing on the stages of New York City and all across the country. It was a tale of two men from different worlds who were being prepared for a rare breed of friendship.

The response to Linda's article was nothing short of overwhelming and deeply humbling. Friends and acquaintances alike were continually commenting, some leaving tearful messages on our answer phones about the story of Prentiss and our friendship. Some said that it was one of the most touching they had ever read.

This was something beyond the two of us or our gifts and abilities. It was the hand of our Creator, forging a unique bond between a black man and a white man—for His purposes. All I knew was that, after meeting Prentiss Barnes, my life was never the same.

~ 4 ~

HALLELUJAH!

The first things one would notice about Bill Pinkney were his signature smile and that full head of curly white hair. When also wearing a white tuxedo, he was a force to be reckoned with. That was the sight that greeted my eyes on a humid August evening when I drove over to Vicksburg, Mississippi, to hear Bill and his Drifters perform at the Ameristar Casino. The four other singers were exceptionally talented, and Bill's distinctive voice still sounded as good as ever. After a moving performance before a packed house, I went backstage to see him.

He threw out his arms to hug me, then asked how Prentiss was doing. I gave him a copy of the article Linda Temple had written and told him I would like to bring Prentiss over on the weekend to visit. He was so pleased, and I jumped at the chance to get these two greats together again.

By mid-morning on Saturday, I picked up Prentiss at his apartment, and we sang all the way to Vicksburg, about thirty-five miles west of Jackson. It happened to be Bill Pinkney's birthday.

When we pulled up in front of the Delta Inn where Bill was staying, there in the parking lot was the Trailways-sized bus with "Bill Pinkney and The Original Drifters" boldly emblazoned on the side. This was the perfect setting for this meeting of old friends. A lazy Saturday morning in the South. The mighty

Mississippi River rambling by. Laughter and light-hearted banter punctuating the scene like the refrain of a beloved old song. This time I was not going to make the same mistake I had made at the earlier meeting I had negotiated between these two. I was going to record every minute. And so I did—posing Bill and Prentiss with the bus in the background, careful not to obscure the The Drifters' name or the wide Mississippi reflecting the rays of the sun.

The Drifters and The Moonglows probably constituted two of the most impressive vocal groups in all of rock 'n' roll history. To have the privilege of being in the presence of these two wonderful men was pure joy. Once again, I marveled as I listened to them discussing old times. I had the recorder going too. But this time I didn't hear much more about the tough years—with the exception of one statement made by Prentiss: "We Moonglows got paid only twenty-five dollars apiece for each of three movies," he explained.

In spite of all the hardships they endured, the thing that seemed to permeate this moment was gratitude—how deeply thankful both men were to be alive and to know that people really did care. Bill was particularly vocal about this, his positive attitude transcending any negativity he might have experienced throughout his singing career. I can still hear him saying, "But, you know, God is so good." And Prentiss echoing, "Yes, He is."

About that time, I felt such a sense to turn off the recorder. Prentiss, Bill, and I began to pray. Once again, I knew something profound was happening. I would not know the full depth, height, and breadth until several weeks later.

In the early afternoon, the three of us were getting a little hungry, so we found a restaurant that served barbecued ribs. Feeling plenty satisfied and with some time on our hands, we got in my car and rode around Vicksburg. I pointed out various sites of historical interest, including the military park in the city cemetery, where the bodies of fallen Union and Confederate soldiers were buried. Pausing here, we could almost hear the sounds of battle—the roar of cannon fire, the cries of the dying—and realized that this was sacred ground. Boys in blue and gray—sons and brothers, black and white—had spilled their blood on this soil. But on both sides of the conflict, their blood ran red.

"I Need Thee"

Bill and I stayed in touch, and our friendship continued to deepen. In November, I was asked by Dale Ludwig, an executive at Connecticut Mutual Life, if I would help arrange the entertainment for the Leaders Life Insurance Underwriters meeting to be held a few months later in Cancun, Mexico. My first thought, of course, was Bill Pinkney and The Drifters. Upon that suggestion, Dale asked if I could get a tape from one of their recent gigs. I called Bill and to my delight, he sent me the tape of their final Vicksburg performance of a few months earlier.

Prior to sending the tape to Dale, I listened in my car on the way to work that morning. At the end of the tape, Bill said, as he typically does at his performances: "God has been so good to me. Would you mind if I closed this show with a gospel number?" In response, there was spontaneous applause, and Bill began to sing a hymn that his mama taught him in the cotton fields of South Carolina when he was just a little boy. He told the story behind this song:

"We'd be out in the field pickin' cotton, and the sun . . . it was so hot. We didn't have no shoes on our feet. We didn't have no shirts on our backs. That's when my mama realized we needed the Lord. We needed Him ev'ry day. We needed Him ev'ry hour. We needed Him ev'ry step of the way. That music helped us make it through the day."

> I need Thee, O I need Thee.
> Ev'ry hour I need Thee.
> O bless me now, my Savior.
> I come to Thee.

Hearing Bill's rich voice singing these timeless words brought tears, and I wiped them away as they trickled down my face. And that's when the seed of an idea sprang to life.

As soon as I arrived at my office, I called Bill. "I was just wondering . . ."

"Yeah, Bill?" he asked, already attentive and eager to hear whatever his friend had to say.

"Have you ever considered cutting a gospel CD?"

"Well, no, I guess I really haven't."

"Then let's both pray about it and see what happens a couple of months from now . . . if you get the deal in Cancun."

★   ★   ★

The Drifters got the deal. They were invited to perform in Mexico, and I was there to see them. From the first note of the first song, I knew beyond a shadow of a doubt that they would put on a magnificent performance. They did not disappoint. Throughout the evening, the crowd was mesmerized as The Drifters performed such all-time greats as "Dance with Me," "This Magic Moment," "Up on the Roof," "Under the Boardwalk," and many others. Toward the end of the performance, Bill Pinkney had just completed the lead on a song and began to share a little bit of the history of The Drifters and The Moonglows.

"And that reminds me," he said, "there's a 'young man' here tonight who's been a friend to me and a 'specially good friend to one of the original Moonglows. I'd like to call him to the stage right now to do the lead on a song."

I must say that for not ever having rehearsed the song with The Drifters, it seemed to come off very well. Bill completed the set with the song his mama had taught him—"I Need Thee." With a portable microphone in his hand and the spotlight following him, he moved through the audience, singing this hymn. When I saw this well diversified audience embrace the words Bill was singing, I knew the time had come to further discuss with him the concept for a gospel CD.

When Bill and I talked about the idea again, he was enthusiastic—if I would agree to be involved in the project.

Hallelujah Productions

In early August, exactly a year after our get-together in Vicksburg, I got a call from Bill Pinkney. The Drifters would be performing in Greenville, Mississippi. He wanted to know if I might be able to book them somewhere in the vicinity the following evening.

"Sure, Bill," I replied. "Go ahead and count on it. I'll take it from here."

Friends from the Odd Couples Dance Club, of which Camille and I were members, were elated when they found out we would be having The Drifters for our annual summer party. Right away, we made arrangements with Hal and Mal's restaurant and lounge to hold the event.

This facility is located in a turn-of-the-century red brick warehouse that has been converted into a popular gathering place, about a hundred yards south of the old Capitol building in downtown Jackson. Known for its down-home cooking and inviting atmosphere, this venue has attracted international figures—politicians and other dignitaries, including many in the artistic community—journalists, musicians, authors. In fact, Malcolm White, one of the owners, is the president of the Mississippi Arts Council and was responsible for founding the annual St. Patrick's Day Parade. To Mississippians, he is a treasure.

One of my all-time favorite writers, Willie Morris, celebrated his sixtieth birthday here, and I was privileged to be invited to attend his big bash, hobnobbing with many of the greats in attendance. At that party were David Halberstam, a well-known writer; Johnny Majors, the football icon, and other notables. Willie, formerly the youngest editor of *Harper's Magazine* and the darling of New York society, wrote beautifully of the human spirit. When he retired, he returned to Jackson to live and write. We became good friends. And now, some of my other friends—Bill Pinkney and The Drifters—would be performing in the same venue. The party was on!

Gosh, they sounded wondrous that August night! As usual, midway through the show, Bill started up with a now familiar request: "There's a 'young man' in the audience tonight. . ." By now, singing a song with the guys was becoming a regular routine, so I shouldn't have been surprised. I noticed, too, that I was more comfortable on the stage and could enjoy hearing the others harmonizing in the background.

Following The Drifters' performance, Camille and I took Bill to the Waffle House on High Street, not far away. It was late—typical for musicians on the road—and this was one of the few places still open. There, while enjoying a very early-morning breakfast, we mapped out further plans for our upcoming recording venture. This called for more hands on deck.

It was decided that my attorney friend Mike Frascogna and I would serve as executive producers, and Melvin and Doug Williams, owners of Blackberry Records of McComb, Mississippi, as the in-studio producers. In other words, Mike and I would put up the money, and the Williams brothers would handle the technical sessions and coaching during the recording process. I was also involved in selecting the songs to be recorded and, to some degree, the production, along with documenting the project with my ever-present camera. Our CD would come out on the Blackberry label, with Malaco Records of Jackson as the distributor.

I knew we needed to form a business entity, and Mike encouraged me to come up with a name. "I'll let you know tomorrow," I told him.

The name that kept surfacing was "Hallelujah Productions, Inc." So on October 25, 1995, a new company was formed, with yours truly as its president. Excitement—yes!

Signed, Sealed, Delivered

At last. The day arrived—a day in late October.

Typically, the recording sessions would begin at 1:00 p.m. and run until eight or nine o'clock at night. I couldn't believe how hard Doug and Melvin Williams were making these guys work to finesse the slightest nuance in the vocals of the gospel hymns. They rehearsed some notes over and over until they finally achieved the effect they were after. Hoping that this gospel recording would be of the highest quality possible, I was fortunate to have the technical and musical skills of the Williams brothers as they coached the talented singers. These two Grammy-nominated studio veterans were able to bring out the very best in the group.

The four days passed quickly. Now it was time for the business end of things—signing the contracts. Mike and I had been pumping money into this deal—by now, in excess of $40,000—without having anything in writing except for a verbal agreement among friends. This whole thing was done in a leap of faith.

Before lunch at the University Club atop the Regions Bank building in downtown Jackson, we worked out all the details, and Bill Pinkney and I signed our three copies of the agreement. Now it was time to try to please the group, which would not necessarily be easy. Many of these musicians had been "messed over," so to speak, time and again. Naturally, they were trying to safeguard their royalties as best they could. But Mike Frascogna did a masterful job of laying out everything on the table. (It also taught me a great deal about the recording business—how many hands the money has to pass through before it finally reaches the singers themselves.) When we finished, everyone was happy.

We closed out the session Thursday night with a lot of hugs, many photographs, and all of us singing together in the studio. I still had to pinch myself and ask, *Is this really happening?*

The next recording session was set for the last week in November, right after Thanksgiving. We were hoping to have everything completed by December 15, for an early March release.

That Is Why I Love Him So

At the second recording session in late November, The Drifters arrived at Terminal Studios in Ridgeland in the early afternoon. Shortly after that, we began recording again. This time, there was a new face in the crowd—Paul Porter, a singer/songwriter from Memphis. The group would be singing a song he had written—"That Is Why I Love Him So."

What a voice! Bill commented that if Paul ever wanted to go on the road with them, they would be very happy to have him. I predicted that this song would soon be a real favorite on the CD.

The next night, the group would be taking time off in order for Melvin and Doug to lay some new tracks. This was the perfect time for me to have the guys over to my house for dinner. Prentiss Barnes was also invited.

Late that afternoon, The Drifters pulled up in their big bus and parked in front of our house. Not long after that, a reporter from the *Northside Sun* showed up to interview the guys. By now, I was sure the neighbors were talking! It wasn't every day that a group of celebrities park their tour bus in our tranquil neighborhood. What made this visit especially newsworthy was the fact that The Drifters were the first to record at the brand-new Terminal Studios.

"I'm goin' gospel," Bill told the reporter when he asked about the new album, *Peace in the Valley*. "The whole idea touches me. When Bill Morris came to me, it almost knocked me off my feet. I was just roamin', wanderin', and driftin.' I wasn't doing bad, but I just couldn't make up my mind. And it looked like when he came along, everything just came together."

It surely made me feel good to hear Bill Pinkney telling the reporter how much I meant to him and how this CD was becoming a reality.

After the reporter left to write his story, the guys and I listened to the previous night's recording. Although by no means complete, the rough cut was outstanding. There was much laughter and joking around as we anticipated how good the finished product would be.

When Camille announced that it was time for dinner—a delicious meal of ribs, slaw, and baked beans—I led off in prayer at the table, and Bill Pinkney wrapped it up. Prentiss told me afterward that he noticed Bill had been crying during the prayer. No surprise there. I already knew Bill to be a deeply grateful and humble man. Later that evening, as we harmonized and shared, our bond grew deeper still.

Huntin' with Daddy

By the time I got to the studio on Wednesday, Bill and the guys were really knocking it out. "Bill," he told me when they paused for a break, "I don't know that I have ever enjoyed anything in my life as much as I'm enjoying doin' this CD. Fact is, we may go entirely gospel from now on."

I laughed. "Well, I'm afraid you'd have some mighty disappointed fans if you did that. They'll want to hear your old songs too."

"Oh, Bill, don' need to worry 'bout that. I'll do it—you know I will."

By the last night, we were all pretty tired, as the guys had been recording since Monday. (The public has no idea how much work goes into producing a top-quality CD. Nor did I . . . until this project.)

Catching another break, Bill and I had a chance to talk for a bit, one on one. So, we ducked into another room, and I set up my video camera on a tripod. For the next couple of hours, we talked about how The Drifters got their start. I wanted to hear the entire story from Bill's perspective since there were a number of versions circulating. While the camera rolled, Bill gave me the facts. It was a long story, but the gist of it was that, ultimately, the singers just "drifted" together, mostly from gospel groups.

One comment Bill made during that evening stands out in my memory. "Bill," he said to me, "I just wanna tell ya again, you can *sing!*"

"Oh, Bill," I retorted, feeling he might be offering the compliment as a means of showing his appreciation for my work on his behalf.

"No! I mean, you can *really* sing!"

It felt good, of course, but I wasn't about to quit my day job.

From there, the conversation took a different turn as Bill Pinkney recalled his childhood. "When I was a little boy, Daddy would take me and my little brother huntin'," he began. "We'd stand beside him with our croaker sacks while he'd throw a stick to shoo the blackbirds up and then fire his shotgun into the flock. He'd bring down a whole slew of 'em. That's when he'd say, 'Go get 'em, boys.' And we'd run out into the field and scoop up all the birds in our sacks. We'd fill 'em with cotton one day and blackbirds the next.

"My grandma . . . now she was a mighty fine cook. Blackbirds weren't the only things she'd cook. We'd go out and shoot a rabbit or a squirrel, and she'd fire up that old woodstove. She'd stir up some cornpone, some sweet 'taters and turnip greens from the garden, and we'd have us a feast!"

When Vernon Young, the lead tenor, entered the room, Bill began teasing him about all the deer meat in his freezer. "You know, Vernon . . . he hunts a lot. Down where we live in South Carolina, along the coast, many deer are killed on the road at night. If you find one of 'em quick enough—while they're still warm—you can cut 'em and let 'em bleed, and the meat will be alright. If I call Vernon, and I know he's in town but isn't answerin' his phone, I'll know where he is. He's out on the highway, lookin' for some of that deer meat!"

Now, there was hearty laughter all around as the rest of the guys tuned in on our discussion. Vernon took the ribbing good-naturedly, but I still recall that look on his face that told the story—he'd been caught!

Celebration

On New Year's Day, I received a call from Bill Pinkney, informing me that Vernon, who was lead on many of the songs, was in intensive care in Lake Charles, Louisiana, with a bleeding ulcer. I figured it was most likely from excessive cigarette smoking, plus drinking, along with the hazards of life on the road. The doctors had advised him that he would not be able to sing for a while. I imagine they advised him of some other things too!

Now we were scrambling to see who might replace him for the coming week of recording. We were considering Paul Porter of Memphis, along with perhaps the Williams brothers. Everyone would pitch in to fill the gap while Vernon recovered. Richard Dunbar would take the lead.

On the way to the studio, I had begun to get a little emotional just thinking about these guys and how much I was going to miss them. Of course, I figured that I would be seeing them again, but we would not necessarily be working so closely together. This season would soon be ending.

When I got home from the studio, a couple of my daughters' boyfriends were there. The girls had been teased a little that their daddy, who was known primarily in the insurance industry, was producing a record album. But when I played my tape for them, they were intrigued—even excited. To celebrate, Camille and I took them all to dinner at the Mayflower Cafe, Jackson's oldest and most historic restaurant, now also known as one of the settings for the filming of the Academy-award-winning movie, *The Help.*

After dinner, I called Bill Pinkney and left a message on his voicemail (as they would still be traveling), telling him how much I loved them and how blessed I felt to be their friend.

Now I was yearning for guidance as we moved into the marketing phase of this project. I was also thinking of Vernon. We needed wisdom for Melvin and Doug as all made some final decisions.

~ 5 ~

SOME KIND OF WONDERFUL

In the next few months, my life took on a dizzying pace. During the week, I was managing the affairs of my expanding insurance business. Weekends frequently found me championing my new brothers at some gala or function held in their honor.

The next such event was the forty-third anniversary of Bill Pinkney and The Drifters in Sumter, South Carolina. This event, a fundraiser, would hopefully support the building of a park and a statue in Bill's likeness. It was quite an honor—for Bill and for me—for he had asked me to introduce him by sharing the liner notes I had written for our gospel CD.

On a Friday in May 1996, I flew in to Columbia, South Carolina, and rented a car for the drive to Sumter. The countryside was at the peak of its springtime splendor, and I reveled in its beauty on the way.

After checking into my hotel, I drove over to the Civic Center to see Bill, who was looking authoritatively sharp in a white shirt, white pants, and a white straw hat. "Bill," I teased him, "at one time you were planting cotton, and now you look like the plantation owner." Indeed, he did! Normally, I would not have made such a comment had Bill not been such a dear and close friend. Deep inside me, I envisioned the little boy with a meager background who had become a man greatly revered and respected, not only for his musical talent but for his character.

When The Drifters completed their sound check and Bill had left to rest up before the evening's performance, I decided to explore the area with Gregory Johnson, first tenor with the group. I knew that Sumter was Bill Pinkney's home. I was curious about where he lived. Gregory found the place easily enough—a two-story brick home with a spacious green lawn, surrounded by a white wooden fence, in a lovely neighborhood. I was so pleased to see that Bill, having grown up with nothing, had obviously done quite well for himself.

Riding around, Gregory and I listened to the mastered version of our gospel tape soon to be released. He was impressed by the quality of the recording once Melvin and Doug had put their finishing touches on it. The cover was strong—distinguished and inviting—and we felt that the project was almost ready for the public.

All Shook Up!

When we returned to the Civic Center about thirty minutes before the show started, I found Bill trying to manage everything. I do mean *everything*—from the order of the performances—*which* band would go onstage *when*—to who would pick up plastic forks for the food that was being served to the artists behind the scenes. It was complete chaos!

Since I was dressed in a tuxedo, band members were coming up to me, asking what time they were supposed to go on. It was hard for me to believe that Bill did not have some type of pit boss to direct the proceedings backstage.

The evening's agenda was to be divided into two categories: first, the gospel singers would perform; then, the rock 'n' rollers. That, in itself, was going to be quite a challenge. Gospel singers, I have found—like some preachers—do not abide by the clock very well. With at least ten gospel groups on the program, one can imagine what was about to transpire!

There were many fabulous groups in both the gospel and rock 'n' roll genres. Some of the more famous gospel groups were Slim and The Supreme

Angels, Tommy Ellison and the Singing Stars, The Dixie Hummingbirds, Thelma Isaac, Flossie and the Singing Sisters, The Traveling Echoes, and, of course, The Williams Brothers, including Doug and Melvin, with Henry Green and their band. And finally, there was Bill Pinkney and The Drifters, and the fifty-member choir from his local church.

Rock 'n' Roll stars were Carl Gardner, original lead singer of The Coasters; The Bay Street Blues Club; Subway; and Clifton Curry ("She Shot a Hole in My Sole"). Clifton also wrote the song "Drifting Along" for Bill Pinkney.

As people were filing into the auditorium, we were playing The Drifters' gospel music over the sound system and handing out fliers announcing the upcoming release of the CD. Predictably, due to lack of organization, no one was following any type of schedule. Once the show finally got underway— approximately thirty minutes late—several entertainers were getting nervous, not knowing when they were to go onstage. Some of the local singers performed more than one song and didn't want to leave. Backstage, excitement mingled with uneasiness.

I, for one, had no idea when I was supposed to introduce Bill for the presentation in honor of his forty-third anniversary with The Drifters. I was not too worried about it, though, as I was getting a kick out of meeting so many of the stars whose music I have loved over the years.

Every performer had the crowd hopping. The very air was pulsating as the bands played dynamic praise songs, rocking the Civic Center. The atmosphere was unlike anything I had experienced during rock 'n' roll festivals. There seemed to be a deeper dimension—something extra.

The moment neared when I would introduce Bill.

Whole Lot of Shakin' Going On!

Around 9:30, a local disc jockey, O. E. Martin, who was emceeing the gospel portion of the event, called me to the stage along with Bill's children. One of the highlights of the evening came when his daughters presented him with a beautifully engraved plaque, telling him how much they loved and admired him. Bill just stood there with tears in his eyes as one of his daughters read the inscription on the plaque.

Someone from the governor's office then stepped forward and issued a proclamation officially declaring Bill Pinkney the "Ambassador of Music for the State of South Carolina." It was a solemn moment, and it took all of us a while to absorb the momentous announcement that had just been made.

And then it was my turn. What a great honor it was for me to introduce my dear and esteemed friend. Before I began, I invited The Drifters, dressed in their cream-colored suits, to join us onstage. Surrounded by Bill's family and colleagues, I read the liner notes I had written in tribute to this musical giant.[1]

The introduction was very well received, but it was not without its problems. Bill's keyboard player was completely out of sync with the performers. In fact, he started warming up the keyboard in the middle of my introduction. I even stopped once and said, "Hello, Bobby," thinking he might get the point, but he did not. A couple of times, he was over the edge. As I would get to a certain place in the introduction, all of a sudden, a single, loud, jarring note would come through the sound system. It was unnerving. As I look back on it, I think perhaps Bobby had some medical issue that had not yet been diagnosed. He had known Bill for years, and Bill was loyal to him. Bill loved Bobby, and his patience was beyond exemplary.

During The Drifters' performance, Doug Williams came out at the end and took the lead on "Amazing Grace." It was staggering, with a choir singing background and Pete Hamilton, a fabulous saxophone player, using his skill on that instrument to take the classic hymn to a whole new level. Melvin Williams later joined the group on "Drifting Along."

As the evening progressed—with its delays and snafus—more of the groups were complaining. For example, The Dixie Hummingbirds were scheduled to leave that night for their next venue in another city. When one of the bands that was set to go on began to move toward the stage, Bill personally stopped them and brought on The Hummingbirds so they could make their next engagement on time. This group was particularly enjoyable.

If I understood correctly, the lead singer, Ira Tucker, and one or two of the others had actually been performing for nearly seventy years.

Throughout the event, I photographed the singers in each group as they performed. Then I would rush back to the dressing room to visit with those who had not yet been introduced. With each backstage visit, I sensed a little more tension. Now that we were transitioning from the gospel portion of the show to the rock 'n' roll segment, it was definitely late. Past midnight, the crowd was still remarkably large. But by then, the gospel groups had stolen the show. The rock 'n' rollers now came out with only a couple of hours to showcase their acts.

Shake, Rattle, 'n' Roll

A disc jockey from Atlanta, Harry Turner, known as "Dr. Rock," took over as emcee. Harry also headed a major rock 'n' roll and vocal harmony celebration slated for June of the following year in Charleston. The event would be entitled This Magic Moment. Before the show, we had talked for a while, and Harry asked me if I would consider becoming a member of their advisory board. I agreed.

He also gave me a heads-up about one of the rock 'n' roll acts. "You are not going to believe this guy, Little Hamilton. He looks and sounds exactly like James Brown—about 5'8" and a very similar build. He even wears his hair the same way James does. He is purported to be a very close relative—maybe a half-brother."

As soon as Little went into his act, doing his one-leg struts across the stage, I was a believer. Harry was right!

Up until then, I had not heard of Little Hamilton, but I was quite familiar with the next group—Archie Bell and The Drells—who performed their popular "Tighten Up." I loved hearing it live.

At the finale, all of the rock 'n' roll singers gathered onstage with Bill Pinkney and The Drifters at the center to a final round of enthusiastic applause. I, of course, was down front, shooting pictures of the unfolding

Bill Pinkney and Prentiss Barnes—Vicksburg, MS

Ali-Ollie Woodson, Bill Morris, & Bill Pinkney at Bill's home following a recording session

The Williams Brothers and Bill

Bill Pinkney (The Drifters), Bill Morris, Steve Cropper (Booker T & The MGs), Tim Hauser (Manhattan Transfer)—Pioneer Awards in LA 1996

Carl Gardner of the Coasters shaking hands with Archie Bell (hat)—Bill Pinkney Celebration Sumter, SC

Ira Tucker and The Dixie Hummingbirds—Bill Pinkney celebration—Sumter, SC

Tommy Ellison (Singing Stars)—Bill Pinkney Celebration—Sumter, SC

Little Hamilton—Bill Pinkney Celebration—Sumter, SC

Bill singing with The Drifters at Hal & Mal's—Jackson, MS

Johnnie Taylor—Jackson, MS Jubilee Jam

Bill Pinkney of The Drifters (left) and Bill Morris (right)—Bill loved to hear me hit that note at the end of "Daddy's Home" so he made me do it again

Following our recording of The Drifters CD—we celebrated at Bill's home (Left to Right) Prentiss Barnes (The Moonglows), Richard Dunbar (Knight Brothers/Drifters), Bill Morris, Bill Pinkney, Gregory Johnson, and Chuck Cockerham

The Original Drifters posing for me in Jackson, MS with their blue suits

Counselman Kenneth Stokes presenting Bill Pinkney and The Original Drifters with the certificate from the Governor declaring it "Bill Pinkney and The Original Drifters Day" in Mississippi. Bill's response, "If my Mama could see me now."

(Left to Right) Eugene Tompkins (The Mellows), Maurice Williams (The Zodiacs), Billy Scott (The Prophets), Grace Satterfield (Dale and Grace), and Bill Pinkney (The Drifters) – Press Conference Charleston, SC

Maurice Williams (formerly of the Gladiolas and the Zodiacs) "Little Darlin" and "Stay"

The Governor's wife (Mrs. Pat Fordice) and Prentiss Barnes receiving the Ageless Heroes Award

tribute—over 200 photos in all! It was around 3:00 a.m. before the festivities concluded.

Exhausted, I drove back to the hotel, but it was another hour before I finally turned off the light. I didn't go to sleep right away. With all these rapid-fire decisions and knotty problems whirling in my head, I finally drifted off.

★　★　★

Up again around 9:30 a.m., I found myself in the lobby, visiting with Doug and Melvin Williams and others in his group. Before checking out, in walked Bill Pinkney.

"Bill," he began, chuckling in that deep-throated laugh of his, "I was comin' by to see you before we left for our next performance in Hick'ry, North Carolina."

"Then this is perfect timing," I returned. "I wanted to see you too."

It was noon—time for all of us to part. Bill and The Drifters were headed to the Tar Heel state for a Saturday night performance and on to Chicago for a Mother's Day Special. I was on my way to Hilton Head to meet my daughters—my older daughter, Camille, and my younger daughter, Kathryn—who were working at the island resort that summer. Family time was always sweet. But then I was beginning to feel like Bill Pinkney and The Drifters were family, too.

~ 6 ~

TAKIN' CARE OF BUSINESS

On Sunday, a month after the Bill Pinkney celebration in Sumter, I received a call from Harry Turner. He had already become a friend. As a true aficionado of rock 'n' roll, Harry was a music historian, author, speaker, and winner of numerous awards and accolades, including "Beach Music Radio DJ of the Year" and a recipient of the "Industry Appreciation Award." He served as president of Beach Music Association International and, among other prestigious titles, was a consultant to the North Carolina Music Hall of Fame.

During our conversation, he asked me, as a member of the advisory board of This Magic Moment Festival, to come to Charleston on the next Thursday for a press conference. At this conference, they would announce the event to be held there the last week in June of the following year.

"Harry, do you know where I am going to be on Thursday?" I asked him.

"Nope. I have no idea."

"Strangely enough, I'm flying to Charleston and will arrive at 4:20 in the afternoon to speak to an insurance office the next morning."

"Well, could you make it a little earlier? The press conference begins at 2:30."

"Not sure I can do that, Harry. We have a lot of moving parts in transition right now."

Nevertheless, the idea intrigued me . . . and I tucked it away in the back of my mind.

Decision in D.C.

On Monday, the very next day, I received a call from Tom Wamberg, president of AALU (Association for Advanced Life Underwriting), and its executive director, David Stertzer. AALU is considered by many to be the most influential of all the insurance industry organizations and is comprised of the most widely respected professionals in the country. The organization meets annually in the nation's capital to share ideas and to keep abreast of current changes in legislation impacting the industry. I have had the privilege of speaking before this group on several occasions.

Tom and David wanted me to set up a Thursday meeting in D.C. with Senator Trent Lott, the majority leader of the Senate and a member of the Senate Finance Committee. There were some concerns about the language in a proposed tax bill that would have negative implications for our clients.

They knew that Trent was a friend of mine, both of us having graduated from Ole Miss. We had stayed in touch through the years. Consequently, I was now, unofficially at least, one of the insurance industry's chief unpaid lobbyists while Trent was in office. This was why they tagged me to arrange an appointment with him on Thursday.

But it wasn't that easy.

"Don't see how, guys. I'm slammed that day. Besides, Trent would give us an audience on the phone, I feel sure. . ." Then, recalling my conversation with Harry Turner of the day before, my mind took off at lightning speed. *If I could make arrangements to see Trent in D.C., then could get down to Charleston by two o'clock for the press conference, I could work in all three appointments.*

"OK," I backtracked a little. "If I could make it to D.C. on Wednesday and schedule a meeting with Trent on Thursday morning, I would still need you to figure out a way for me to get to Charleston by 2:00 that afternoon."

To my astonishment, they were not fazed. "No problem," Tom said. "We can arrange that."

But there *was* still a problem. "Well, I don't even know if I can get an appointment with Trent on such short notice. That's not a given."

Sure enough, when I called Trent's office and spoke to his scheduler, she verified my concern. "Oh, Mr. Morris, there is no way Senator Lott could meet with you on Thursday. They are going to be sequestered."

After pleading a bit more, I said, "Tell Trent that the only reason for my trip to Washington would be to discuss an extremely important matter with him! Please see what you can do."

About ten minutes later, she called back. "The Senator said he will meet you in the majority leader's office at noon."

When I relayed this information to Tom and David at AALU, they booked a Delta flight for me to arrive in Washington on Wednesday afternoon. Things were moving rapidly. With Tom indicating that he would fly me down to Charleston via his private jet, I notified Harry Turner that it looked like I might be able to make that press conference, after all.

★   ★   ★

When Tom and I arrived at the majority leader's office that Thursday morning, we were escorted into a room where Trent was waiting with the attorney who advises the Senate Finance Committee.

"Trent," I began, "we have great concern about some of the language in this legislation. We understand that it is now in the Joint Committee on Taxation. If the bill passes as it reads now, there could be serious consequences for our small business clients."

We then explained the specifics.

Trent listened attentively, then directed a question to the attorney. "Is this correct?"

The attorney nodded. "Yes."

"Fix it!" said Trent.

With that, he picked up the phone and called Representative Bill Archer, chairman of the House Ways and Means Committee, and informed him of the problem. "We have resolved the matter on our end. You take care of it in your committee."

With an affirmative response from Chairman Archer, we thanked Trent for his leadership. As a private citizen of this great country, I was also personally grateful to be of assistance in crafting a piece of legislation that would benefit Americans, small business owners in particular.

We finished with our meeting and headed to Washington National Airport where Tom's pilot was waiting for us. The flight was exceptionally pleasant on this early-summer day, and we were off to our next destination, feeling satisfied that we had achieved our goal in D.C. We arrived in Charleston at approximately 2:20 p.m.—just ten minutes before the press conference was scheduled to begin.

Just in Time

With a taxi already standing by, the driver took me directly to the Dock Street Theater in downtown historic Charleston. I parked my bags at the ticket desk downstairs and hurried up to the room where the conference was underway. The press conference was about twenty minutes in, with television cameramen and photographers recording the announcement of This Magic Moment Music Festival.

The moment I entered the room through a side door, Bill Pinkney spotted me. He stepped up to the microphone. "I think you know that The Original Drifters have just recorded a gospel CD," he said. "I want you to meet my executive producer, who has come all the way from Jackson, Mississippi, to be here today." There was brief applause, and announcements continued.

Ultimately, we all converged at the front of the room for a photo session. There I was able to meet one of my favorite singers, Maurice Williams of The Zodiacs (originally The Gladiolas), the first to release the Excello label hit "Little Darling." I can still hear the raw, rhythmic beat of their rendition of this song drifting to me through the airwaves from Nashville's WLAC. The melody carried me far away to places unknown—a part of the mystical experience of the vocal group harmony of that era. This song was later covered by The Diamonds—a bit different version, yet both fabulous. Another one of Maurice Williams's songs was "Stay," which Jackson Browne later covered with verve.

Also present at the press conference were Billy Scott; Eugene Tompkins of The Mellows; Grace Satterfield of Dale and Grace ("I'm Leaving It All Up to You"); my friend Harry Turner; Joe Riley, the mayor of Charleston; Earle Morris, comptroller general of South Carolina; and various disc jockeys and media representatives. I was then introduced to the man who is purported to be the originator of "the shag," a dance made famous in Georgia, the Carolinas, and throughout the Low Country, claiming devotees as far north as Newport News, Virginia, and as far south as St. Augustine, Florida.

To close the event, Bill and the group of singers who were assembled at the front of the room did an a cappella version of "This Magic Moment" and finished with The Spaniels' hit "Goodnight, Sweetheart, Goodnight."

After the media dispersed, several of us joined Bill Pinkney outside the Dock Street Theater. I captured the moment by flagging a tourist walking by and handing him my camera. He proceeded to take a photograph of Bill, me, Harry, his wife Jean and Eugene Tompkins in front of the theater with St. Phillips, one of the most iconic churches of Charleston, in the background. Its majestic steeple, piercing the sky, seemed to be relaying a message from our Heavenly Father: *I have orchestrated all of this.* Chills ran down my spine, and I knew this was not about me. Something far greater was developing.

I went back to check in to my hotel, The Planters Inn, in the heart of Charleston. It did not take long for me to freshen up, and I was soon on my way to the Hilton, where the party was in full swing. I learned that every Thursday evening, one of the local radio stations hosted a gathering there for shag dancing and fellowship from 5:30 until 10:00 p.m..

The spacious room was overflowing and pulsating with energy left over from the press conference. Several times during the course of the evening, the DJ, Leo Wyndham, asked Bill to lip-sync "America the Beautiful," "White

Christmas," and "Drifting Along" as he played our CD. The crowd was exuberant. They loved Bill Pinkney in these parts. Rightfully so, for he was so much a part of their lives.

Bill and I laughed a lot that night. Then, in a rare moment, we found some seats in the back of the room. Bill was enjoying a glass of orange juice when I made a request.

"We are so close, I don't often ask for your autograph," I told him, "but I would really appreciate it if you would sign this. Just your name will be sufficient."

Bill grinned and took the brochure from me, pulling out a pen from his inside coat pocket. When he handed me the piece of paper, I saw that he had scrawled much more than his name. I read: "To Bill Morris—my very best friend. Sincerely, Bill Pinkney of The Original Drifters."

I could barely make out the last words for the tears that sprang to my eyes. I felt exactly the same toward him. While I couldn't verbalize the emotion at that instant, I'm sure he could read my heart. When God forges a friendship, words are often unnecessary.

The mood shifted once again, and Bill began to open up about something that had been bothering him. "I've got an appointment on July Ninth to see a doctor who is a thyroid specialist," he began. "I've had some swelling in my neck that's been worryin' me some."

"Bill, are they concerned about cancer or anything like that?"

"Yeah. My first doctor said it might be just the beginnin' of a cancer. . ."

I must say, this announcement came out of the blue. Immediately, I put my hands on Bill's neck to feel the swelling and to silently offer a prayer. I wanted my friend Bill Pinkney to live for a long, long time.

Havin' Some Fun

There were some lighter moments in the evening too—such as the time I turned over a glass of wine on Grace Satterfield! Fortunately, it was white wine. She squealed and jumped up to avoid being completely drenched, mopping up the moisture with her napkin.

"Oh, Grace, I am so sorry!" I apologized. "Please . . . send me the cleaning bill."

"Oh, that won't be necessary," she said, laughing it off.

"Yes, but I won't have any evidence that I was really with you unless I have a cleaning bill to show for it."

Oh, how we laughed! She was such a good sport about the incident.

It was a marvelous evening, and I had fun crooning with Grace, Maurice Williams, Eugene Tompkins, and Herb Hardesty, the marvelous sax player associated with Fats Domino's band out of New Orleans.

Later, as Bill Pinkney and I were visiting about the events of the day, I recall that he quietly repeated what he had written on the brochure. "You know, Bill, you are one of the best friends I have in my life."

This time, I had the composure and presence of mind to reply, "Bill, you are one of my best friends too."

The evening ended early for me as I headed back to my hotel. I intended to be well prepared for my presentation the next morning. Although music feeds my soul, insurance is my business. It was important that I get to bed, for I had some eager minds that deserved my best. My daughter Kathryn, who was working on Hilton Head Island that summer, would be joining me in Charleston for the weekend, and I was looking forward to spending it with her after addressing the insurance agency.

★ ★ ★

Following the marvelous time with Kathryn—enjoying the Lowcountry cuisine and shopping on King Street—my action-packed week concluded. On the flight home, there was time for deeper reflection. There had been many unforgettable moments—our success with the tax bill in D.C., seeing Bill Pinkney again in Charleston, mingling with the musical giants and hearing their heart expressed in unforgettable lyrics and that ever-present rhythmic beat.

A couple of days later, Doug Williams told me he had recommended that our CD be nominated for a Grammy. As executive producer, that was music to my ears. But that thrill was not to be compared to the deep, deep satisfaction of Bill Pinkney's words to me: "Bill, you're one of the best friends I have in my life."

~ 7 ~

LET THE GOOD TIMES ROLL

Surreal. *A moment suspended in time, captured by my camera, The Drifters in their royal blue suits, leaning in to a single microphone as they had many times before in the fifties. Stage lights bathing them in a luminous blue wash as they croon the music that has thrilled thousands through the decades.*

It was the night of the Jackson Music Awards when Bill Pinkney and The Original Drifters were again to be honored—both Sunday night, in the Gospel category, and Monday, in R&B. The event was held at the Harvey Hotel (now a Marriott) in downtown Jackson.

The foremost order of business the first evening was a television interview I had arranged with the NBC affiliate WLBT's Rosalyn Anderson, who asked probing questions that allowed Bill to be at his best. He answered in his warmly personal way.

Throughout the evening, various church groups performed. Camille was with me this time, and while she does not share the same intensity of my passion for music, she was fascinated throughout the entire proceedings. So many outstanding gospel artists. I was in my element.

"If She Could See Me Now!"

After a few hours' sleep Sunday night, Monday morning dawned, clear and bright—a day we had been anticipating for some time. At ten o'clock, a news conference was held with the ABC affiliate, WAPT. Various local government officials spoke, offering kudos to some of the performers who were to be honored that night. Councilman Kenneth Stokes read a proclamation from the city council honoring The Drifters. Then, Jesse Thompson, executive director of the Jackson Music Awards, on behalf of Governor Kirk Fordice, proclaimed July 22, 1996, "Bill Pinkney and The Original Drifters' Day" in Mississippi.

"Oh, if my mama could see me now!" Bill exclaimed with his endearing chuckle. As usual, Bill went on to acknowledge all of the people who had helped him achieve this distinction, "especially my executive producer and manager, Mr. William Morris." Of course, I was not his manager, but he thought of me in that way.

I had set up a meeting for Bill and his group with WMPR, one of the black gospel radio stations in Jackson. The meeting was scheduled for a little after eleven o'clock that morning. DJ Robert Hatcher conducted a fabulous interview and played quite a number of the songs from our CD. With several irons of my own in the fire, I had left the remainder of the afternoon open for the guys to get some rest before the big night.

A little before seven, I found my dear friend Prentiss Barnes waiting for me on the mezzanine level of the Harvey Hotel. I had invited him to join us for the evening event—the R&B portion of the Jackson Music Awards—and it was good to see him. But I was feeling ill-prepared to deliver the introduction for Bill and his crooners a little later when they would be receiving the Legends Award.

Asking Prentiss and Camille to excuse me for a few minutes, I found a quiet spot and isolated myself until I could jot down a few thoughts in conjunction with the CD liner notes I had used in previous introductions. Having done enough public speaking to know the importance of adequate rehearsal, I wouldn't feel confident until I had more of an idea how to proceed.

It's Just a Matter of Time

A few minutes later, I rejoined Prentiss and Camille and settled in to enjoy the evening. The show was spectacular, with singers such as Willie Clayton and Johnny Taylor performing some of the songs that had catapulted them to stardom.

Shortly before I was scheduled to go onstage, I told the people in charge that I would need a light on the podium. But no sooner had a stagehand complied with my request than someone else approached me, saying, "You won't be able to use the podium, Mr. Morris. You'll have to make your introduction from a single microphone out on the stage."

To make matters even worse, I got a frog in my throat and had trouble clearing it. That was the last straw!

At that moment, I heard, "And now William Morris, president of Hallelujah Productions, will introduce Bill Pinkney and The Original Drifters!"

Stepping to the microphone at the far end of the stage, the bright spotlights almost blinded me. I could see nothing in the audience but inky darkness. But feeling peaceful, I relaxed and began to speak from my heart about the man of the hour—Bill Pinkney—musical legend, pacesetter, warm human being, and my good friend. About that time, Bill himself strolled across the stage, followed by Gregory, Richard, and Vernon. I put my hand on Bill's shoulder and continued to speak into the mic, pausing at one point to introduce our mutual friend, Prentiss Barnes.

During the introduction, I began to pick up more and more steam—almost as if I were announcing a major athletic event, with momentum building toward a crescendo. As I told about Bill's participation in World War II, emerging as a highly decorated war hero with four bronze stars and a presidential citation, the crowd was wildly enthusiastic—applauding, yelling, and whistling. "You should hear his sincerity when he sings 'America the Beautiful,'" I added. More whistles and shouts.

When the applause died down, I shared a little of our early encounter. "When I met this man in the 1960s in Oxford, Mississippi, where I was a college student, I had no idea of the path our lives would take . . . or that we would reconnect years later. Nor did I know how richly God would bless our relationship or that one day, I would have the privilege of being not only his friend, but his producer. So, tonight, it is my great honor to confer upon Bill Pinkney and The Original Drifters the Legends Award for Outstanding Success in the field of Rock 'n' Roll."

I began handing out the awards. Soon after I left the stage, the group swung into a soaring medley of favorites, beginning with "What Ya Gonna Do?"

I have heard these Drifters many times, but nothing approached the magnitude of their scintillating performance that night. They must have struck a chord with their listeners, too, for the audience response inspired an even greater effort on the part of the entire group, and the guys poured their hearts into each song. "This Magic Moment" . . . "Dance with Me" . . . "Up on the Roof" . . . "Under the Boardwalk" . . . and Sam Cooke's "Chain Gang." Every note, every close harmony, every nuance of sound was pitch perfect. And the crowd loved it—jumping to their feet, screaming, waving throughout the entire performance—exceeding our utmost expectations!

Afterwards, several people came up to me to tell me how much the introduction had meant to them. One man said, "It was all I could do to keep from crying." Then Malaco Records executive Tommy Couch Jr. rushed over to me, wanting to book The Drifters for New Year's Eve in Destin, Florida.

Ultimately, there came the time when it was necessary to say farewell. Bill and his guys were headed to Virginia to perform the next night and then on to upstate New York. And once again, I could dream about all that had transpired on this special evening—the memories we were making and the unique friendships we had been given.

At Last

On a weekend in early 1997, Bill Pinkney's Drifters performed at the newly re-opened Ameristar Entertainment Center in Vicksburg. The show was sold out for all performances both nights. Camille and I went over Saturday and took Bill Purdy and his wife, Suzie, with us. Bill is a Carolinian and a true fan of this music—especially beach music. He and Suzie love to dance the shag, showing off their well-executed dance steps.

We found our seats, compliments of Bill Pinkney—right down front near the stage. The pre-show featured a couple of new people in addition to Frankie (Bill's female singer). Joining him were Toni Williams, formerly with Bill Dogget ("Honky Tonk"), and Roscoe Robinson, who appeared to be maybe seventy-five years old and had sung with the Five Mississippi Blind Boys. Toni sang "At Last," made famous by the great Etta James, and Roscoe did a fine job on "I Who Have Nothing," originally a hit by Ben E. King, a lead singer of a later set of Drifters.

Then Bill's group took the stage. Their performance that night was over the top. And the crowd was monstrous. Energized by the electricity in the room, Bill danced, he gyrated, he grooved to the music, thoroughly entertaining his audience. The applause rarely ceased from the first song to the last—over an hour later.

Toward the end of each act, Bill would come down off the stage into the audience with his portable mic and complete whatever song The Drifters were doing at the time. He would then begin to testify as to what God has meant in his life. By then, I had heard his testimony many times, but I was completely unprepared for what came next.

"Some of you may know that I been feelin' a little poorly lately. The doctor told me I might have the beginnin' of a cancer in my thyroid gland. Well, I believe I'm healed through prayer and a better diet, because I don't want to take any surgery. But the doc thinks I only have 'bout a year to live. . ."

You could have heard the proverbial pin drop as the room went completely silent. At this point, Bill was standing in front of me when he began telling the story of the gospel CD and our friendship. With tears forming in my eyes and the spotlight fully on us, I rose to my feet to help him back onto the stage. The audience broke into thunderous applause.

I sat down, and Bill went into the song "Candlelight," followed by "I Need Thee." As he continued to make his way through the audience, the people got up to shake his hand or hug him. Ladies—black and white alike—as well as many of the men, were deeply moved.

All of the singers then converged onto the stage, and Frankie began to proclaim, with volume, as she did at the end of each show: "The only surviving member of The Original Drifters . . . Rock & Roll Hall of Fame member . . . Mr. Bill Pinkney!" The entire group exited the stage, returning twice to take their bows.

With Frankie announcing Bill one last time, he broke down in tears. As he left the stage, I saw him cover his eyes with one hand and knew what he must be feeling. The audience obviously adored him, and he still had trouble comprehending just how much. I only knew that he always considered it something of a miracle that God had used him so powerfully to reconcile the races. Oddly enough, Mississippi—once a hotbed of racial prejudice in the deep South—embraced him perhaps as much as any place he performed.

I raced backstage, eager to find Bill, and was told he had gone over to the other side to sign some autographs. I caught him as he was just about to walk over. We wrapped our arms around each other in a wordless embrace. I didn't know what to say. It didn't matter. Words were unnecessary.

~ 8 ~

THE WONDER OF YOU

New York, New York! What a wonderful town! Camille and the Big Apple go together like "love and marriage," "horse and carriage," and "Bill Morris and Rock 'n' Roll." In February 1997, Camille and I were off to NYC on an excursion that would take us to the Rhythm & Blues Foundation's Eighth Annual Pioneer Awards—my third year to attend and her first—and a shopping trip for her to scout out some additions to her antiques and design business.

As is the case with so many wives in our era, Camille worked tirelessly while our children were young, devoting herself to our family. When our younger daughter, Kathryn, finished high school and left for college at Ole Miss, Camille and I were empty nesters. With more time on her hands, I knew my wife needed something else on which to focus her creative gifts, so I encouraged her to explore interior design. Consequently, whenever possible, she would accompany me on trips, seeking out antique dealers, fabric design shops, etc.

Flying into LaGuardia a day early, we checked into the Hilton Hotel on The Avenue of the Americas where the event was being hosted. At the hotel counter, I asked the clerk if Bill Pinkney of The Drifters had arrived. To my disappointment, she informed me that he wasn't registered as a guest, nor was he expected.

Since Camille needed every available moment for shopping, she struck out on her own, and I went to our room to relax and make a few calls. The first number I dialed was Bill Pinkney's, but he didn't answer. A nagging doubt gave me a momentary twinge of concern: *Is he out with the guys at a gig . . . or is he ill?* A further check with Maxine revealed that he was indeed on the road performing. Relieved, I decided to surprise Camille by unpacking her bags. When she returned to the room, laden with packages and completely exhausted, she found her clothing and accessories neatly organized in the closet and drawers.

"Darlin', that's one of the nicest things you've ever done for me!" she said, her speech flavored with Southern sweetness.

Hmm, I thought, making a mental note. *Maybe I should do something like this more often.* It was a first for me, but, judging from the warm reception this good deed had rated, it would definitely not be the last.

When No One Else Can Understand

Opening day of this celebration would bring a never-ending parade of my favorite R&B artists, and I didn't want to miss a single moment. Not all wives would understand this kind of obsession, but as I have said before, my wife is different. She has always encouraged me to pursue my passion and simply be myself. But I knew she would not enjoy the pre-awards activities—such as the press conference and photo session. So I urged her to take a cab and visit a few more shops while I attended these scheduled events.

"Just be back in time to put on that gorgeous outfit you brought along for the reception tonight," I reminded her. "You'll look fabulous!"

She blew me a kiss and hurried off, eager to discover more unique items for her design clients.

One of the first people I saw at the news conference was Little Milton Campbell, a native of Mississippi, who used to play at our fraternity house back in the early 1960s. The Dekes at Ole Miss were known for extraordinary bands and parties. "Man, what are you doing all the way up here?" he asked, strolling over to greet me. I explained my involvement with the foundation; he seemed pleased.

During the photo session, there was a steady stream of celebrities whom I had the pleasure of capturing on camera—David Crosby, Duke Fakir of The Four Tops, Little Milton, Ruth Brown, and Suzanne Jenkins, the executive director. Shortly after I had shot some film with these greats, I spotted Bonnie Raitt and gave her a copy of our CD. "By the way, the invitation to do a duet with Bill Pinkney is still open, if you're interested." My tone was teasing, but I meant every word.

Camille was back with an hour to spare when I reached our room. I could hear her in the bathroom, spraying her hair. When she stepped out, she turned for me to zip her dress. I did the honors. "Darlin', I love that dress on you!" I said, holding out both her hands and twirling her about to get the full effect. "With your red hair and blue eyes . . . and that dress—you're a knock-out! I'm going to be so proud to introduce you to my friends."

I changed into my tux in record time. Camille straightened my tie, and we were off to the ballroom on the third floor. At the door, the registrar laughed. "Sorry, but you can't get in with *these.*"

Much to my disgust, in my haste I had picked up the VIP coat-check tickets! The kind lady did allow Camille to enter, and I rushed back to our room to retrieve the proper admittance forms.

With tickets in hand, I hustled to catch the next elevator down. And when the elevator door opened, I was surprised to see Ruby Nash of Ruby and the Romantics ("Our Day Will Come"). On the ride down to the venue, we had a short but pleasant visit, which charged my energy and got it flowing.

Upon my second appearance in the reception area, I found Camille visiting with Diz Russell of The Orioles and his wife, Millie. Diz and his group had a close relationship with The Moonglows.

As we began to chat, Diz offered some fascinating facts about some mutual friends. "Prentiss Barnes and I shared an apartment at one time way back," he said. "And Bobby Lester and Harvey Fuqua used to do other more labor-intensive jobs before they became famous singing stars! Back then, it was tough to make ends meet."

Diz seemed quite excited when I mentioned that I had helped produce The Drifters' latest CD. I then gave him a copy.

At that point, Millie spoke up. "Diz, give him one of the tapes of that new thing you guys did."

"Well, it hasn't been released yet, but will be shortly," he explained and handed me the tape.

When I listened later, I could tell that this one was a winner. I soon had a favorite off the album—"Let Them Talk"—originally cut by Little Willie John. It is a song with real emotional pull.

Moving on, Camille and I followed the crowd into the next room to get a bite to eat from the sumptuous buffet, then sat with Henry Fambrough and his wife, Norma, and daughter Heather. Henry is with the famed group The Spinners. I can recall vividly when I first heard their initial song recorded in 1961—"That's What Girls Are Made For." As members of The Spinners and others joined us at the table, I noticed that, time after time, Henry would get up to find chairs for everyone, making sure that all were comfortably seated. He is what I call "a class act."

With Camille absorbed in conversation with Norma, I made my way through the room, speaking with many singers whose music I love: Earl "Speedo" Carol of The Cadillacs, Clarence "Gatemouth" Brown, and Chuck Jackson, famous for "Any Day Now." Chuck thought he knew me. We had met before, perhaps in L. A. Upon striking up a conversation with William Bell ("You Don't Miss Your Water"), George Benson arrived and joined in. Next I saw Gene Chandler, most famous for "Duke of Earl." We had fun talking with Billy Vera ("At This Moment") and Wolfe Stevenson, senior vice-president of Malaco Records. Wolfe is a great guy—very gifted too. I was always glad to see a fellow Jacksonian at these events.

Just before the awards ceremony was about to begin, I spotted Bonnie Raitt again and called to her: "Bonnie, I want to get a picture of you and my wife together. I think you two redheads should look really great."

Bonnie took a good look at Camille and exclaimed, "Oh, you're *beautiful!*"

So was the shot!

★   ★   ★

No sooner were we seated at our table, comprised of people from Polygram Records, *Billboard Magazine*, and others, then Gladys Knight dropped by to chat for a moment.

Suzanne Jenkins kicked off the program by explaining the purpose of the Rhythm & Blues Foundation in helping deserving artists receive recognition and remuneration for years of work in the R&B field. A sensational orchestra was once again assembled, including Steve Cropper and led by the great saxophone player Maceo Parker, originally of the James Brown Orchestra.

The program began, recognizing this year's award recipients. Among them were William Bell, Gary "U.S." Bonds, Gene Chandler, Gloria Lynne, Smokey Robinson & the Miracles, Phil Upchurch, and Van "Piano Man" Walls, along with others with whom I had socialized during the evening. The Lifetime Award—the "granddaddy" of them all—went to The Four Tops.

Each individual recipient or group then performed one or more of their top songs. But it was Gene Chandler who stole the show with his rendition of "Duke of Earl." He appeared onstage wearing a black cape with a red lining and holding a black top hat and cane in one hand and a portable mic in the other. I knew that Camille was caught up in the mood Gene was creating when, several times, I saw the sheen of tears in her eyes. I was so glad she was able to live in the moment as deeply as I.

Later, while receiving their awards, many of the singers teared up, recalling years of pent-up emotion—hurt, disappointment, and frustration. Yet, virtually all of these pioneers expressed gratitude to the industry for giving them the privilege of using their talent to benefit the public. As we lingered in the presentation hall to chat with Stevie Wonder, Smokey Robinson, Gloria Lynne, and others, the evening eventually wound down—but not until 2:00 a.m.! I always hated for these moments to end. Yet even though another event was over, it felt like it had just begun.

You Give Me Hope

After seeing Camille off on her flight home to Jackson, I went on to the AALU meeting in Washington, D.C., where I delivered the opening invocation. The closing speaker was General Colin Powell, a man with a commanding presence. I was privileged to meet him afterwards and give him one of our CDs. In the past few days, so much had taken place in such rapid succession, I felt I was in the eye of a hurricane.

My first morning back in the office, I opened up a package that had arrived in my absence. Enclosed were four chalk renderings of an oil painting John Carroll Doyle, an artist friend from Charleston, was completing for me. The subject was a quartet of black singers out of the 1950s. It was an absolutely masterful piece, the very essence of the spirit of that era! As I sat at my desk, imagining the splendor of the finished product, I was reminded of how this art project had begun.

Back in the spring of 1995, Camille and I had taken our daughter Kathryn to visit the campus of the College of Charleston, where she was considering applying. With our daughter's extraordinary gifting for art, we felt that this city of rich history and romance might offer her everything she would need to excel in her field.

In the process, we were directed to a local artist of renown, John Carroll Doyle, whose studio was located on King Street. Climbing the stairs and stepping into his spacious, second-story studio, with natural light from the skydomes overhead, I was immediately captivated by the quality of the artwork displayed throughout. One could feel the passion and energy pouring from his paintbrush onto the canvas. This man produced museum-quality work, and today, many of his pieces hang in boardrooms across the country. He had some strong words of encouragement for Kathryn to continue pursuing other institutions, as well, and we left deeply moved by the entire experience. A few years later, Kathryn was a featured artist at one of Charleston's fine art galleries.

Although she ultimately chose Ole Miss, where she received scholastic and art scholarships, the impact of John Carroll Doyle's work had made its mark on Kathryn and on me. Now I longed to own one of these masterpieces—despite the high price tag! But which one? The answer came to me in a dream: the passion of my heart, the black vocal groups of the 1950s. Would it be possible to commission John to do a painting of one of these groups—preferably Bill Pinkney and The Original Drifters—set back in the earlier days when they had clustered around a single microphone? Camille urged me to put in a call to John.

When I told him what I had in mind, he was eager to tackle the job, but warned me he was booked ahead by six months with commissions for several nationally known corporations. Secondly, although he did not paint portraits, he would be glad to use The Drifters or photos of other groups as models, so to speak, but that his painting would be more generic in feel. And I knew just the photograph he could use as a reference—the one I had shot the night of the Jackson Music Awards the previous year!

Almost exactly six months later, a sizeable container arrived at our home. It was what I had been waiting for. When I finally opened the large parcel—well-packaged and crated—I was overwhelmed! Seeing the oil painting itself—a dramatic thirty- by forty-inch piece—I knew that it exceeded everything I had expected. It was Camille, my wonderful wife, who purchased it for me. A song made famous by Ray Peterson—"The Wonder of You"—sums up my love and esteem for her. After several decades of marriage, I continue to discover new facets of her personality and character. She is, truly, a wonder!

Her gift to me, John's painting, now hangs in the most prominent place in our home, alongside a few of our daughter's beautiful works, reminiscent of some of the most joyful moments in our lives. John had scribbled a tentative title for the work on the back of the painting—*Doo Wop*. But with Harry Turner's upcoming music festival in June, the answer was clear. The painting should be called *This Magic Moment*, also later to be used as the title of this book.

Meanwhile, as a member of Harry's advisory board, I would be in touch with him about details of the festival. It occurred to me that one way to advertise the event would be to commission posters and T-shirts bearing the slogan "This Magic Moment." He agreed. Done.

~ 9 ~

DOIN' THE SHAG

On Thursday, June 26, 1997, Camille and I planned to head to Charleston for the big event for which Harry Turner and his committee had been preparing for over a year—This Magic Moment Festival. As had been our custom if traveling by air, my wife and I would go separately. Our plan was to arrive in time for the VIP reception on Thursday night for sponsors and various contributors.

When I set out for the airport in Jackson, stormy weather was forecast and it was beginning to rain. As a result, my flight was delayed by an hour. But Camille, who was booked on a later flight, had to wait around for five hours as the front closed in. Her story was bizarre. In addition to rain delays, she had to endure further missed and aborted flights. As always, though, she was a trooper. When her plane finally landed and I was able to pick her up at the Charleston airport at approximately 11:00 p.m., we both burst out laughing. By now, of course, the reception was drawing to a close. But we were both too exhausted from our travels to take in the festivities, and we turned in "early"—if you want to call it that.

Since the show on Friday was not scheduled to open until 3:00 p.m., Camille and I spent the morning strolling down King Street, poking around in the quaint antique shops, and cultivating some good professional connections for her. Leaving Camille to continue shopping—we agreed that she would join me at the entrance gate at 7:00 p.m.—I made my way to the festival venue.

Brittlebank Park is situated beside the beautiful Ashley River, a couple of miles from the very heart of downtown Charleston. A covered bandstand had been erected on a large grassy area overlooking the river, with great live oaks standing sentinel over the grounds. Here, Harry had estimated, would be the ideal spot for the fans to gather. They could bring folding chairs or blankets to sit on, while others listened to the music from the comfort of deck chairs on their boats, docked along the banks of the river. Behind the bandstand were tents and trailers where the entertainers could change their outfits or relax between sets. It was quite a setup—one that had required months of thought and planning, with Harry Turner taking the lion's share of the responsibility.

Apparently, the weather front had followed us from Jackson, for a light rain began to fall intermittently as I was enjoying the music of The Flamingos, Maurice Williams and the Zodiacs, The Impressions, and Pure Gold. We soon learned that this was an omen for the weekend. Still, the misty rain did little to dampen the spirits of either performers or audience.

As chairman of the festival, Harry was kind enough to give me a VIP pass so I could have access to the back, where I could mingle with those heroes of mine. Not wanting to miss a note of this mystical music or a moment of fellowship, I found myself dashing back and forth from the audience, where I was able to photograph the groups during their performances, and backstage again to visit with the singers, one on one. As a bonus, I met so many outstanding attendees—people whose love of this genre of music matched my own. Camille and I later commented on the fact that the audience for this event was exceptional—kind, courteous, and thoroughly engaged in the proceedings. They did not seem to mind the rain that had now escalated to a steady downpour.

Promptly at 7:00 p.m., Camille arrived at the gate. To avoid being drenched, we darted for the car and huddled there for a while to allow time for the storm to blow over. Harry hopped into the car, too, and finished a plate of pasta and chicken that he had grabbed on the run. We commiserated with him for a few minutes before he left us to resume his duties.

With nothing further I could do to help Harry, Camille and I decided to drive into town and have dinner; we would come back later, when the rain had subsided, to catch some of the final acts of the evening. We dined at Carolina's, protected from the elements. All the while, the wind was whipping the rain sideways through the bandstand, threatening to damage the musical instruments and sound equipment. The bands could not go on. As we learned later, the entertainment ended early while the crowd scattered to find shelter.

Unaware of this dilemma, Camille and I enjoyed our fabulous meal at the fashionable restaurant, where we met Nancy Snowden, the new owner. Afterward, with the rain still pelting the pavement, we decided to wait for the weather to clear before returning to the festival venue. Maybe by morning.

When we awoke on Saturday morning, it was still raining. As the show would not resume until noon, Camille opted for some more shopping and ventured out on her own, leaving me to look up Harry and some other friends to assess the progress of the festival. With all of the planning, we had not factored in the weather—to this extent, anyway.

In spite of the soggy conditions, to my surprise, there was a fairly sizeable crowd at the festival that afternoon. The people of South Carolina, in particular, have a passion for beach music, and the rain was not going to stop them. I continued my same routine—strolling back and forth from the front of the bandstand to the rear of the entertainers' tent to visit with these legends. I particularly enjoyed chatting with Maurice Williams of The Zodiacs; Sonny Turner, who sang lead with The Platters for twelve years; and Frankie Ford, who did "Sea Cruise," recorded on the Jackson, Mississippi record label—ACE Records.

Frankie's song triggered a thought: *If this rain doesn't let up, we'll be cruisin' all the way to the sea on the beautiful Ashley River!*

Doin' the Shag

Another casualty of the persistent bad weather was the giant Shag dancing lesson that was to be offered for those who were interested. Camille and I were definitely interested! We had always wanted to learn this dance, much like the traditional bop we had enjoyed in Mississippi, but with its own distinctive steps.

Alas, the dance floor—provided for just this purpose—was too slick from the rain, and the lesson was called off in the interest of safety. Nonetheless, some intrepid souls did get out and dance at their own risk. I watched for a while, noting the intricacy of some of the fancy footwork as the dancers kept time to the upbeat music—their feet flying, the men twisting and twirling their partners with exuberance. Their joy was contagious, and if Camille had been there, I would have been tempted to try it, as we knew some of the more basic steps.

Since 1984, the Shag, also known as "beach dancing," has been the official state dance of South Carolina, originating many years earlier at Myrtle Beach. Since then, the dance has evolved somewhat, and there are still Shag clubs, Hall-of-Fame shaggers, and national competitions.

While looking on, wondering if at any moment the energetic dancers were going to slip and slide off the now muddy platform, I spotted my buddy Clifford Curry from Nashville and Clarence "Frogman" Henry from New Orleans. Clarence's nickname seemed appropriate on a day like this! He remembered me, and we exchanged greetings. Meeting old friends and making new ones is half the fun at these gatherings. But Camille and I were still determined to learn how to do the Shag, even if we had to postpone the lessons.

With the rain now showing no signs of abating anytime soon, I made my way back to the hotel to meet Camille and arrived about the same time as she. Once more we decided to opt for dinner and then if the rain slacked off, we would go back again. It did not slack off; it only increased. How disappointing! Now the weather forecaster was talking about flash flood warnings. This meant that potentially the river could rise and flood the festival grounds. If so, the rest of Harry's well-laid plans would grind to a screeching halt.

On this dismal thought, Camille and I went to bed, not knowing if we would be packing up early the next morning to check out of our hotel and head for home.

Some Sunny Day

We will always believe that Bill Pinkney brought out the sun on that Sunday morning, the final day of the festival. Camille and I awoke to a brilliant sunrise. No ominous dark clouds hovered over the horizon. Although light showers were forecast for the afternoon, we could see nothing but blue skies.

With Bill and his Drifters scheduled to go on at 10:00 a.m., we arrived early, in time to hear an amazing solo voice singing "Any Day Now" and "I Don't Want to Cry." It was Chuck Jackson, an extraordinary performer with a marvelous talent. At the end of his program, I was backstage waiting for him, along with Harry, who was literally in tears. I'm sure Harry's show of emotion was partly from relief that Chuck had been willing to stay over one more day. But I knew that Harry, too, had been deeply moved by the performance.

Although the grounds were a complete mess from all the rain, and we were forced to tiptoe around large mud puddles, the crowd grew. Their dedication was a tribute to the performers, to the many people who had put forth the effort to bring this event to Charleston, and to the music genre itself.

When it was time for Bill Pinkney and The Drifters to begin their set, I hurried around to the front of the bandstand. I had been backstage, bantering with Bill and the guys—Vernon, Richard, Gregory, and Harold Jackson (a member who used to sing with The Drifters for years and had now rejoined the group). The long-awaited moment came. Bill and the guys filed onstage, backed by a band that played for them on their gospel set only.

The soothing sounds of "Peace in the Valley" settled over the crowd. With no further introduction, the group moved into Bill's signature "I Need Thee," and I could almost hear his mama singing to him.

With the sun now at its zenith, the humidity rose with the temperature—typical of summer in the South. Amid the applause that was somewhat subdued because of the reverent theme, Bill stepped away from the group and stumbled off the stage. Perspiration was rolling off his brow, and his shirt was soaked. He had to sit down. Paramedics who were standing by rushed over to offer him water, then doused him with a full bottle. As others realized what was happening, they, too, raced over to help.

One of the paramedics called an ambulance. I still remember the bewildered and disoriented expression on Bill's face as he was loaded into the emergency vehicle. We were reassured by the medics that this was likely related to overheating and would be temporary. But, with Bill's medical history, I was worried.

Unaware of their friend's condition, the rest of The Drifters finished their performance and left the stage. We then stood around out back, wondering about Bill's true state and if he would be able to return.

About that time, I heard a hauntingly beautiful voice. It was Ray Peterson, singing "The Wonder of You," made famous by the inimitable Elvis Presley. Never having met Ray in person, I knew him only by name and reputation for his many songs, including "Fever" and "Tell Laura I Love Her." I had heard that Ray had worked with Dick Clark, putting shows together on a national level, and that he was truly an industry icon. The sales of his songs have reportedly totaled in the millions.

Ray began by singing songs of praise, telling how as a broken man—one filled with pride, yet greatly discouraged and sinking into soul-deep darkness—he had been rescued. Our diverse audience was swept up in his story. Camille recalls those moments as her favorite part of the entire weekend.

Following Ray's stirring set, the show moved along with the Coastline band playing, then The Crystals, singing "Da Doo Ron Ron," "He's a Rebel," and "He's Sure the Boy I Love." The ladies looked fabulous in their red sequined dresses, shaking and shimmying as they had throughout their performances all these years.

Never far from my thoughts, though, was Bill Pinkney.

Stand by Me

Backstage again, I visited with Rick Sheppard, Charlie Thomas, and Ben E. King, all former lead singers with The Drifters. Meanwhile, spotting Jerry Butler wandering around, I called him over and we stepped outside the tent for a breath of fresh air between rain showers. With Jerry having a primary role with the foundation, as well as emceeing most of the musical specials on PBS—not to mention being a great singer in his own right—I presented him with a proposition.

"I don't know if you remember this, Jerry, but several years ago, I wrote a letter recommending Bill Pinkney for a Pioneer Award with the Rhythm & Blues Foundation. Considering that his career has spanned fifty-five years in South Carolina, he has been a part of the very fabric of this area. He has sung for weddings, graduations, Fourth of July celebrations, and on and on. He's an industry legend, and I think it's time we honored him again on the national stage. I don't care how it's done—as an entertainer, entrepreneur, songwriter, or whatever—let's just highlight his lifetime of achievements . . . while we still can."

Jerry nodded. "We should do that, but let's honor him for who he really is—one of The Original Drifters."

"I could not agree with you more," I said. "I just want to make sure we do it."

Seeing Ben E. King heading for the stage, I left Jerry and took my place in front of the bandstand. Ben E.'s vocal range is impressive—from tenor to bass-baritone. That afternoon, before an appreciative audience, he showcased his full range on such great songs as "Stand by Me" and "Don't Play that Song Again." He was a member of The Five Crowns before the group took over the name of The Drifters during the controversial transition.

The Tokens followed with "The Lion Sleeps Tonight." Jerry Butler was next, performing "For Your Precious Love." I couldn't help noticing several couples dancing, one locked in an embrace, most likely inspired by the romantic melody. I caught that magic moment on camera.

General Johnson and The Chairman of the Board turned in a stellar performance with "Give Me Just a Little More Time." General had a fine voice and was quite a showman, even singing some of The Drifters' songs just before they came back on. Then came the long-awaited moment when Bill Pinkney and The Original Drifters took the stage for their final set, joined by Charlie Thomas and Rick Sheppard.

Bill, now apparently revived after an IV at a local hospital, rocked out with the other guys on "What'cha Gonna Do?" and a couple of other early numbers. He then led in "America the Beautiful" as we had recorded it on our CD. Looking around at the audience, I recall seeing many a teary eye as The Drifters transitioned effortlessly into the "Battle Hymn of the Republic." Bill encouraged the crowd to sing along, and we responded with enthusiasm.

By now, his strength and energy were depleted. He lasted only for those three songs before he had to leave the stage and rest. At this point, Charlie Thomas and Rick Sheppard stepped in and took over Bill's spot, finishing with "Up on the Roof," "On Broadway," and other classic Drifters songs.

★   ★   ★

Camille had left around 3 o'clock as she couldn't put up with the mud any longer. I decided that I should join her back at the hotel. She had been a great sport—patient, tolerant, and so caring—when at times she may have felt ignored. I remember her now, waving at me at different times from afar. I didn't think it would be right to impose on her any further. How lucky I am to be married to this redhead who loves me so!

But before I left the grounds, I wanted to express my appreciation to those performers who had persevered through torrential rain, threatened flash flooding, mud, and heat to bring us these magic moments. First, I found Bill, embraced him, and told him how thankful I was for our treasured friendship.

One by one, I sought out the other singers, shook their hands, and looked them in the eye. "I just want to thank you for all the joy you have given me and millions of others over the years."

For several of them, it was like a light came on. They paused, returning my steady gaze, then replied, "You don't know how much it means to hear you say that."

It was as if they understood that my comments were not trivial words meant to impress. They came from the depths of my heart. In each case, I was seeing the essence of the person behind the performer. I was seeing the long road many of them had traveled—from humble beginnings to this present day. From pain and poverty to the applause of thousands of eager fans. I, personally, was applauding their steadfastness perhaps more than their showmanship.

Later, as I was leaving the festival grounds, I preserved the idyllic scene forever in my memory through the lens of my camera. Blue sky punctuated with drifts of puffy white clouds. Majestic oaks, their leaves riffling in a playful breeze. Boats swaying to the rhythm of the lazy river. The band was still playing the finale, "Shout," with all of the entertainers onstage for one grand performance. The crowd went wild—hands raised, feet tapping or jumping on the still muddy platform—until the final note sounded. I just had to take one last look before I left, never forgetting from whence this journey originated.

~ 10 ~

WHAT A WONDERFUL WORLD!

If you have made your way thus far into my recollections, you know that I am an aficionado of art and music and a lover of people. All kinds of people—black, white, down-and-outers, up-and-comers, faith-filled, secularists, Republicans, Democrats, Libertarians, and undecideds. As a result, I have quite an assortment of friends—none more precious to me, of course, than Prentiss Barnes and Bill Pinkney.

In early December, having spoken with Jerry Butler about Bill in Charleston last summer, I called the Rhythm & Blues Foundation in Washington, D.C., to find out the exact date of the next event, as well as to learn whom the foundation would be honoring. As the list was read, the voice on the other end of the line continued: "...and Bill Pinkney, Charlie Thomas, and Johnny Moore of The Drifters." I was elated! This honor for my friends was overdue. I couldn't miss this and made my reservations right then and there for the annual gala to be held on February 25, 1999.

★   ★   ★

As the date approached, Camille and I flew to Austin to attend the National Financial Partners meeting. I was to go on from there to Los Angeles for the Pioneer Awards ceremony.

Bill and Willie Morris (Dear Friend and author of *North Toward Home*)—book signing at Lemuria Bookstore Jackson, MS

Duke Fakir of the Four Tops and Bill—Press Conference in NYC

Stevie Wonder (center), and Fred Cash (right—The Impressions)—Pioneer Awards Press Conference NYC

Johnnie Taylor—R&B Pioneer Awards LA 1996

Bo Diddley Pioneer Awards LA 1996

Bill and Bonnie Raitt—R&B Press Conference NYC

Jerry Butler and Camille Morris—Pioneer Awards NYC

Henry Fambrough (The Spinners) and his wife—Pioneer Awards NYC

Bill and the Duke of Earl—Gene Chandler—Pioneer Awards NYC

Gladys Knight and Bill—Pioneer Awards NYC

Camille Morris with Bonnie Raitt—Pioneer Awards NYC

Smokey Robinson of the Miracles with Bill—Pioneer Awards NYC

Sonny Turner (lead singer of the Platters)—This Magic Moment Festival—Charleston, SC

Bill and Billy Scott (The Prophets)—TMM Festival Charleston, SC

Harry Turner (Chairman of TMM Festival) and Chuck "Any Day Now" Jackson

Jerry Butler, Herb Hardesty (Fats Domino's Sax Player), Ray Peterson—TMM Festival Charleston, SC

General Jackson (Chairman of the Board)

Bill and Ernie K-Doe ("Mother-In-Law")—Pioneer Awards NYC

Bill at Prentiss' church Morningstar
Baptist Talent Show Jackson, MS

During our visit, we had the joy of seeing our daughter Kathryn, now a student at the University of Texas, doing further work in her field. There was one breathless moment that still draws me to that time and place. Kathryn and I were sitting on the deck overlooking Lake Austin at a place called Mozart's—a coffee shop where the students often gathered. Surrounded by the best of God's fine art—the placid waters of the lake mirroring the azure sky above and a green cathedral of trees lining the shoreline—the young people could study while sipping their coffee. All this, accompanied by a chorus of birdsong and old favorites from the 1940s coming over the sound system.

I had found a spot a couple of tables away from the place where Kathryn was seated right next to the rail by the water. So as not to disturb her while she was studying, I tended to some insurance paperwork. Just then a song came over the speaker—"Heart and Soul"—sung by an enchanting female voice. Glancing over at Kathryn, I noticed a silky strand of chestnut hair falling over her face as she was reading, one hand tucked under her chin. She looked so sweet and vulnerable, and I was tempted to go over, take my daughter in my arms, and dance with her while the music played. But I wouldn't have wanted to embarrass her in front of the other students. Nevertheless, the song and the scene have remained in my heart to this day.

That tender moment set the tone for my trip to L.A. the next day. When I walked into the hotel lobby of the host city, where the stars were staying, there were my dear friend Bill Pinkney and Charlie Thomas, chatting with Johnny Keyes and Reggie Gordon of The Magnificents. When they introduced me to Judy Adams, who was also to be honored at the event, I learned that her husband, Johnny, had passed away only a few months earlier. My heart went out to her, and I couldn't help softly singing some of the lyrics to her late husband's classic "I Won't Cry."

Then along came Maxine Porter, inviting us all to Bill's room to view a video, which had been filmed five years earlier. The video featured Charlie Thomas's trip to the Civic Center in Sumter, South Carolina, where Bill was performing, celebrating his forty-fifth year in the rock 'n' roll genre. On the video, Charlie speaks of Bill being his number-one idol in music and sings to him the touching words of "What a Wonderful World."

After viewing this piece of Bill's history and feeling the camaraderie in that room, we all relaxed and surrendered to the mood. There was much laughter and reminiscing before adjourning to get ready for the press conference, which was slated to begin at noon.

Hello, Stranger!

This press conference is always one of the most exciting times for me because of the opportunity to interact with so many of the entertainers. As we were gathering in the lobby, in walked Mickey Baker, who is half of the duo Mickey & Sylvia, best known for their song "Love is Strange." Mickey was also the main guitar player in many of the most famous songs recorded on the Atlantic label. Bill Pinkney beamed a sunny smile when he saw him. I was able to get a quick photo of Mickey with Bill, Charlie, and Lloyd Price before moving into the main area for the press conference.

Here the stars were filling the room with their incandescent glow. Most all of the honorees were present, and spotting Mabel John—Little Willie John's sister—I walked over, thanked her for nominating Bill for the award, and gave her a tape of our *Peace in the Valley.*

As I moved around the room, I bumped into Barbara Lynn, whose alluring voice made her song "You'll Lose a Good Thing" a favorite of mine. "And that pleading sax that comes in about halfway through sends me to the moon," I told her.

"Hello, Stranger," I called out to Barbara Lewis, alluding to her famous song by that title. "You know, that song really tugged at my heartstrings as an ROTC cadet just after my junior year at Ole Miss. I was spending the summer in the red clay hills of Ft. Benning, Georgia, training with a few thousand other cadets. When I heard that number playing on someone's radio in the barracks, it sure made me homesick for my girlfriend back home in Mississippi."

Stylish Brenda Holloway ("Every Little Bit Hurts" and "Just Look What You've Done") then caught my eye and gave me a hug and a copy of her new CD, about to be released. After that, it wasn't long before I met Isaac Hayes and David Porter, his songwriter. And there were The Manhattans, famous for "There's No Me without You." I visited with Winifred (Blue) Lovett, along with the other original members, and then 23-year member Gerald Alston, who did the lead on most of their hit songs.

In the center of the room was a guy being interviewed by several reporters, jockeying for position, their mics extended on long poles. A long line of people waited to speak with him and get his autograph. I, of course, was intrigued and wanted to know who he was.

"Oh, that's Larry Graham of Graham Central Station," I was told by someone near the end of the line.

So, *this* was the fabulous singer who had recorded the song "When We Get Married," also released by The Dreamlovers several years earlier. Couldn't help myself. I broke into a few bars of the song, and a precious lady standing beside Larry stepped away and moved closer to me to hear a little better. She was smiling. I soon learned that she was Larry's wife, Tina, and when she introduced herself, we chatted while her husband was completing the interview with the reporters covering the story.

Later that night, when Larry saw me outside the main event, he told me that he had overheard me singing his song. "Man, you sounded *good!*" he said, giving me a high five.

"Got my inspiration from *you* and The Dreamlovers," I replied. "I heard you singing that song on TV several years ago. You had on a white suit."

When the press conference began to wind down, I retired to my room for a quick nap. We would reconvene around five o'clock for a ride back to the big event. The time couldn't come soon enough for me—that moment when one of the best friends I have on this earth would be saluted by the industry and foundation.

★ ★ ★

Gathering downstairs were all the stars, but my focus was on Bill Pinkney, Maxine Porter, and Eartha (Bill's daughter). We took some pictures in the lobby, and then we were on our way.

Others who joined us in the limo were Dee Dee Warwick, Dionne Warwick's sister and Whitney Houston's first cousin. With her were her two male backup vocalists—guys who also choreographed her numbers. As the limo began moving slowly toward the event, which would be held at Sony Studios in Hollywood, the traffic became congested and Bill was getting a little impatient. To ease the tension, I smiled at Dee Dee, who was sitting next to me, and began to sing "Oh, What a Night!" This seemed to help, and I continued my serenade—one ballad after another—all the way to our destination.

When we arrived, we proceeded into the main Sony building where a silent auction was underway, to be followed by dinner. In a section reserved for the VIPs, I saw many of my friends, including Cissy Houston, Whitney's mom. I also noticed a poster I had donated to the Rhythm & Blues Foundation—"This Magic Moment" (same image as the cover of this book). Ray Benson (Asleep at the Wheel) and Billy Vera ("At This Moment") were checking it out. Every second seemed magical.

Under the Boardwalk

Around seven-thirty, it was time to move over to the big tent for the main ceremonies. As far as I know, this was the first time the foundation had ever hosted such an auspicious occasion in a tent, although the area was quite spacious with fifty-foot ceilings. The honorees were seated throughout. Behind me was Sam Moore of "Sam and Dave," with Andy Williams at the table in front of us. I also had the pleasure of sitting next to Bill's niece, a beautiful young lady named Terese, who was an aspiring actress in Hollywood. At our table was an interesting gentleman, Michael Walker, Wolfman Jack's manager. Michael related to me that he had over 7,000 signed photographs of singers in his collection, with access to almost every record one could want.

Marty Stuart, the famed country singer, stopped by the table and we talked for a couple of minutes. "You know, I'm from your neck of the woods—Philadelphia, Mississippi, to be exact," Marty reminded me. "Fact is, I'll be doing some shows back home before long."

A few tables over was Bonnie Raitt, her flaming red hair making her a standout in any crowd.

As the meeting unfolded, Smokey Robinson took charge as the master of ceremonies. He did an outstanding job with his humor and wit. Most of the performers gave us their current rendition of their most famous song.

Judy Adams (Johnny Adams's widow) gave a plea for the plight of the singers and musicians who had never been paid. To illustrate her point, she said, "My husband, who cut over one hundred records, never received one cent of royalty." At that remark, a hush fell over the crowd.

When they brought Bill Pinkney and Charlie Thomas onstage to introduce them prior to receiving the award, the band was playing "Under the Boardwalk"—a song made famous by the second set of Drifters, featuring Charlie Thomas.

Due to unresolved copyright issues regarding The Drifters' name, Bill and Charlie had been cautioned not to perform that night. But as the two were being honored at the podium, Charlie's pent-up frustration burst forth, and he would not be denied. He grabbed the mic in front of him and launched into the song. Bill could do nothing but join in, carrying the bass harmony in his inimitable style. I felt so much compassion for them.

The other performances were splendid, including The Manhattans singing "Kiss and Say Goodbye." But I was particularly thrilled to hear Dee Dee Warwick singing "I'm Gonna Make You Love Me." A couple of hours earlier, *I* had been singing to *her.*

Bill was ready to leave before the entertainment was over, as he had to catch a six o'clock flight the next morning. He had promised one of his daughters that he would play for a party being sponsored by her business.

But there was one further delay. As we were leaving, a number of people out back rushed up to Bill and wanted photos with him, including the singer, Sinbad and the CBS *60 Minutes* star, Ed Bradley. We missed Ashford & Simpson and John Lee Hooker and Isaac Hayes, although we did get a photograph with Smokey Robinson's wife.

Soon after, I encouraged Bill and the guys to go on ahead. I caught a ride in a limo back to the hotel with Barbara Lewis and her manager, along with Johnny Keyes and Reggie Gordon of The Magnificents. And that word described the entire evening—"magnificent"!

Heart and Soul

The next morning at breakfast, everywhere I looked were stars from the evening before. This time, though, the celebrities were not wearing tuxes and tails, or satin and sequins. Dressed more informally, they were letting their hair down in more ways than one, and for an hour or more, I stepped into the real world behind the scenes.

Everyone was reliving the previous night's event, and the energy in that room was palpable. At one table, Jerry Butler, his wife, and manager Benet MacMillan, one of the foundation trustees, were laughing at some private joke. Seated nearby were Gene Chandler, Lloyd Price, and Judy Adams. Gene, the Duke, was one of my all-time favorite singers. I could see Ray Benson at yet another table, slapping his knee in response to a comment. As someone would mention a highlight of the evening, someone else would sing a snippet of a song.

With a second round of coffee, the conversation grew more serious, and I heard again the real-life struggles of many of these top-flight singers and musicians. This was not news to me. I had walked with some who knew only too well the bittersweet life of a professional musician. I would not have wanted to be anywhere else. For all the pomp and circumstance of the main event, this morning's conversation over coffee would remain as one of the most memorable moments I would experience. To be included in this fraternity of singers was an honor I could never have anticipated. I truly felt I was one of them.

Just then, Mickey Baker strolled in, and we visited for a little while. He owned his own publishing company in Southern France and had obviously done quite well. I also saw Joyce and Sam Moore and connected with them again.

After breakfast, I listened as Cindy Birdsong of The Bluebelles told me about her entry into the ministry. Then Nick Ashford of *Ashford & Simpson* came by and shared something about their latest foray into television. About that time, along came my friend, Harvey Fuqua of The Moonglows. What a man! What a singer, songwriter, and arranger! After conversing for a while, the inevitable occurred. It was time to pack.

★　★　★

As I came down to head to the airport, I saw Mary Wilson of The Supremes standing at the front door of the hotel. "Mary, do you want to catch a ride to the airport together?"

Unfortunately, she needed someone to drop off her car at the rental car kiosk. She asked me, but to do so would possibly have caused me to miss my flight. Reluctantly, I bade her farewell until the next year.

Turning, I noticed a precious young lady standing behind me, wearing a hat and sunglasses, and asked her the same question. When she replied, I realized that it was Dee Dee Warwick, the same woman I had been singing to the night before. We hopped in a cab, and I began to relate to her all the blessings that God had given me in my involvement with music. I proceeded to sing to her all the way to the airport, including "Heart and Soul," "Zing! Went the Strings of My Heart," "Devil or Angel," "Daddy's Home," finishing up with "My Girl" as we rolled onto the departure ramp.

Dee Dee was one of several singers who encouraged me very strongly to record. Maybe . . . someday.

The Today Show

The re-release of the CD by The Original Drifters featuring Bill Pinkney entitled *True Love* was the week of July 4th. A mere ten days later, on July 15, 1999, Bill and his Drifters, also featuring Charlie Thomas, were on the *Today Show* for a full two hours. They performed three numbers, closing the segment with a fourth.

Katie Couric, the TV anchor, promoted the CD, holding it in her hand as she gave a glowing review. She capped off the hour by saying, "The reason for this special on Atlantic City is because I absolutely love the song 'Under the Boardwalk'!" No singer, songwriter, or group could have asked for more!

~ 11 ~

YOU'RE THE ONE

Since much of my passion for life is set to the music of my youth, it is not unusual for some haunting melody from the past to be playing in my mind. For many years, my mental replay button was stuck on "Daddy's Home." Over and over again, I moved to the sentiment of this song by Shep and The Limelites.

For quite a while, Prentiss Barnes and I had been discussing the possibility of teaming up to sing a number at his church—Morning Star Baptist on Albemarle Road. It was this song—a love ballad out of the 1950s—that I "heard." Hmmm. Maybe I could write some new lyrics—something spiritual, something appropriate for an audience of worshippers on a Sunday morning.

Inspired, I set about to write my first "gospel" song, entitled "You're the One." But first, Prentiss and I would try it out at a talent show to be held at *my* church on a Sunday afternoon in late March. We would rehearse at my home the preceding Saturday.

With his vast experience in recording, Prentiss brought so many valuable insights to the table as we worked out our arrangement. We must have rehearsed for a couple of hours until we felt that we had it down fairly well. The song was to be done a cappella, with only one chord to start us off in the right key.

We were both nervous about the whole affair. Prentiss said that he had not been able to get it off his mind for several weeks. Nor had I!

On the afternoon of the talent show, Prentiss and I met at the church for a final rehearsal before the show was to begin at four o'clock. For the first time, we worked out at a mic in the fellowship hall, then joined the other participants in the sanctuary to await our turn to perform. It was quite a line-up—a dozen or so acts preceding ours.

Near the end of the event, Prentiss and I were called to the stage. To brief the audience on our relationship, I quickly shared our story. How I had met this member of the world-famous Moonglows indirectly through a later composition of the singers, led by Bobby Lester, then through an article about Prentiss himself in the *Clarion-Ledger*. And how, moved by his troubling life experience—both personally and professionally—I had reached out to him, beginning a deep and abiding friendship.

With this introduction, I hit the play button on the jam box to give us the chord, and then back to pause. From that moment, we were unaware of anything but the music as we poured out our hearts in harmonious praise, singing the new lyrics to the song that had become a part of me. When we reached the soaring climax, Prentiss and I were able to crescendo with such volume and intensity I was literally shaking all over.

When we finished, the crowd rose to their feet in a thunderous ovation. I could tell that Prentiss was thrilled. There were tears in his eyes. I must admit to some moisture in mine as well. This warm reception merely fueled my resolve to repeat this performance in Prentiss's church. In fact, I had "seen" this very scenario played out in a dream. In my vision, I was singing at Morning Star Baptist, looking into the eyes of his people. I wanted them to know that this white guy loved them.

Home at Last

Unexpected news the first week of August brought a much different cause for emotion. Profoundly shaken by the death of my beloved friend Willie

Morris, I struggled with his loss. I had read every book Willie had written. He was revered not only as a writer, but as a raconteur and a lover of the human spirit. Willie paid homage to his fellow man in eloquent prose. Not only that, but as a native of my home state, he could transport readers to our earthly paradise when he described the entrance into the Mississippi Delta he knew so well:

> Half an hour north of Jackson on U.S. 49, not far beyond the Big Black River, the casual rolling land gives way to a succession of tall, lush hills one after another for . . . miles. . . . Beyond these hills, if you follow the highway as it forks north and slightly west, the hills suddenly come to an end and there is one long, final descent. Out in the distance, as far as the eye can see, the land is flat, dark, and unbroken, sweeping away in a faint misty haze to the limits of the horizon[2].

My friend had reached "the limits of the horizon" and had stepped over into eternal Paradise. But he would be sadly missed on this side.

The day after he passed, I made my way to Willie's home. The house was already overflowing with family, friends, and luminaries from his past.

While visiting with his widow, JoAnne, she told me that one of Willie's favorite pictures of himself was one I had taken while he was sitting at the Mayflower Café. At the time, Willie had been writing a memo to Jerry Kountouris, the proprietor, on the occasion of the birth of Jerry's first grandchild. JoAnne wanted to display a larger copy of that photograph in the rotunda of the historic Mississippi State Capitol where he was to lie in state. I was thrilled to oblige and immediately left to have the photo enlarged.

When I returned the oversized image to JoAnne, she asked me if I would be willing to sign it. I was deeply honored to do so. A few days later, displayed on an easel next to a large flower arrangement, the picture looked quite appropriate as it rested near the body of only the third person in Mississippi history to be so honored. Having written of the tumultuous 1960s, when feelings were tender and conflict erupted over human rights, Willie had not always been held in such universal high esteem. At one point, when racial tension was still thick in the air, he had left the rolling hills of Mississippi for the concrete canyons of New York City, where he soon became the youngest editor of *Harper's Magazine* and the darling of the intelligentsia. Yet, frustrated with the rising tide of animosity between the races, he found himself writing his epic *North Toward Home.*

★   ★   ★

The morning of the funeral, JoAnne received the many guests in the old Capitol rotunda—everyone from governors to waitresses, since Willie had known no class distinction. With the funeral at four o'clock in Yazoo City at the Methodist Church, I left promptly to be sure to get a seat. When I arrived an hour early, I spotted the red hair of Sherry Lucas, journalist, heading toward the parking lot, which was nearly full as was the church, although I was fortunate enough to find a spot a couple of rows back in the balcony. Like the rest of us, she loved Willie too.

As I scanned the sea of people in the sanctuary, I recognized some well-known dignitaries—Charles Evers, civil rights icon; Pulitzer Prize winners David Halberstam and Richard Ford; Dr. David Sansing, noted historian and author; revered former Governor William Winter; best-selling novelist John Grisham; and countless others.

The service was quite moving as testimonies were given of Willie's impact on multifarious lives. At the conclusion, Reverend Will Campbell called for a standing ovation for Willie, and it was all I could do to keep my grief under control. I settled for biting my lip while tears streamed down my face.

As we left the church at the conclusion of the service, we all stood around outside and visited while they brought Willie's casket to the hearse. Then began the half-mile, slow, silent procession up to the old Yazoo City Cemetery, one of Willie's favorite haunts.

This spot had always held a special fascination for him, particularly the old witch's grave. Interestingly—perhaps on purpose—he was buried thirteen paces away. As a teenager, Willie would play the echo bugle on a hillside overlooking the cemetery, honoring the fallen soldiers of the Korean War who had made the final trip home.

A couple hundred people gathered around the tent and surrounding area to hear the last words over Willie's body before his interment. Prior to that, however, a combo consisting of Raphael Semmes and his group performed several songs in honor of Willie. Jill Conner Browne, the Sweet Potato Queen, offered another touching testimony, as did Winston Groom, author of *Forest Gump*.

Finally, Reverend Campbell stepped forward to utter the words of committal:

> For as much as it has pleased Almighty God to take out of this world the soul of our brother, Willie Morris, we therefore commit his body to the ground, earth to earth, ashes to ashes, dust to dust, looking for that blessed hope when the Lord Himself shall descend from heaven with a shout, with the voice of the archangel, and with the trump of God, and the dead in Christ shall rise first.

I was standing beside William Styron in the dusty Delta heat of that late afternoon in early August, when Willie was laid to rest in the soil he had loved so dearly. The last person I spoke to as I was leaving was my friend Richard Ford, the writer. There is a fraternity of sorts of those of us who choose to write. We hope our written works are worthy of our readers' time and money. Willie was truly worthy.

Bourbon Street Beat

I wasn't able to stay around long to visit with Willie's many friends and admirers, for I had another very important mission. My younger daughter Kathryn and I were to leave for New Orleans on our annual father/daughter trip as soon as I returned from the funeral. She was packed and waiting for me when I arrived. We grabbed a quick bite and, at dusk, headed on down I-55 to the Big Easy as my melancholy heart was transmuted to one of eager anticipation.

Upon reaching our destination some three hours later, we checked into the Royal Orleans in the heart of the French Quarter. (Daughter Camille would be making a similar trip with me the following weekend. Since the age of eight, each of my girls has enjoyed this outing with me, their proud dad, and I wouldn't have missed it for anything!)

At breakfast with Kathryn the next morning at the Bluebird Café on Prytania Street, I was leafing through a local newspaper. To my amazement, there was a picture of Bill Pinkney and The Original Drifters (the same picture that graced the cover of our first CD) with an ad for an upcoming performance scheduled in New Orleans for Sunday night. I quickly called Maxine Porter for more info. She told me that the guys were, indeed, in town for a gig. Bill's family was also gathering for a reunion, staying at the Royal Sonesta, only a block away from our hotel.

For a couple of days, Kathryn and I enjoyed our usual marvelous experiences in New Orleans—wonderful dinners, shopping, and perusing the antique shops and art galleries of Magazine and Royal Streets. These trips always provided the opportunity for a deeper bonding with my daughters.

While walking to one of the city's legendary restaurants for dinner on Friday night, we stopped by the Royal Sonesta and slipped into the room where Bill Pinkney and his kinfolk were gathering. We were thankful to get in this short visit with Bill and some of his family members before moving on. But we promised we'd see him again on Sunday before we left for home.

After resuming our walk down Bourbon Street, Kathryn and I made our entrance into Galatoire's, a favorite dining spot for the gourmand crowd. Our taste buds were craving the world-class cuisine. We started off with an appetizer of fried eggplant and soufflé potatoes, served with a generous portion of béarnaise sauce and powdered sugar. Kathryn loved dipping the delicacies in first the sauce and then the sugar to create a tantalizing taste treat. This was followed by crabmeat maison. Our entrée was trout meuniére, celebrated by chefs the world over. We planned to top off our fresh seafood meal with their iconic chocolate mousse—a must when in the Big Easy. *Bon appetit!*

Sitting there with Kathryn, I was reminded of a time when Camille and I were dining at Galatoire's. I was contemplating why I loved this restaurant so much. Granted, the décor was elegant—illuminated by wall sconces and overhead lighting, and bright tile flooring; the food, superb. But it was more than that. It was the anticipation of excellence, the expectation of a rarified experience, with the waiters dressed in tuxedos. Even the clinking of glasses, the lively conversation, and continual bursts of laughter across the room delighted me. I could sense, in the very atmosphere, the energy, a *joie de vivre,* the camaraderie of those who appreciate grand dining. At Galatoire's, we were never disappointed.

★   ★   ★

Sunday morning, after we were packed and ready to return to Jackson, we pulled around to the Royal Sonesta. There, in front, was the big tour bus with "Bill Pinkney and The Original Drifters" splashed across the side. That sight never failed to stir my soul. I left my flashing lights on and went in to visit with the man himself. None of the other Drifters had arrived yet. Only Paul, the bus driver, was there with all of their equipment. The others would be arriving separately.

Bill and I harmonized for a while in the lobby, and the thought occurred to me that I would really like to record my new song, "You're the One," with Prentiss and Bill. It would be a natural for the second gospel CD we were considering. With Kathryn capturing the moment on camera, we said our goodbyes and departed for Jackson. Bill Pinkney and I would meet again.

★   ★   ★

Back home, I faxed Bill a letter in care of Maxine Porter, who was hosting a seventy-forth birthday party for him in Las Vegas. I had been invited but could not attend. Still, I wanted him to know I was thinking of him.

Happy Birthday to Mr. Bill Pinkney!

Bill, you are truly one of the dearest people in my life. You have blessed me more than I can ever tell you. Even before I knew you, I loved your music. That God should bring us together in a deep friendship is beyond my fondest dreams and imagination. I hope and pray that you have many, many more years of health and happiness. Most of all, I pray that you keep "drifting along and singing your song."

With much love, I am *sincerely* yours,

William H. Morris Jr.

Sincerely . . . that song by The Moonglows encompassed so much of the genuine respect and esteem I held for these singers from an earlier era. And now, back in my office, my mind reeled with the enormity of the charge I had been given—to help guard their legacy so that future generations might enjoy the unique sound of their music.

A greater charge had also been given to me, and the reminder came with the next phone call.

You're the One

"Brother Morris, it's Prentiss."

I smiled at the sound of the familiar voice. "Well, hello, my friend. Hope you're well." For a split second, I was concerned that his old ailment might have flared up in my absence.

"Doin' fine, doin' fine. Jus' wanted you to know that my church is asking us to sing together this coming Sunday night. It's part of a musical program they're puttin' on."

We agreed to meet again at my house on Saturday. After a brief rehearsal, we were pleased with the harmony. Prentiss tweaked a few places, and we were ready. More than ready.

★　★　★

Morning Star. . . Camille and I loved the name of Prentiss's little Baptist congregation. Hugging the hillside, the red brick building was neat and well-kept. I was impressed with its stately look.

When we approached, we could see the doors were open, welcoming all who entered. We hadn't been inside long before we realized we were among friends.

As people began to filter into the fellowship hall, I noticed a glow about them. On each face was a warm smile that seemed to emanate from deep within, and we returned the smiles. By the time everyone had arrived, including the various singing groups from different churches in the area, Camille and I felt right at home. It was a joy to be in the presence of these people. It felt good and right . . . and overdue.

I recalled my vision of earlier in the year, when God awoke me from a dream in which I was looking out into the faces of a black congregation. He was saying, "I want you to sing to My people." That time had arrived.

The master of ceremonies, Ray Robinson, an eloquent and delightful young man of around thirty, informed Prentiss and me that we would be last on the program. As a result, we could relax behind the scenes as the various groups performed. From my vantage point, I could see that Camille was enjoying the event more and more as the entertainment progressed.

When it was time for Prentiss and me to perform, Ray introduced us, referring respectfully to Prentiss as "Mr. Barnes." Prentiss, in turn, made a few kind remarks about me. Stepping up to the mic, I spoke of our friendship and how God had divinely merged our paths, weaving together two distinctly different backgrounds and experiences. Our attentive audience responded with loud "amens" and much clapping.

Our song seemed to make a hit with the crowd, and when we were able, once again, to reach the towering crescendo, they erupted with enthusiastic applause. By the time we finished, they were cheering!

Following the service, we were able to shake the hand of almost everyone in the congregation. "You gentlemen oughtta cut a record with that song on it," I heard more than once. Unfortunately, there was no recording equipment available in the church at that time. But we got the message.

The Tie that Binds

Jutting twenty-two stories into the skies above Jackson, atop a regional bank building, was the prestigious University Club. Here deals were made, business plans laid, and men met and prayed. For, among other things, this was the location of the monthly meeting of Mission Mississippi, a racially mixed group of approximately forty or fifty men spanning the political spectrum and the racial divide. Many of the black members were former civil rights leaders who had done time in Mississippi jails and suffered physical violence and emotional trauma. On the other hand, there were successful businessmen of both races who embraced one another with no racist overtones whatsoever. It was this group, led by philanthropic oil man Victor Smith, Rev. John Perkins, and Rev. Dolphus Weary, that had invited Prentiss and me to provide a musical program for the meeting. It would be my great privilege, as a member of the mission, to introduce Prentiss Barnes.

When it came time for the program, I attempted to set the tone by playing some of The Moonglows' famous songs on a jam box. I wanted my colleagues to understand the significance of Prentiss's singing career and the magnitude of his musical gift. Repeating much of what I had shared with the members of our two churches, I ended with an explanation of the genesis of our gospel CD, *Peace in the Valley.* Then I introduced Prentiss, who took the mic and told his story.

"If you have children or grandkids, be real sure they get a proper education and don't do what I did," he said. "Wouldn't be in the shape I'm in today if I'd kep' on with my schoolin'. And what happened after I started singin' and writin' songs wasn't right, either. I've been at this music business a long time. But all the songs I helped to write—well, somehow my name jus' got left off the credits."

I could hear a few sympathetic groans from the audience.

"If it wasn't for this brother here"—Prentiss choked up a little, then turned to clap me on the back—"who came along when I was really down and out . . . well . . . don't know what I woulda done. But it's more than the money. I mean, he's been a real friend to me. Like I tell 'im . . . he's been better to me than some of my own people."

Somehow, after those emotional moments, we managed to sing our song. It was well received, and afterwards, we were surrounded by our appreciative audience. Some of them questioned us about our availability to perform in other venues, including Mission Mississippi's state-wide rally coming up in October. We agreed, gratefully.

~ 12 ~

DANNY BOY

Like most red-blooded American males, I love football. However, it's somewhere down the line from faith, family, friends . . . and music. But when I can combine two or more of these passions in one evening, count me in!

In the fall of 1999, the Arkansas Razorbacks would be playing the Ole Miss Rebels in a nationally televised game in Oxford, 150 miles north of Jackson. On the same weekend, in Vicksburg—less than an hour to the west—there was to be a reunion of The Red Tops, the spectacular orchestra featuring Rufus McKay. As previously mentioned, Rufus has to be one of my all-time favorite lead singers, known best for his inimitable rendition of "Danny Boy." In my adolescent years, like so many others of that era, my soul had been branded with his signature sound. I knew, too, that of the eleven original band members, only five of them were still living. To hear Rufus again was an opportunity I could not afford to miss. He would be performing with a local band, and the surviving members of his orchestra would be honored.

One major dilemma: our firstborn, also named Camille, was recovering at our home from foot surgery. As a result, she was physically limited for a while, and her mom or I needed to be with her at all times. That meant only one of us could travel to Vicksburg. Knowing Camille, she would probably insist on my going. But that would be quite selfish of me, I felt.

So . . . what to do?

I was pondering this problem the Saturday morning of the event, sitting in the swing out back in our arbor—a favored place for some quiet time and hashing out decisions in prayer. My phone rang. Deep in thought, I almost didn't answer. But something nudged me. On the line was a dear friend of ours—Kathie Moore.

"Bill, Irene Mangum said that I should call you because you might be going over to Vicksburg for The Red Tops' reunion," Kathie said. "If you are, I'd like to catch a ride with you."

I filled her in on my dilemma, concluding, "Let me check with Camille. If she agrees, I would be delighted to take you over to the reunion . . . but only after the Ole Miss game."

She laughed and said she'd wait to hear from me.

Typical of her thoughtfulness, Camille encouraged me to go. It would be a quick trip, though. The televised game did not begin until five o'clock and would likely not be over until around eight or so.

I called Kathie with the news. She was thrilled.

★   ★   ★

The game was a shoo-in. Ole Miss dominated Arkansas from the first play, a hundred-yard kickoff return by Deuce McAllister, and it was virtually over by the end of the first quarter. The final score: 38-16. They got us back in later years, however. It happens.

To honor The Red Tops, I donned my red sport coat and black trousers, similar to the outfits The Red Tops always wore when performing.

Camille teased, "All dressed up for your big date?"

"Darlin', you know I wanted you to come along. . . ." After twenty-seven years of marital fidelity, she knew I meant that.

Camille smiled and gave me a kiss before waving me off. "Have fun and be careful," she called as I left the house.

On the short drive over, I popped a Red Tops CD into the dash, and the mellow sound of Rufus McKay's voice filled the atmosphere.

The band was just warming up when we arrived a little after nine o'clock. Kathie joined a group of her friends, former classmates, and I made my way down front to visit with the great musicians—Rufus's Red Tops—who were seated offstage.

One by one, I shook their hands, thanking them for the gift they had given so many of my generation. Jesse Hayes, a fabulous guitar player, was in a wheelchair, but his mind was sharp. Lewis Spencer, one of the sax players, showed the same affable personality I remembered. We chatted a bit, remarking that since he lived so close, we really ought to get together more often. There was still time for a few camera shots before the evening's entertainment kicked off.

But where was Rufus? I knew that he, backed by a local band, was to be the headliner tonight. While former band members were still living in Vicksburg, Rufus had to fly in from his home in Carson City, Nevada. Had he missed his flight?

And then I looked up and saw him striding onstage, this time in his white tuxedo with the white satin stripe down the side of his pants' leg, red bow tie and cummerbund. As he began singing, his pure, sweet voice flowing over the audience like warm honey, the years rolled back.

Long Ago and Far Away

Rufus McKay was first ushered into my life around 1954, when I was entering the seventh grade at Bailey Junior High in Jackson. My classmates and I were learning to dance the fox-trot, the waltz and the bop at the Arthur Murray Studio on North State Street.

Midway through the series of lessons, an invitation arrived in the mail, addressed to me. Enclosed was a card with the name of the young lady I was to escort to a dance. Some committee—or maybe the mothers of the dance students—had listed the young ladies and selected their escorts. All I recall is that I never knew who my dance partner would be until that little envelope arrived. That night, I wore a white sport coat with a red boutonniere in my lapel. My mother drove me to pick up my date. This would be the first of many such evenings until we were of driving age.

I recall arriving at the King Edward Hotel on Capitol Street in downtown Jackson and taking the elevator to the second-floor ballroom. And there he was—Rufus McKay, accompanied by ten black musicians, his Red Tops, wearing red coats and black formal pants with satin stripes down the legs. He was singing "Stardust." The girls in their semi-formal dresses with starched petticoats seemed to be floating across the floor. There were some awkward moments as we boys tried to lead our partners in the dance steps we had just learned. But somehow we made it that night—and many more to come. It was a rite of passage, and Rufus and his music accompanied us on our journey.

For a while, the ubiquitous Red Tops turned up at venues throughout the Mississippi Delta. After high school, when I enrolled in Ole Miss, I still followed Rufus whenever possible. He and his fabulous orchestra were the hottest ticket in town after town. But in the late 1960s, Rufus and his group disappeared from our lives. We didn't know where he had gone. Some thought he had moved west to join The Ink Spots in Las Vegas. Someone else claimed to have heard him in some faraway place like Jakarta, Indonesia. We only knew that he was no longer a part of our lives and lived only in our memories.

And then the music had changed. Our beloved genre shifted with the invasion of the British rock era—good, though not the same. I yearned to hear "my" music . . . which was now unfolding again at the reunion in Vicksburg, Mississippi.

Somewhere in Time

Tonight was the night. The words Rufus was singing were familiar. So were the feelings they evoked, carrying me all the way back to my teenage years in the 1950s. Once again, I could almost see the girls in their light summer dresses, their hair pulled back in ponytails or swinging, silky and free, around their sun-kissed faces. Could almost catch the scent of White Shoulders or Shalimar as I held my dancing partner in my arms . . . until some other guy would "break in," tap me on the shoulder, and whisk her away. In those days, it was popular for the guys to switch off with as many girls as possible per dance. I remember the girls well—and fondly.

Then Rufus began to sing, smoothly, effortlessly:

"Oh, Danny boy, the pipes, the pipes are calling. . ."

Everyone on the dance floor paused, eyes riveted on the man behind the mic. His own eyes were closed, his head tilted back as he crooned:

"From glen to glen, and down the mountainside. . ."

Couples remained locked in place—no changing partners—swaying to the music. Spellbound, we listened as the sublime sound, like liquid velvet, poured from the throat of this musical giant. It was a moment suspended in time.

As the song came to an end at last, rising to a crescendo.

"I'll be here in sunshine or in shadow,

Oh Danny boy, oh Danny boy, I love you so-o-o."

On the final note, his voice would ascend three octaves.

Shaking off the mood, I suddenly realized where I was. Over forty years later, I could still be transported from earth to heaven when I heard Rufus sing this song . . . except for one thing. Camille, my "earth angel," was not with me.

Looking around, I realized that the people in this audience apparently felt the same. No longer dancing, they were just holding each other, standing in awe of the gifted man on the stage. I have not heard such music—before or since. Perhaps there will never be another singer who can match this one. Certainly not another who can put so much emotion and soul into this particular song, reviving our memories.

As the band struck up the next tune, Rufus was wiping tears from his eyes. And I was wiping tears from mine.

Thanks for the Memory

Throughout these years, there was a sprinkling of guys and gals who had always made it to Red Tops' dances. They came from all over the Delta—from Belzoni, Vicksburg, Rosedale, Greenville, Clarksdale, Greenwood, Indianola, Lexington, Yazoo City—a hundred miles in various directions, spanning what was the fertile Mississippi alluvial plain. As the night wore on, I enjoyed dancing with several old friends—Kathie, of course, and Lynn Orkin, plus a few more.

Between numbers, several came up to me, recalling those high-school and college days when I used to throw the dance parties after the football games. One fellow said, "Bill, those were the best dances I've ever been to in my life. I'll always appreciate what you did." I felt blessed by those words.

At intermission, I was one of the first to get down to see Rufus. He may have aged, but I let him know that his voice sounded as fine as ever— even more beautiful, if that were possible. I gave him one of my CDs. (I had already given one to Walter Osborne, the manager and drummer of The Red Tops, who was celebrating his ninety-third birthday!) And for the next few minutes, I talked to Rufus about the possibility of his singing with Bill Pinkney and The Original Drifters.

"Yeah, Bill, I'm very interested. Just let me know what you're thinkin'."

Before Rufus returned to the stage, he wrote out his address and phone number on a Red Tops brochure. The stage was set. Recording Rufus McKay singing "Danny Boy" would top almost anything I had yet achieved. If only we could pull it off. With my business, time was always a big consideration.

I continued to listen to the band as they played the songs of The Red Tops, including "Swanee River Rock," which Rufus had not sung since the 1960s. Strangely, this was one of only four songs ever recorded professionally by this group.

After midnight, people were beginning to clear out. Rufus had finished his last set, and we visited for a few more minutes. But I wanted to leave while the band was still playing. There is something almost mystical about leaving a venue with the music you love still ringing in your soul.

On the ride back home, their sounds were encircling our heads from the car stereo . . . and in my heart. It would always be so.

~ 13 ~

UNFORGETTABLE

Funny how some people never entirely leave your thoughts. They reside there in some treasured memory—a haunting melody, a warm conversation, a magic moment shared.

Such was the case one evening in late 1999. For some reason, Harvey Fuqua, the renowned baritone of The Moonglows, was on my mind when the phone rang. To my astonishment, it was the man himself!

"Hey, Bill! Harvey here. Great news! Looks like we're definitely goin' into the Rock & Roll Hall of Fame this year. Just talked to Prentiss, and he's pretty excited!"

Man, was I elated for Prentiss and the guys. How fitting, after all these years, that The Moonglows should receive the top recognition awarded by their industry. But I really wasn't expecting his next comment.

"Now, you'll be with us, of course, sittin' at our table at the Waldorf Astoria in New York. Just wanted to be sure I had the right address for the invitation. They will be paying for your airfare and hotel room for three nights too. "

Once again, I was in awe of the way things were evolving. Who would have thought—when I was in junior high, hearing the sounds that would shape the remainder of my life—that I would be mingling with these greats on a somewhat regular basis. Now . . . at the very height of their recognition.

When Harvey hung up, I immediately dialed Prentiss and found him ecstatic about the upcoming honor and award. But, first, he would be traveling with his brother Houston to Chicago for the funeral of another loved one. With seventeen siblings—and only a couple of years between them—it seemed that someone in the family was always reaching heaven's gates, leaving the others to celebrate the life of the departed. And Prentiss, loyal brother that he was, never missed a funeral. These events were extremely important in this family-oriented culture—perhaps even more so than Christmas and Thanksgiving—when people who don't often see each other can get together and reminisce about old times.

Before we signed off for the night, we discussed our program for the Mission Mississippi annual Christmas Party. Then, before we knew it, we were harmonizing on "The Ten Commandments of Love," "Sincerely," and "When I'm with You."

Prentiss laughed. "I sure am enjoyin' myself. You've jus' absolutely made my night. We oughtta get us up a group and go on the road."

Tempting. But two or three things hindered us. Prentiss's age, his fragile health . . . and time. No. I would have to be content to enjoy these rare friendships and the perks they afforded only on occasion.

Just the Way You Look

In early 2000, several weeks before Prentiss and I left for New York City, I vowed to do everything in my power to make this important event—his induction into the Rock & Roll Hall of Fame—as positively memorable as possible. To do so, I would need to make sure he was properly outfitted for the occasion. With this in mind, I knew just the places to go—the Rogue men's store, one of the best in the entire South. I called the founder and proprietor, Billy Neville, and told him about Prentiss's big night and asked if he would like to have the honor of dressing this legendary singer.

"I would be happy to," he said. "Just bring your friend by the shop some afternoon, and I'll see what I can do—complementary."

At around three o'clock on Saturday, I took Prentiss to The Rogue. The owner brought out a beautiful dark brown, double-breasted suit, along with a shirt and tie. While we were upstairs getting the suit fitted properly, Prentiss and I broke out into song and sang several numbers.

Such a special occasion called for a brand-new tuxedo with patent leather shoes. I quickly called Jimmy Edwards, owner of Tuxes Too at Banner Hall in Jackson, and asked if he would like to be a part of paying tribute to Prentiss. He readily agreed to do it—again, at no charge.

Located in the heart of a popular retail center in town, Banner Hall is an imposing three-story building with exclusive shops. Among them are Broad Street Bakery, Tuxes Too, Barnett's hair salon, a bridal salon, and the nationally known Lemuria Books, one of the top-rated privately owned bookstores in America.

Prentiss and I sang a song for Jimmy while the measurements for the tuxedo were being made. When Prentiss stepped out of the fitting room, he looked splendid in his new formal attire. At the awards ceremony, he would be able to hold his own with the best of them.

Stand by Me

As the final week approached, I made it a priority to shield Prentiss from any stress associated with preparing for a major trip and the excitement that would follow. Therefore, when I called to check on his progress, I kept the conversation light. Inevitably, we closed our time on the phone with a song or two in anticipation of the good time we were going to have together in New York. Therefore, Prentiss never knew about some of the hassles along the way.

Because of an issue with logistics, our flights were not confirmed until the Wednesday before we were to depart on Friday. This last-minute arrangement was an unnecessary holdup, but Prentiss never suspected. Nor would he have to worry about expenses as the foundation had generously covered our airline tickets and room reservations, along with the $2,500-per-plate dinner for the awards ceremony. I would be there to pick up the tab for any miscellaneous items he might need. Just another opportunity for me to stand by my friend in order to guarantee that this would be an unforgettable experience

★   ★   ★

On Thursday morning, *I* was beginning to feel the strain. Not only did I have Prentiss to think about, but I had my own business affairs to put in order before we left for the weekend. Fortunately, I was able to slip out with Camille for an early dinner during which I began to relax a bit. By ten o'clock that evening, I was packed and ready to go. With so much on my mind, however, I was still awake at 12:50 a.m. and didn't get more than an hour of sleep all night. My alarm went off at 4:00 a.m., at which time I called Prentiss in case he had forgotten to set his clock.

I called him again before leaving home, informing him that I would be by at 5:15. It was closer to 5:20 before I pulled up in front of the Albemarle Apartments. I dialed his number once more to let him know I was waiting. A drowsy Prentiss answered and, just as I suspected, he had gone back to sleep. When I saw him peeping out of his second-story window, I knew he was not ready.

Meanwhile, I felt a bit uneasy as I waited in the car, wondering if we would make our flight. It was at least fifteen minutes later before I saw him emerge from his apartment building, carrying the nice piece of roller luggage I had given him. But I had failed to explain how to release the extension handle. Now he was attempting to lug that heavy suitcase down the sidewalk with his one good arm!

This was only the beginning of the comedy of errors to come.

All Shook Up

Prentiss and I arrived at the airport only a half-hour before our flight was scheduled to depart—instead of the hour I had planned—and quickly ran into another problem. The ticket agent checking our bags informed us that my name was listed, but not Prentiss's. This was turning out to be a fiasco! I had left the car at the curb, checked in, and now had to go park while the agent looked into the matter. When I returned, he had found the problem: Prentiss's name had been listed as "Barnes, Prentiss."

We hurried down the corridor to Gate 19—or as fast as Prentiss's infirmity would allow. As luck would have it that day, this gate was the farthest from the ticket counter. We barely made it for the final call. Out of breath, I presented our tickets to the gate agent and was able to tell her about Prentiss and the great honor he would be receiving in New York.

Once seated, we settled in for the first leg of our flight that would carry us to Atlanta before taking a connecting flight into LaGuardia. After the flight attendant's routine checklist, the voice of the pilot came over the intercom. "We are pleased to have on board with us today Mr. Prentiss Barnes of the famous vocal group, The Moonglows. He is to be inducted into the Rock & Roll Hall of Fame this weekend. Everyone, please make him welcome. Congratulations, Mr. Barnes! And thank you for choosing Delta."

There was a hearty round of applause, and three flight attendants appeared with a gift bottle of wine for Prentiss. I accepted it on his behalf, or rather, I confiscated it. All we needed now was an inebriated honoree!

Headed to Washington via Atlanta for spring break that day were thirty or so kids from Clinton Junior High. Many of them started asking for Prentiss's autograph and wanting photos with him. He was happy to oblige. Then they asked Prentiss to sing, and he insisted I join him. It was another one of those fun moments.

One of the young ladies sitting behind us leaned over and said, "Mr. Barnes, I learned about you when I was in the sixth grade. We were studying famous Mississippians, and you were one of them."

Our early-morning mishaps faded, and we began to relax.

★   ★   ★

At Hartsfield in Atlanta, the world's busiest airport, once again we found ourselves racing to make our connecting flight. Our gate was quite a distance away, requiring a tram ride and a long walk. With Prentiss's injured hip, he could not cover the territory very rapidly. It soon became apparent that I would have to run ahead so we would not miss our flight. They had already made the final call when I arrived, but I explained to them about Prentiss's condition and that he was on the way. We were gratified—and a little surprised—when they held the plane for him.

A little over two hours after boarding our flight, we arrived at New York's LaGuardia Airport. Not finding anyone at the gate to meet us, Prentiss was a little confused. We had chatted the entire trip—thus, no rest after our sleepless night—and now his bum hip was giving him trouble. He was limping by the time we reached the luggage area. To my relief, I spotted a man with a sign reading, "W. Morris."

"There he is, Prentiss," I said, and we were escorted to a town car for the ride into the city.

When we arrived at the Waldorf, Prentiss entered the lobby with confidence, pulling the roller luggage behind him. Our rooms were not quite ready, but by now, we were somewhat expecting the unexpected. Exhausted from our strenuous travels, Prentiss and I sank down into a plush couch in the grand lobby and promptly fell asleep. When we were finally able to check into our rooms, we freshened up and headed over to MSI studio for rehearsal.

There we met all of the members of the Hall of Fame Foundation office. Paul Shafer, the orchestra leader on the "Late Show with David Letterman" show, hit some fabulous strokes on the piano, and The Moonglows took their cue and started into a medley of "The Ten Commandments of Love" and "Sincerely." As the four singers—Harvey Fuqua, Pete Graves, Gary Rogers, and Prentiss—leaned in to the mic, I got some great shots. Gary had been in the original group that I had sung with in Washington, D.C., back in 1980.

Paul Shaffer, James Taylor, and Carolyne Fuqua —Rock N' Roll Hall of Fame Rehearsal NYC 2000

Harvey and Prentiss greeting Ray Charles at the R&R Hall of Fame Rehearsal

The Moonglows rehearsal R&R Hall of Fame

James Taylor and Bill—Rock and Roll Hall of Fame Rehearsal NYC 2000

Prentiss Barnes's R&R Hall of Fame trophy which he gave to Bill years later as a token of his love and appreciation of their friendship shortly before he died

Bill is the guest of The Moonglows for their R&R Hall of Fame induction ceremony at the Waldorf-Astoria NYC in 2000

Bill Pinkney in his white tails with Harvey Fuqua (right) for Bill's 75th Birthday celebration Columbia, SC

Eugene Pitt (lead singer of The Jive Five), Bill, and Billy Scott (The Prophets) at Bill Pinkney's 75th Birthday celebration Columbia, SC

Howard Kramer—curator (left), Terry Stewart—President of the R&R Hall of Fame Museum in Cleveland, Ohio, Prentiss Barnes, and Bill

Carl Gardner (The Coasters), Prentiss and Bill

Vocal Group Hall of Fame induction ceremony—Bill Pinkney (1st set of Drifters), Ben E. King and Charlie Thomas (2nd set of Drifters), and Mary Wilson (The Supremes) co-MC of the event

Herman Santiago and Jimmy Merchant (Frankie Lymon's Teenagers) and Mary Wilson (The Supremes), Vocal Group Hall of Fame in Sharon, PA

Bill taking a bow after singing with The Moonglows at The Vocal Group Hall of Fame Induction ceremonies—Sharon, PA

Tommy Hunt (The Flamingos) overwhelmed with emotion after receiving an award at the Vocal Group Hall of Fame in Sharon, PA

Bill Pinkney—The Drifters performing at The Vocal Group Hall of Fame in Sharon, PA

Rock and Roll Hall of Fame Museum—Prentiss Barnes standing beside his signature on the wall along with his fellow Moonglow members

Howard Kramer fitting a Rock and Roll Hall of Fame coat on Prentiss at the museum

Prentiss Barnes, Bill Morris, Julie Butala, Harvey Fuqua, and Tony Butala ("The Letterman" and Founder of Vocal Group Hall of Fame)

Bill Morris and Mary Wilson (The Supremes)—Vocal Group Hall of Fame Ceremony in Sharon, PA

Bill presenting a gift to B.B. King—A CD The Drifters recorded, Jackson, MS

But I had caught a whiff of alcohol on Pete's breath and wondered how he was going to fare.

At the conclusion of The Moonglows' session, I was delighted to meet and talk with James Taylor. I had loved his music for many years and found him to be genuinely likeable and approachable. At one point, I overheard him say to Harvey, "Well, I'm just going to relax and enjoy this thing. No need to get uptight."

James Taylor . . . uptight? It had never occurred to me that such a professional—after years of celebrity status—would ever feel nervous about a performance. Another lesson for me: Even celebrities are just ordinary people with the same apprehensions we all feel.

Ain't It a Shame?

After getting back to the hotel at around five o'clock, Prentiss and I both retired to our rooms, which were conveniently contiguous. At 6:30, Prentiss called. "Brother Morris, I can't find my arm—the one with the hook. I need it to get dressed in my tuxedo. You ain't got it by any chance, have ya?"

Prentiss had two prostheses—a functional one with a metal hook on the end that he used for most daily activities; the other, a plastic and more aesthetically pleasing one, resembling a real hand, that he wore when performing. I recalled that he had hurriedly exchanged the hook for the hand when we pulled up curbside at the airport. Realizing that it was possible I could have picked it up and packed it in my carryon in our haste to check in at the ticket counter, I searched my luggage, but came up empty. Still, I also vaguely recalled seeing the hook on the backseat of my car . . . or even on top of the car. I wasn't sure.

If the latter were the case, I would need Camille's help. I called, but she wasn't home, so I left her a voice message. When she returned my call, she was upset. "I tried to tell the policeman at the airport what had happened, but all he said was, 'Lady, this is a police officer, and if you think this is funny, we don't have time for prank calls. We have not seen any "black hand" or "hook" or whatever you think you've lost . . . what's your name anyway'?

"Bill, I'm so sorry, but I didn't get anywhere with him. Sure hope you can find what you need and wish I could help." She had hung up, still agitated with the officer's apparent lack of concern.

I assured Prentiss that, no matter what, even if we couldn't find his hook, I would help him get dressed. It would be a first for me, never having helped a grown man put on a tuxedo. But the show must go on.

★   ★   ★

Prentiss had told Harvey Fuqua about his missing prosthesis, and early Monday morning, Harvey buzzed my room. "Bill, I've talked to a Mr. Clayton at the United Prosthesis, in lower Manhattan, and the guy can help you if you hurry up and get down there by 10:30."

Prentiss and I jumped in a cab and hurried to the address given. Although close to Greenwich Village, we ended up in a district that didn't look entirely wholesome. We had to press a buzzer in order to be allowed in, and then only after careful scrutiny by the clerks inside. We felt like we were in some two-bit Mafia movie!

When I explained the situation, we were escorted into an examining room. The gentleman Harvey had spoken to came in and took a look at Prentiss's hand.

"Hmmm," he said. "I thought you just needed me to tighten a cable or something. I don't have any hooks here. We don't carry that kind of thing. We can order it, but you're not likely to find anything quite like what you're looking for." He shook his head. "What a shame."

Prentiss and I thanked him, got back in a cab, and headed to our hotel in central Manhattan. It was a beautiful day, and the only thing we had lost was a little time and the round-trip cab fare. Well . . . with the exception of the hook, of course. It had been a wild goose chase, but we'd seen a little more of the city and enjoyed some good laughs together.

"Don't worry, Prentiss," I told him. "I can help you get ready for the awards show tonight."

Patent Leather Shoes

When we got back to the Waldorf, the momentum was building. The very atmosphere was charged with the anticipation of the evening's activities. Harvey, Pete, and Gary rehearsed several times as Gary was having some difficulty with his part. I got to sing a little with them—just for fun—then took lots of photographs. From there, we went to the rehearsal area where Harvey began to bang out some fabulous sounds on the piano, including "The Ten Commandments of Love" and "Sincerely," which they were to perform that night. Harvey then left for radio interviews while Prentiss, Pete, and Gary rehearsed a little more on their own.

When time came for the formal rehearsal, we reconvened in the main hall, the Vanderbilt Suite, a multi-storied grand hall reminiscent of a European theater with many private balconies. Chatting again with James Taylor, I asked him if he would have any interest in recording some songs for a CD with Bill Pinkney and The Original Drifters. He was interested and gave me the number of his manager. Spotting Melissa Manchester, I got a picture with her as well. I wanted to mingle with all of them.

The Moonglows sounded marvelous when they were rehearsing on the main stage. I was pleased to see that Prentiss, looking confident and handsome, outshone them all in his new brown suit. While the others were more casually dressed, he had chosen to wear his new outfit. Later, he told me had received countless compliments. "I owe it all to you, Brother Morris." But I deserved little credit. We knew Whom to thank. Prentiss was always grateful.

In the next few minutes, I could feel the electricity sizzling through the room. There was the world-famous Ray Charles talking with Blanche McDaniel-Valentine. At the time, Blanche was involved in marketing several vocal groups, including The Spaniels. I couldn't resist photographing them.

When Prentiss and Harvey joined them, laughing and hugging each other, I got some more great shots. After being matted and framed, several of the photos hang in my office today.

I was then able to speak to Ray, to touch his hands and thank him for his contribution to my life and to his millions of other fans the world over. He seemed so appreciative, laughing and rocking back in his characteristic style. I told him there was one other person who would want to thank him, too, and that was Bennett Chotard, one of my close friends, who played the piano and sang Ray's music constantly.

While Ray rehearsed, I listened, stunned by the man's talent. I also met Larry Dunn of Earth, Wind, & Fire and his wife, Luisa. Larry was the original keyboard player for this great group. Melissa Etheridge, who would be playing with Bonnie Raitt a little later, was also there. Basking in the glow of these stars, I felt deeply thankful that Harvey and Prentiss would include me.

★　★　★

Somehow, I managed to get myself dressed and Prentiss, too, in time for the cocktail hour that began at 6:00 p.m. in the ballrooms adjacent to the main presentation room. It was a black-tie affair, of course, and all the ladies looked lovely, dressed in their full regalia.

The Moonglows were to be the first inductees, with Paul Simon doing the honors. With the exception of Harvey and me, the others did not realize who Paul Simon was—a pop star of the first magnitude. When he came over to greet us during cocktails, wearing a baseball cap, he introduced himself simply, "Hi, I'm Paul."

Unaware that Paul was to introduce The Moonglows a little later and not recognizing him in his signature cap, I am embarrassed to admit that I had to ask, "Paul who?"

He smiled. "Paul Simon."

I felt a little silly, but he, being a gracious sort, seemed to understand.

As folks began filtering into the main hall for the dinner and awards presentation, we joined them and found our table. All our guys were there, some with their wives. Seizing the opportunity, I left my seat and wandered around, snapping photos of the many celebrities assembled in this one room. When I returned a bit later, dinner was being served.

Sometime between the appetizer and dessert, Harvey asked, "Where's Pete? We're scheduled to go on in a few minutes!"

We assumed he had gone to the men's room, but when he didn't return right away, his wife left to go look for him.

They showed up a scant five minutes before The Moonglows were to go onstage. With one too many cocktails under his belt, Pete had wandered out onto Park Avenue, and it was a miracle that he had been found . . . just in the nick of time!

Fortunately, he came through. When the guys took the stage for their performance, it was clear they felt confident that they were ready to wow the audience. And wow them, they did! The Moonglows looked dashing in their tuxes, Prentiss proudly wearing his fine tuxedo and his new patent leather shoes. They sounded as sensational as they looked, and they finished to a deafening standing ovation. Well deserved. They had worked hard this week.

Since Harvey offered the acceptance speech on behalf of the entire group, Prentiss later expressed his disappointment in not being able to have said a few words of his own. "I wanted to tell 'em 'bout *you,* Brother Morris," he said. "How you took care of me and helped me." His thoughts were appreciated, but helping him was entirely my pleasure. Nevertheless, Prentiss still had some frustration with Harvey.

Next was Earth, Wind, & Fire, who performed at the decibel level of an airport runway, a volume that rattled my sternum. I had to wonder how someone with heart trouble must feel when hearing such loud music with its vibrating bass. Nevertheless, I loved every moment, particularly seeing my new friend Larry Dunn on the keyboards. Among others being inducted into the Hall of Fame, some posthumously, were The Lovin' Spoonful, Nat King Cole, Billie Holiday, and Clive Davis. The list of luminaries goes on and on.

Diana Ross came out to do a couple of numbers with Ray Charles, who also paid tribute to Nat King Cole. "Nat was one of the greatest influences on my early career," he said. Eric Clapton, a guitar player with The Yardbirds, was the next to receive his award. Eric had definitely spiffed up his act, wearing a suit and tie to play "If I Saw You in Heaven," followed by a hot lick-type guitar duet with Robbie. Melissa Etheridge then introduced Bonnie Raitt, and they performed some sassy guitar numbers also. The place was hopping.

The last person to be recognized was James Taylor, introduced by none other than Paul McCartney. James performed "Fire and Rain," his signature song. Knowing a little about a tragic loss in his life, I felt for him as he sang, ". . . but I always thought I'd see you again." That poignant line captured much of his painful journey.

The grand finale brought all the performers together onstage for one last stupendous jam session. Watching Eric Clapton, James Taylor, and Bonnie Raitt knocking out the guitars right next to each other was a sight I shall never forget. All in all, it was a sublime show, with such outstanding talent deserving of recognition. But uppermost in my memory will be seeing Prentiss in his new tux, patent leather shoes, and a transformed countenance. This is what happens when one knows they are truly loved—they feel valued. And Prentiss was relishing this newfound knowledge.

★　★　★

Too soon, our adventure in New York was drawing to a close. On the day of departure, we were scheduled to fly out of Newark, New Jersey. Not to be outdone by all of the other mishaps over the past several days, there were a few more in store.

When the town car assigned to take us to the airport pulled into an area of the Waldorf where we were waiting, the porter asked us to get in and assured us that he would "take care of everything." Following his instructions, we slid into our seats and buckled ourselves in. My normal procedure when leaving on a trip is to personally supervise every piece of luggage being loaded into a car. Shortly thereafter, I was to regret not having paid attention to my instincts.

We arrived at the Newark airport after the drive over on a halcyon-like afternoon. Serene blue skies. Cotton candy clouds. No ominous sign belied what was in store.

When the trunk was popped, I checked the contents. "Where are our hang-up bags?"

"What hang-up bags?" the driver asked.

The answer was clear: They certainly were not *here!* They must still be on the luggage cart back at the hotel!

When we inquired at the Delta desk if someone from the hotel could drop off the bags to be sent on a later flight, we were told that passengers were required to accompany their luggage. Needless to say, we missed our original flight while the bags were retrieved from the Waldorf.

Prentiss and I were then booked on the next available flight with a precarious connection in Atlanta. We were unable to make the connection, causing another long wait. After trekking what seemed like miles, we took a tram to reach our gate in Concourse D, a good distance away. By this time, poor Prentiss had missed a meal and, with his diabetes, combined with his other physical limitations, he was extremely weak and near exhaustion.

"Brother Morris," he said in a shaky voice, "I ain't never walked this much in all my years put together."

A little supper perked him up. But it was nearly nine o'clock before we boarded our flight to Jackson, and Prentiss was asleep the instant he plopped down and leaned back against the headrest. When our plane landed and we left the jetway, he was happy to be home, cradling his cherished statue in his arms.

Retrieving our luggage at baggage claim—hang-up bags and all—I left Prentiss to watch over them while I went to get my parked car to drive him to his apartment. When I slid behind the wheel, I saw—nestled between the passenger seat and the console—the missing hook! That discovery, along with a little monetary "happy" I handed Prentiss for all his trouble, seemed to give him almost as much pleasure as his induction into the Hall of Fame.

★   ★   ★

At my suggestion, Chris Walters drafted a letter to the foundation, requesting a grant to help Prentiss with the necessities of life. Shortly thereafter, I was delighted to receive the news that he would be awarded a grant of approximately $300 per month. Since now he received about $650 per month from Social Security and approximately $50 a month from his newly found royalties, this would represent almost a fifty percent increase in his income. My hope was that these funds would be a blessing to Prentiss and give him some peace. After all, each day was a struggle for him.

~ 14 ~

THE BEAT GOES ON

Friendship is a mysterious thing. Sometimes it springs up suddenly from the seed of a common interest. Storms of misunderstanding may batter the seedling. The heat of conflict may scorch it so that it withers and dies. But true friendship roots deeply and endures past seedtime and harvest, clocks and calendars—for a lifetime and beyond. Such was the friendship of the five of us—Prentiss, Bill, Rufus, Harvey, and I. Each had something of value to share as our lives intermingled over the years, bringing a harmony of souls.

In the spring of 2000, I called Rufus at his home in Carson City, Nevada. "Rufus," I began, my enthusiasm ramping up at the sound of his voice, "My fortieth high school reunion is scheduled for early June, and we'd love to have you come sing for us. Oh . . . and maybe we could do some recording at Malaco Studios. You know, for a long time, I've been wanting to cut a CD with you singing 'Danny Boy.'"

"Well now, Bill, I believe I could do that."

We chatted some more, recalling how sad it had been to lose Walter Osborne, The Red Tops' manager and drummer, who had passed away well into his nineties, just three weeks after their own reunion in November. At one point in the conversation, we discussed the possibility of Rufus singing the lead on "Sincerely" with Prentiss Barnes and The Moonglows. He was definitely interested.

"Before I sign off, Rufus, I want to tell you again how deeply you are appreciated here in Mississippi. You and The Red Tops have made a significant musical contribution even beyond Mississippi."

A long pause on the other end of the line. "Hmm . . . guess I didn't know that, Bill. But I thank you for telling me."

Such humility was typical of the man. Just one of the many reasons I regarded him so highly.

Spinning, Spinning, Spinning

In the next few weeks, things transpired so quickly my head was spinning. The class reunion was set for June 9, which happened to be my fifty-eighth birthday. Rufus and I kept the wires hot between Jackson and Carson City as I updated him regularly on the progress of plans for recording at Malaco. He would fly in for a few days, arriving on June 5 and return home to Carson City on the tenth.

★   ★   ★

As planned, on June 5, I picked Rufus up at the Jackson International Airport to begin what was to be a delightful and inspiring week. We drove first to Vicksburg to the home of his sister, Elizabeth Harper, singing together in the car and playing music by artists he had not heard in years. As we headed for this storied city, crossing the bottomland of the Big Black River and making our way into the hill country, we let our minds wander. There were recollections of the past and high hopes for the future. I recalled names and faces of old friends and fans who will never be forgotten—Roger Stribling, Wilton Hinds, Al Povall, plus so many others, especially those gorgeous Mississippi girls.

We talked more about the upcoming recording session. As the time drew near, I was growing more and more excited, hoping I had covered all bases thoroughly. For one thing, we had assembled a group of professional musicians from around the state to lay the musical tracks for Rufus.

He spent the first day in the studio rehearsing with Ben Shaw and some of the members of his band. We all met the following afternoon at Malaco Records to begin phase one of the recording. Tommy Couch Sr. was so generous to let us use the Malaco Studio without charge. We had only to pay the engineer.

The guys laid down the tracks, yielding an exceptionally good rhythm section arranged by Ben. But I wasn't satisfied with the take on Rufus's voice. The studio version just did not measure up to the sound he could deliver in a live performance. There is something about the sterility of a booth and headphones in a studio that limits some recording artists. Maybe that was our problem.

As producer, it was my job to try to remedy the situation. Since Rufus seemed to do better on a stage in front of an audience, I figured we could broadcast the tape into the studio and let him sing from a hand-held mic. It would be our version of a "live" performance and should accomplish a great deal of what I had been looking for.

Rat-a-Tat

The few days Rufus and I spent together were not all work and no play. I took him to the Mayflower Café and introduced him to some of the locals, along with the savory fish that is the trademark of Jackson's oldest restaurant. On another day, we went to Brent's drugstore for hamburgers and tuna fish salad. Brent's, like the Mayflower, was also featured in the movie *The Help*.

By Friday, we had covered most of what we had hoped to accomplish in the studio and could turn our attention to the class reunion. Besides, it was my birthday, and I was in a celebratory mood. Just seeing old friends arriving from all over the country brought a rush of nostalgia.

Rufus's performance on the opening night of the reunion was spectacular. Everything was on key, and, just as I had expected, his vocal presence—live—was mesmerizing. At one point, he and the band sang "Happy Birthday" to me and then called me to the stage to do—you guessed it—"Daddy's Home." As

I was singing, I heard a familiar "rat-a-tat." I glanced over my shoulder. Rufus was backing me up with the sound I loved. Classmates gathered on the dance floor as we sang. I could think of no more perfect ending to my birthday.

The next afternoon, I took Rufus to the airport to board his flight for home. Later that night at the banquet, just before my good friend Guff Abbott gave the main presentation, I delivered greetings from Rufus with this great news: "Rufus McKay has decided to move back to Mississippi just as soon as he can wind up his affairs in Carson City."

The cheer that went up warmed my heart. It would be so good to have him back home where he belonged.

The Beat Goes On

A month later, Rufus was back to do a final take of his vocals. Because he had a very late flight, we grabbed a quick dinner at Copeland's, one of the only restaurants still open at that hour. While we were there, I called Wilson Stribling at WLBT-TV, Channel 3, to alert him that we would be recording at approximately ten o'clock the next morning. Wilson, the news anchor for this NBC affiliate, was the son of Roger Stribling, whom Rufus had known in the past. I knew that he would enjoy renewing their relationship.

Jerry Masters, the engineer, was waiting for us at Malaco when we arrived at the studio. But Rufus had not had a good night's sleep, nor had he eaten properly the day before. With his diabetes, he felt he was having an insulin reaction. Consequently, his voice was way off—shaky and hoarse from lack of sleep and insufficient energy. When Jerry told me that the studio was considering buying a new piece of equipment called an intonator, which would take a flat note and bring it into key, I relaxed a little.

About the time we were wrapping up our session, Wilson and his cameraman from Channel 3 arrived to interview Rufus. The interview went well.

Then Rufus turned the questions on Wilson. "Did you ever hear about the time your dad rode on the top of a car all the way from Jackson to Vicksburg to attend a Red Tops dance?" Rufus chuckled. "You know, folks always said that Roger was a real daredevil."

Wilson grinned. "So I've been told."

Roger, Wilson's dad, a West Point grad, had died while still in his twenties, when Wilson was just a baby. Everyone had expected that Roger would "fly high" someday—become an executive in some major company . . . or own one himself. He was just that kind of guy. The sad truth was that he had died in a private plane crash with a group of business executives just after takeoff from Hilton Head Island, South Carolina. They had overloaded the plane.

They were winding up the interview when Jerry reminded me of something I had asked him much earlier. "If there is room at the end of the master, I would like to record 'Daddy's Home.'"

There was . . . and I did . . . in one take. I had given Jerry a karaoke tape as back-up, and we made quick work of the recording. I was somewhat nervous, but Jerry Masters was very pleased and said that my pitch was exceptionally good. When I played it for Camille that afternoon, she liked it so much that she sent copies to our daughters.

That night, I took Rufus to Walker's Drive-In, an upscale vintage restaurant of the 1930s and located in the Fondren district of Jackson. We celebrated with a fine dinner before he left for Carson City the next day.

★　★　★

"Bill, I think I've got something we can run with here," Jerry said when he gave me a call the following afternoon.

"Not surprised, Jerry. I was praying about it just this morning."

"Well, it must have been your prayers that caused me to go back into the studio and extract enough segments for the desired effect," he went on. "Most of what we got was from the very first take, but we can do something with this."

I was relieved, of course, but still not completely satisfied with a couple of spots. If they got the intonator machine, we would be in better shape.

Wonder why things are never quite as good as one's memory might suggest. Perhaps we would never be able to duplicate the magic of those early years when I had first heard Rufus and his Red Tops at their peak.

The six o'clock news that evening featured the studio session where Wilson and the WLBT team gave us a five-minute spot. For several weeks, we continued to receive positive comments from so many of Rufus's fans. This encouraged me not to give up on the CD. His appreciative audience was still out there, still intrigued with this aging Mississippi singer.

Remember When

On August 15, I left for Bill Pinkney's seventh-fifth birthday celebration, to be held at the Sheraton Convention Center in Columbia, South Carolina. Maxine, his agent, had promised an "eleganzia," so I had packed my tux for the occasion.

Preceding the party was a seated dinner with many dignitaries and other entertainers in attendance. Various musicians from Bill's band were there, along with such singers as Diz Russell of The Orioles. And there was my dear friend, Harvey Fuqua, whom I was always delighted to see.

My dinner companion was Ruth Brown, a great singer in her own right, who worked with the Rock & Roll Hall of Fame Museum in Cleveland. She was a wealth of information about the industry, and I drank it in. Others at the head table were Bill, the honoree, Maxine, Billy Scott, and a couple of others who would be announcing and introducing.

About thirty seconds before the program was to begin, Maxine leaned over and asked if I would open the event with prayer since the preacher had not arrived. I am never uncomfortable praying extemporaneously. All we have to do is thank our heavenly Father for His manifold blessings and lay before Him our heart's desire.

Many of Bill's friends and fellow musicians told of their appreciation for him. Then it was time for my roast:

"Bill Pinkney, my friend and fellow music-lover I first met you backstage at Ole Miss in 1963. I remember it well: you were changing from a red tuxedo into a white one, dancing around on one foot while attempting to insert the other in your pants leg. . ." At that thought, there was a ripple of laughter around the room, punctuated by a few guffaws. "But it was twenty-two years later before I saw you again."

For the next few minutes, I highlighted events in Bill's life that had impacted mine. As I recounted our mutual experiences, I felt myself reliving them and hoped he did.

Bill was touched, and he got up and hugged me. He was dressed to a tee in white tails and a pair of white patent leather shoes. After the moving testimonials of so many people who revered Bill, he cut through it all when he whispered to me at the end of the program, "Man, these shoes are killin' me! I've got to hurry up and get out of 'em! I wear a size 13, and these are 11!"

★   ★   ★

The main show was to start at eight o'clock, so Maxine was anxious for the roasts to conclude. Several awards were bestowed on Bill that night, reminding us of his many achievements. It was an honor to be a part of recognizing this remarkable man.

Throughout the evening, we heard one outstanding group after another perform—all of them here at their own expense to pay tribute to a colleague they loved and admired. Harvey Fuqua sang "The Ten Commandments of Love" and "Twelve Months of the Year." The Orioles were next, dazzling everyone in their red suits and red patent leather shoes. Then Barbara and Rosa Hawkins from The Dixie Cups in New Orleans, along with Gloria Jones of The Shirelles, did a couple of numbers, including their hit song, "Chapel of Love." Now Eugene Pitt and his group came onstage. With all the great performers at this event, it was Gene who stole the show for me when he sang "My True Love."

After a brief intermission, Bill Pinkney and The Original Drifters performed. It was hard to believe that Bill, at seventy-five, was still jumping around with such energy and vitality. Their first number was "I'm Going to Go Across the River," then Bill stepped offstage, and the rest of the group did their thing—the usual show that I've seen so many times and always enjoy.

When Bill came back onstage, he felt that he should give credit where credit is due. "God has been mighty good to me, and now you're here to help me celebrate." With this, the gospel groups who had come to honor Bill began their set, with Tommy Ellison leading off. In no time, his group had the stage rocking. The whole building was shaking so that the huge speakers, stacked one on top of the other, almost tumbled over. Several of us had to rush over to steady them!

At the finale, Bill Pinkney took the lead, performing the rendition of "America the Beautiful" we had recorded in Jackson. Joining in was Skipp Pearson, a superstar saxophonist with extraordinary industry awards. He was given the Palmetto Order Award and is the South Carolina ambassador for jazz. How good it felt to be a part of another milestone in Bill's life.

★　★　★

In early September, I headed to Malaco Studios to pick up the master tape and three cassettes of Rufus McKay's "Danny Boy" and my own "Daddy's Home." I listened with gratitude for the wonderful job that Jerry Masters had done. It was not everything I had hoped for, but the project was complete.

I took a copy of the tape and the liner notes to Ann Abadie, head of the Center for the Study of Southern Culture at the University of Mississippi. It was my fervent wish that it would be a great blessing to thousands, perhaps even millions of people.

Most of All

Shortly after, I received a call from Harvey Fuqua. The Moonglows were scheduled to be inducted into the Vocal Group Hall of Fame on October 20 in Sharon, Pennsylvania. Harvey and I deliberated about whether or not they should perform at the ceremony. The primary concern was Pete and his drinking habit. Harvey thought one of the reasons they weren't getting more requests for performances was because of the way Pete had acted in New York at the Rock & Roll Hall of Fame induction. Harvey decided to check with Pete's manager to see what they should do about it. In the meantime, Harvey was going to send me a CD of one of his recent releases. I was eager to hear it, knowing that some of the numbers had been recorded with Smokey Robinson.

Harvey was as deeply embedded in the history of rock 'n' roll as any person I have ever known. At one time, he was married to Barry Gordy's sister, Gwendolyn, was a founding member of The Moonglows, tutored The Dells and The Spinners, and was Marvin Gaye's close friend and manager of sorts during the last part of Marvin's career.

★ ★ ★

On the way back from Oxford one Sunday afternoon, I was listening to the CD that Harvey had sent me. The first song was a medley entitled, "When I'm with You," my favorite song by The Moonglows. In the medley, he mentioned all of the original members: Prentiss Barnes, Pete Graves, and Billy "Party Time" Johnson, along with Bobby Lester. It was a great upbeat rendition in which Harvey included "Most of All," "Sincerely," and "Love Is Strange." As I listened to that track, I felt a strong tugging on my heart, imagining Prentiss as a young man first recording that music and performing for audiences throughout the country.

I called Prentiss and played the music over the phone as I drove down the highway. We reminisced for a while and realized that it would only be a couple of weeks before we would be in Cleveland at the Rock & Roll Hall of Fame Museum, and in Sharon, Pennsylvania, for the Vocal Group Hall of Fame ceremony.

I then called Harvey and thanked him for the CD and told him how much I loved the music, particularly the medley. We discussed one of the songs in particular, "The Tracks of My Tears," one of the songs he was performing with Smokey Robinson, his friend for many years.

"Harvey," I said with affection, "I appreciate everything you've done for us. You are one of the top arrangers in the entire history of rock 'n' roll. Your songs are virtually flawless, and the harmony is unequalled. Most of all, though, I want you to know how privileged I am to know you, Harvey, and the others who have affected our culture."

He seemed very touched. "Bill, you know I love you, too, brother."

★   ★   ★

Sometime later, I received a call from Prentiss, informing me that Dr. Pieklik, who was also my personal internist, had told him that he would need to go on insulin for his diabetes. Already disabled, with one arm missing and the other stricken with palsy as a result of the accident, Prentiss would have a difficult time giving himself an injection.

When he relayed this news to me, I said, "Let me call Dr. Pieklik and see what he says about it. Perhaps he will let you increase your oral medication."

"With Mr. Barnes's blood sugar levels, increasing his dosage is not an option," the doctor replied when I put in a call to him.

My heart sank. This was not good news. But being an optimist, I was hopeful that Prentiss would push through this setback as he had so many times before.

~ 15 ~

MEMORIES

Although Prentiss Barnes's health was unpredictable these days, he could have stepped off the cover of *GQ* Magazine as we set out for the Rock & Roll Hall of Fame in Cleveland, Ohio. He looked mighty sharp in a new black and brown hound's-tooth sport coat, tan trousers, and a black shirt and tan tie. This sartorial splendor was compliments of Steve Scott of the Great Scott men's clothing store in Jackson, listed as one of *Esquire* magazine's top fifty men's stores.

Our flight arrived on time, and we showed up around noon at the museum, only to discover that they were also honoring John Lennon's widow, Yoko Ono, and were in the process of rolling out the red carpet. The place was under heavy security, and the police officer in charge would not allow us through the main gate, despite the fact that Prentiss was a member of the Hall. Only momentarily frustrated, I called the president, Terry Stewart, whom I had met on a number of occasions. His assistant cleared us right away, directing us to park in a designated spot beside the building. Terry, along with Howard Kramer, came to greet us and posed for some photos before escorting us inside.

Cleveland's Rock & Roll Hall of Fame Museum was phenomenal! With many of the original outfits, tuxedos, other memorabilia, and even their musical instruments on display, we were swept into the past. And here beside me was one of the greats himself—Prentiss Barnes. It was fascinating to see the technology they had applied to the old records and video scenes of days gone by. In the actual Rock & Roll Hall of Fame, the names and signatures of each artist that had been inducted were inscribed in gold on the black marble wall. A few of the artists' signatures were missing, but Prentiss's was at the very top with the rest of The Moonglows. Although visitors were not normally allowed anywhere in the museum, today—for Prentiss—it was.

Prentiss's nephew, Leonard Barnes, joined us halfway through our time there. He was a delightful young man and obviously admired and loved his uncle very much. As the afternoon moved along, we found ourselves in the gift shop where Prentiss was presented a beautifully embroidered Rock & Roll Hall of Fame leather jacket.

Just as we were leaving, Ruth Brown saw us and came running up to give us both a hug and a kiss. It was clear that the actual members of the Rock & Roll Hall of Fame were cherished.

Faded Photographs

Mid-afternoon, we headed for Sharon, Pennsylvania, in a brand-new mid-sized rental car to join the many fabulous groups being inducted into the 1999 and 2000 Vocal Group Hall of Fame. The scenery on the turnpike was breathtaking. In the glow of the afternoon sun, the trees appeared to have literally burst into flame—fiery reds, deep gold, burnt orange. All across Ohio and into Pennsylvania, the changing colors of the season provided a visual feast.

No sooner had Prentiss and I checked into the Radisson Hotel than Herman Santiago and Jimmy Merchant of Frankie Lymon and The Teenagers were there to greet us. When Prentiss got to his room, awaiting him was a bag of goodies, including a hat, sweatshirt, and other items from the hall of fame. Attached was a luggage tag labeled Inductee. As a courtesy, the same package had been placed in my room.

In the early evening, we gathered in front of the Radisson to be chauffeured to the location of the ceremony in Sharon. As I got into the fancy shuttle they had arranged for us, Duke Fakir from The Four Tops climbed in and stood next to me. We chatted, then started singing and were rocking out by the time we reached the venue.

Also in the van were some members of The Dixie Hummingbirds, Ira Tucker, and several members of The Soul Stirrers. I especially enjoyed talking to Luther Gamble. Then I spotted LeRoy Crume, the only original member of Sam Cooke's old group who was still singing. What a sweet and gentle spirit. He remembered me from Malaco Studios six weeks earlier when I was there recording with Rufus McKay.

When we arrived, Duke wanted to buy me a drink. "Man, I like your spirit!" he said. I, of course, accepted, honored to have received such an offer from the last surviving original member of The Four Tops.

The very vivacious Mary Wilson of The Supremes sashayed over to join us. As we chatted, I noted the obvious camaraderie and a certain spark of long-ago friendship between Duke and Mary. But, of course, they had recorded in the same studio at Motown and had traveled together for several years, along with many other Motown singers, having two of the most successful acts in the history of rock 'n' roll.

During the evening, I met so many others, including Joe Jackson, father of Michael Jackson. Carl Gardner, the original lead singer of The Coasters, shared with me that he had been healed of cancer.

The Moonglows had a reserved table down front, and I was seated with them. Entertainment was furnished by The Lettermen that night. Spectacular! Tony Butala, the only member of the original Lettermen still performing at the time, was now also involved with the Vocal Group Hall of Fame. For the entire two-hour show, he and the two younger singers held the audience in the palms of their hands. The group finished to a standing ovation.

As we began to file out of the venue, I had a chance to speak with two of the Delta Rhythm Boys—René DeKnight and Carl Jones—discussing certain positive changes in the State of Mississippi. I had a number of those discussions that night and took great joy in telling others about my home state—also home to some of the most notable writers, artists, singers, and musicians in history.

One of the more unusual things that happened was the number of singers who commented on my singing. "You should do voiceovers for commercials," said Joe Croyle of The Modernaires. "You know—like that Motel 6 guy, Tom Bodett."

I laughed. "Funny, I've heard that before," I told him. "But as president of an insurance firm, don't know how well that would play."

When I continued to run into Joe during the weekend, he insisted on giving me instructions as to how to go about pursuing that avenue. *Well, we'll see,* I thought to myself. The world of entertainment—and all that accompanied it—was a great place to visit, but I wasn't sure I wanted to live there. Nevertheless, my audio version of this book gives some flavor of what they might have been hearing.

Opening Day

At breakfast the next morning, I met a DJ named Tim Marshall out of New York City and Larry Cotton, editor of a British rock 'n' roll magazine, *In the Basement.* I gave them both CDs, and they promised to print some good reviews. Prentiss and I were already in our tuxes, ready to leave for the late-morning ceremonies. Once the program started, we knew we would not have an opportunity to change.

In front of the Radisson, while we were awaiting our ride, we spotted Pete Graves, the lead tenor, drunk at ten o'clock in the morning. He was not dressed in his tuxedo—far from it! He was wearing some kind of rag-tag clothing with a skullcap pulled down on his head. With no further time to spare, Prentiss and I jumped into the van that was taking us to the venue, a ten-minute drive. As we pulled away, Pete was still staggering around at the front door, puffing on a cigarette. With The Moonglows not scheduled to appear until that night, they would have some time to work with him later.

We arrived at the Vocal Group Hall of Fame a little after ten o'clock to find an impressive three-story building with glass cases filled with memorabilia—old records, posters, publicity photos, 78s, 45s, and 33 ⅓ rpm albums. I shot thirteen rolls of film over the course of the three-day event.

The press conference was low-key and relaxed compared to others I have observed. Normally, the air would be crackling with tension, but this was quite different. I kept expecting things to become stressful, but they never did. Everyone seemed to be enjoying themselves. The reporters were free to roam around and question whomever they wished. A number of them approached Prentiss.

At one time, Bill Pinkney came up to me, looked me in the eye, and said, "Bill, I've got something I want to tell you. I appreciate what you do for Prentiss. It really means a lot to me."

I thanked him and, unable to say anything more, held his gaze for what seemed like a long time. It was in that emotion-packed moment that a reporter snapped our picture, then approached us to ask the meaning of this exchange. As best I could, I explained our friendship. But words were insufficient. I only hoped this reporter could read between the lines.

It was an elegant, midday affair with nearly everyone in black tie and the ladies in their finery. And wonder of wonders—even Pete appeared in his tux! The formal induction ceremony, which started sometime after noon and continued until nearly four o'clock, was exceptionally long because they were inducting both classes of 1999, which included The Moonglows, as well as the class of 2000. The first class in 1998 included Bill Pinkney and The Original Drifters.

Spunky Mary Wilson was one of the emcees, along with Jay Warner, music producer and Grammy award-winner, and both of them were able to sense the moment to be respectfully subdued or to bridge an awkward gap with a little well-placed humor.

The 1999 inductees were then presented with their trophies—one trophy for each group. It was touching to hear the sincere gratitude expressed by inductees or those receiving on behalf of a deceased loved one or colleague. The most moving acceptance speech was by Tommy Hunt of The Flamingos, who had been out of the country for several years and was now living in Holland. This dignified man broke down at the podium upon receiving his award and momentarily covered his eyes with his hand. In response, the crowd erupted in a standing ovation.

The funniest recipient was Prentiss Barnes. Prentiss always said he was not comfortable speaking at a microphone, but it was hilarious to hear him talk about some of the problems of old age. Indeed, Prentiss was a very good speaker, now having developed a great deal of self-confidence.

Harvey accepted for The Moonglows, with the individual trophies to be mailed out some time after the event. For some reason—perhaps some organizational glitch or financial problem—Prentiss's trophy never arrived.

As the preliminary festivities finally concluded, I went downstairs with Bill Pinkney. Prentiss had gone on with Pete somewhere, and Bill took me to a bar where they were rehearsing for the evening event. When we arrived, Jimmy Merchant was running through a new version of "Why Do Fools Fall in Love?" The song started slowly, building to an up-tempo beat. It was eventually Bill Pinkney's turn to rehearse "White Christmas," and I kept wishing he had one of his original tenors with him. The keyboard player with the house band was attempting Clyde McPhatter's part and wasn't quite able to pull off a true falsetto.

Chuck Negron of Three Dog Night walked in, looking cool in his black leather britches, and we talked for a while. When it was time for Chuck's rehearsal, he performed "One," "Easy to be Hard," and "Joy to the World." I kept thinking what people would give to be elbow to elbow with such musical personalities as Chuck, Mary Wilson, Bill Pinkney and The Drifters, The Moonglows, The Flamingos, and so many other fabulous groups.

Later, getting a bite at Donna's Diner down the street with Bill, we looked up to see Harvey Fuqua coming in the door. He joined us at the counter. Bill was on my right and Harvey on my left—two of the most influential people in the history of rock 'n' roll. Once again, I could only shake my head in wonder.

Great Balls of Fire!

At 5:30 p.m. the show began. Unfortunately, Pete's status had not changed. He was still inebriated, and Harvey, Prentiss, and Beryle Easton—whom Harvey had pulled in from another group to sing for the evening—were all upset with him.

They had asked me to do the recitation part of "The Ten Commandments of Love." That meant I would repeat, "Thou shalt never love another" in a very deep voice as the rest of the lyrics were sung by the lead singer and the others carried the harmony. I was growing increasingly nervous now because if Pete messed up, many might think "the white guy" was the cause.

Finally, Harvey and Prentiss confronted Pete and told him that he was off the show and I was on. I wasn't actually going to replace him; I was just going to fill in with some extra bass for the repeated portions of the song. In fact, Pete and I had never had any kind of disagreement, and I certainly wasn't intending to start one now! Harvey and Prentiss loved Pete as he was the "baby" of the group. They just did not know what to do with him.

Nevertheless, Pete was so distraught over all this that he didn't know what to do and began pleading with the guys, insisting that he would be all right. Then he broke out in one of the lyrics, trying to convince them that he could still sing. From what I had heard of his rehearsal earlier in the day, however, he couldn't hit a note, not even a sour one.

Everywhere I went, whether it was the museum itself, backstage, or the audience, energy was pulsating. Different groups were singing in various places. It was an amazing event!

When it was time for The Moonglows to go on, I couldn't help being a little apprehensive, even though we knew the entire audience would be aware of the problem by now. After we got to the top of the stairs to the rear side of the stage, waiting for the emcee to announce us, I began to pray silently with my hands placed lightly on Pete's back, asking God to give him the ability to do the set in spite of his intoxication. I prayed for all of The Moonglows and for myself, that we would do a creditable job.

The first song was "Sincerely," followed by "The Ten Commandments of Love." It went remarkably well, considering what had transpired with Pete. One lady approached me after the show. "Knowing Pete's condition, I could not believe how well he was able to sing!" she exclaimed. "That performance was truly a miracle!"

Others in the audience kept coming up to tell The Moonglows they had loved the show. I cannot count the number of people who asked for *my* autograph—something that was certainly new to me. One guy in a fringed jacket—cowboy style—approached me, sure he had seen me on the "Grand Ole Opry." Even though I told him I had never been on that stage, he insisted he had seen me there.

At the conclusion of our performance, I decided to sit in the lounge and enjoy a moment of relaxation. There, ahead of me, was Beryle—for this night, the baritone of The Moonglows—and we had a moment to visit.

A few minutes later, Bill Pinkney came through the bar. "You know, Bill," he said, "we keep running into each other at these things all over the country."

"I know," I replied. "It's God's work, not ours."

I walked back into the lobby of the museum to find Jimmy Merchant teaching some young white guys how to sing "Why Do Fools Fall in Love?" A sign of things to come?

★   ★   ★

Jim Winter and his wife, along with Tony Butala and his wife, Julie, had been entirely responsible for the museum and the event, which they had pulled off marvelously. At the conclusion of the evening, I was grateful to have an opportunity to thank them in person.

We stayed around, signing autographs and visiting with people until we were the last to leave. On the ride back to the Radisson in a limo with Tony and Julie, Prentiss, Harvey, Luther Gamble of The Soul Stirrers, and others, Julie and I discussed the meaning of all that had taken place and the deep spiritual blessings we were receiving. During the weekend, we had glimpsed far more than an awards ceremony. Our souls had, indeed, been stirred. Just before exiting the limo, I told Julie about the book I was writing that would include the difficult situations of several of these musical giants from another era. Our efforts to remedy their plight would continue.

Home Again

The next morning, as Prentiss and I headed back to Cleveland to catch our flight home, nothing about the pleasant drive past all that glorious fall foliage could have prepared us for the fiasco to follow. It was only when I made my routine phone call to the airline to confirm our travel plans that I learned anything was amiss. Our Delta flight had been canceled!

To compensate, they put us on another carrier, which left earlier, so we were now behind schedule. It was a race to get to the Continental gate because I had to turn in the car at the rental kiosk, which pushed us up to the last minute. Prentiss and I were on the run to get to the other terminal. It was quite a hike. When we got to the other side, the escalator from the basement to the main floor was broken. It seemed there must have been over a hundred stairs, appearing more daunting than the Atlanta airport escalator that runs from the tram cars to the upper level. I told Prentiss to catch the elevator and I would take the stairs.

When he finally dragged himself to the gate to join me about ten minutes later, he looked exhausted. "Man," he said, "that elevator was broke, too, and I had to climb all those stairs." A pretty good jaunt for a seventy-five-year-old man who had the use of only one good leg.

When we got to Atlanta and down to our gate, Prentiss was so tired, he stretched out across several seats, out of sight. When the agent at the counter asked for our photo IDs in order to issue our new Delta boarding passes for the last leg of our flight, I looked around for Prentiss, but he was nowhere to be seen.

"Prentiss!" I yelled. "Prentiss!" After several agonizing minutes, he finally rose from the spot where he had been sleeping—the seats near the windows overlooking the tarmac. His tie was askew and his nice suit coat rumpled. My heart went out to him. He had given his all . . . again.

When our flight into Jackson landed, and we reached the baggage carousel, we learned that our luggage had been checked only as far as Atlanta. By now, Prentiss was literally on *his* last leg.

When I dropped him off at his apartment and helped him to his door, he asked if I would wait a minute while he fetched something. He returned from a back room with his most prized possession—his Rock & Roll Hall of Fame trophy, the one that is recognized the world over as the most treasured of all.

"Brother Morris," he said, handing me his cherished award, "would you keep this for me? I'm afraid somebody might take this thing or break it if we leave it here."

I was honored. There was no doubt in my mind that he would never receive anything that would compare to the prize he was now placing in my hands.

★　★　★

The next morning—very early on Sunday—I slipped out back to my favorite spot on the patio to spend some quiet time recording memories of the weekend in my journal. Once again, I was overwhelmed with the significance of all that had taken place—this sacred journey I was taking with some of the shining stars of yesteryear.

A couple of hours later, I could hear Camille calling me to breakfast. Her sweet voice and the aroma of hot coffee, crisp bacon, and sweet potato biscuits drew me inside. But not before making one last note in my journal: "Give Prentiss that plane ticket from my Delta frequent flyer miles for his next trip . . . and look into hosting a fundraiser for him as soon as possible."

~ 16 ~

AMAZING GRACE

On New Year's Day, 2001, I reached for the phone to call Bill Pinkney at his home in Sumter, South Carolina. When Bill answered, there was much laughter in the background and the sounds of joyous fellowship among family members.

"Bill, I got your message, and it was wonderful," he told me. "And oh, look, man! I've found Christ! I've accepted Him as my Lord and Master!" He went on to tell me how he had been ailing from what sounded like gout. "I've been hobblin' around for weeks. Even with crutches and a cane, I couldn't hardly make it, I was in so much pain.

"My nephew asked me to go to church with him—you know, that Church of Christ Holiness out in the country a ways. So I got myself ready and went with him. I was on my crutches, of course. When I got there, Bill, all the ladies were dressed in white. They looked like angels! Another female relative—a cousin of mine—was in the choir loft, but she came on down to the podium, looking at me, and said, 'Bill Pinkney, I've been waiting a long time for you to come.'

"Bill," he said, "they took me in. Then they poured oil all over my head, and I began to cry. I couldn't stop cryin'. They prayed over me and laid their hands on my side where it hurt. I began to ask God for forgiveness for anyone that I had mistreated, and I received Christ. I was saved!" He choked up and had to pause.

"One more thing, Bill," he went on when he had regained control of his emotions. "When I left the church and got to my nephew's car, my cousin called after me, 'You forgot your crutches!' Just couldn't believe all that was happenin'. I got saved and healed all in one day!"

It's my perception that Bill Pinkney had long been a Christian, but only God knows a man's heart. Maybe what happened was that he had now fully surrendered and was feeling the euphoria of being released from youthful sins, along with the relief from pain and disability.

As he was retelling the story, he began to cry again. "Can't help it," he said. "Every time I talk about it, I begin cryin'."

Moved by his testimony, tears sprang to my eyes too. I had been talking on my cell phone, walking to a neighbor's home to attend their New Year's Day open house, and had to stop to wipe my tears. When I could compose myself, I cleared my throat and said, "Bill, this is one of the nicest New Year's Day gifts I have ever received. The Lord is so good. Happy new year to you, my brother!"

★ ★ ★

A few days later, I called Larry Cotton, editor of *In the Basement* magazine, the European publication. I had sent him some photos of the Vocal Group Hall of Fame ceremony that had been held a few weeks earlier. I had also sent him a recording of my "Daddy's Home" on CD.

Larry and I talked for nearly an hour, laughing and sharing anecdotes. Then he surprised me with this comment. "And by the way, you're quite a writer!"

When I questioned him as to what he meant, he added, "Those liner notes in The Drifters' CD. Unbelievable! How did you do that?"

That's when I told him I had prayed for three hours before I wrote. "God sometimes answers prayer in ways we can't understand."

"Well, can't tell you how much I love it! Been talking about you on my radio program up here in New York . . . and just had an interview with your friend, Bill Pinkney."

★ ★ ★

Ever since speaking with Bill on New Year's Day, his spiritual experience had been on my mind. I called him again and asked him if he would mind my recording this amazing testimony.

He didn't hesitate. "Bill, you go right ahead." He paused, then added, "You know, I've been thinkin' about Prentiss Barnes. Of all the guys, he's the worst off of all of us—losing his arm in that accident and not really being able to work much ever since. I'd really like to do something special for him."

"Interesting that you should mention that," I said. "I've been considering the idea of holding a benefit for Prentiss, and I'd like for you to be the lead act. Prentiss, you, and I could sing together, and we could bring Rufus in from Carson City for the entertainment."

It was a deal. The benefit for Prentiss was an idea whose time had come.

Television Debut

Near the end of February, I received a call from the executive director of Mississippi Educational Television. He was inquiring about scheduling Prentiss Barnes to appear on their Doo Wop 51 Special, a statewide ETV broadcast of a show pre-taped in December 1999 out of New York City. The show would showcase many fabulous groups, including The Dells, Bill Pinkney and The Original Drifters, and the second set of Drifters, featuring Charlie Thomas as lead singer.

"By all means," I told the executive director. "Count on me to arrange it. But is there any budget for Prentiss's appearance on the show? Even a little would help him."

The executive director assured me that they would give me a call and let me know what they could do. As it turned out, Edie Green, producer for this program, checked in with me later that day and agreed to pay Prentiss $200.

In further discussion, Edie was pleased to know that I was willing to work with Bill Pinkney in taping a one-minute voice-over, proclaiming the value of ETV in Mississippi and the need for people to contribute. We had a lot of fun making the tape. Actually, the whole process was hilarious, and we both got so tickled, we could hardly finish! Unfortunately, when Bill and I undertook the taping, the quality of our little effort was not up to their standards, or maybe they didn't have the time to edit it properly.

But as the time drew near for the show, I realized that there *was* something else I could do for ETV—I could donate sixty *True Love* CDs by Bill Pinkney and the Original Drifters that they could give to the first callers.

★   ★   ★

On a late Sunday afternoon in early March, Prentiss and I rode over to the ETV studios. There we were met by Edie Green and escorted into a room where we waited for a few minutes. Shortly, we were joined by the charming and popular local news anchor, Melanie Christopher. Her welcoming smile was infectious and put us at ease immediately.

After meeting Prentiss, she asked if I would be willing to go on the set with him to make him more comfortable. I was happy to do that. She also inquired about Prentiss singing a song, and I tried coaxing him through a couple of lines to see what he might like to sing. Then I excused myself for a few minutes as the upcoming session was scheduled for two hours. Upon my return, I discovered that they had all decided I should sing with him.

"But I'm not a professional singer," I demurred.

"Oh, I've heard quite enough to know that you'll do just fine!" Melanie insisted, her brown eyes sparkling.

The show was on! I knew Prentiss, with his bass voice, would probably not be able to do much without someone to harmonize with him, so I really had no choice. I had never sung on TV before, so this was another first for me. It was a blessing that we didn't have much time to think about it, as twenty minutes

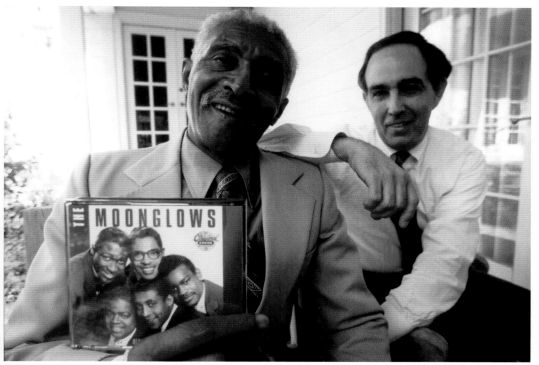

Bill and Prentiss at Bill's Home posing for an article that appeared in The Clarion Ledger 1994—Photo by Tom Roster

Bill Pinkney (The Drifters), Lloyd Price, Harvey Fuqua (The Moonglows), Reggie Gordon (The Magnificents), and Mickey Baker (Mickey and Sylvia)—R&B Pioneer Awards in LA

Larry Graham (Graham Central Station & Sly and The Family Stone) and his wife, Tina—R&B Foundation Press Conference LA

Bill and Brenda Holloway—R&B Pioneer Awards Press Conference LA

Charlie Thomas (Left—Second set of Drifters) and Bill Pinkney (Right—The Original Drifters)—R&B Pioneer Awards LA

Bill and Dee Dee Warwick "I'm Gonna Make You Love Me"—Pioneer Awards LA

Bill, Evelyn Harris (ETV), Prentiss Barnes, and Melanie Christopher (TV Personality)—the night Prentiss and Bill were singing to benefit ETV

THIS MAGIC MOMENT PRESERVATION TRUST

WILLIAM H. MORRIS, JR.
CHAIRMAN

MORGAN FREEMAN
HONORARY CHAIRMAN

March 1, 2002

We are thrilled to announce the formation of the *This Magic Moment Preservation Trust*, under the auspices of the Community Foundation of Greater Jackson, a 501(c)(3) non-profit organization. The establishment of this fund is in response to a need that has been expressed within our own Jackson community.

There are many of the singers and musicians in our region who have given us wonderful music over the years, particularly those of the 1950's and early 1960's. These people were never given credit for many of the songs that they wrote, nor did they receive proper royalties for their music recorded which is still sold today. A perfect example of this situation is our first year's honoree, Mr. Prentiss Barnes of Jackson, MS. He is the original virtuoso bass singer with the world-renowned "Moonglows" group. Prentiss helped write many songs that became famous and he was given no credit for them. He has been more fortunate than most to have received some meager reward, and yet he still struggles to make ends meet while millions of people continue to enjoy his music. In the year 2000 Prentiss was inducted as a member into the Rock and Roll Hall of Fame and the Vocal Group Hall of Fame. He also is a Mississippi Ageless Heroes Award recipient and a Rhythm and Blues Foundation "Pioneer". Prentiss is 77 years old, disabled, and barely able to pay his bills on his monthly Social Security check. He is just one that we refer to, but there are unfortunately many others.

Please help us give assistance to these singers and musicians who have given us the priceless gift of a lifetime of music by becoming a member of the *This Magic Moment Preservation Trust* and attending our inaugural event on April 26 at the Country Club of Jackson. This year's entertainment will be provided by *Bill Pinkney and the Original Drifters*, along with *Rufus McKay of the Red Tops* (performing "Danny Boy"). We anticipate this becoming an annual event and we seek to have many more famous entertainers participate year after year. Becoming a charter member insures your ticket priority for the following year's event.

Tickets to this year's gala are limited, so please respond as soon as possible. Various levels of participation are indicated on the enclosed response card. Fine hors d'oeuvres, dancing, and entertainment will be provided. Please make your check payable to The Community Foundation of Greater Jackson with an indication that the funds are intended for the *This Magic Moment Preservation Trust*.

Thank you for your support and interest in a most worthy cause!

William H. Morris, Jr.

Morgan Freeman

188 EAST CAPITOL STREET, SUITE 1075
JACKSON, MS 39201-2189
601-948-0030/ FAX 601-948-0041

*A PROUD MEMBER FUND OF THE COMMUNITY FOUNDATION OF GREATER JACKSON

This Magic Moment Preservation Trust announcement letter- William Morris Chairman and Morgan Freeman, Honorary Chairman – Jackson, MS 2002

TMM Event – Rufus McKay with Dr. Faser Triplett (Charitable Benefactor)

Photo Op for Publicity Featuring Chris Walters, Lelia Manning, Bill Morris, Prentiss Barnes, Camille Morris, and Linda Montgomery with the Painting "This Magic Moment."

Before the TMM Event began—gathered in the foyer of the Jackson Country Club (JCC)—Bill Pinkney (The Drifters), Bill Morris, Prentiss Barnes (honoree in tails), and Rufus McKay

Prentiss getting a big hug from Bill upon receiving the inaugural "This Magic Moment" award—Jackson MS JCC April 2002

Bill singing the lead with Rufus McKay (Left), Prentiss Barnes (Center), Reggie Gordon and Harvey Fuqua—TMM Event

Reggie Gordon, Harvey Fuqua, Bill Morris, and Prentiss after just having sung the song "Daddy's Home" which Harvey wanted to record

Prentiss giving his appreciation to the large crowd at TMM event—Jackson, MS

Camille and Bill enjoying a dance at TMM event—
Jackson, MS

Bill with Rufus McKay in the background singing his immortal version of "Danny Boy"—
several hundred pairs of shades were given to the attendees

later, we were on the set. Over a period of two hours, we sang segments from the following songs: "The Ten Commandments of Love," "In the Still of the Night," "For Your Precious Love," and "Why Do Fools Fall in Love?"

During one of the breaks, I commented to Melanie that my wife, Camille, was going to kill me.

At that, Melanie burst out laughing. "Oh, no, she won't!" she said. "Let me talk with her."

I dialed the number and handed Melanie the phone. To my surprise, Camille had no reservations whatsoever about my appearance on the show. Quite the contrary. She said she was very proud of me and was enjoying the program, which eased my mind considerably. She also reported that friends were calling the house and commenting about it. I noticed that a number of my friends from around the state were, indeed, calling in to the station to make pledges. It was a heartwarming experience.

After the show, we learned that the station had exceeded their financial goal! A bit of celebrating was in order. Best of all was Prentiss's sense of satisfaction with our performance.

"Hey, Brother Morris," he said to me on our way out to the car later that night, "folks said we sounded really good together." Then, on a more somber note, he turned to me. "You know, if you hadn't found me, I would have been dead in a gutter somewhere. I am just so thankful to the Lord."

"I'm thankful, too, because you have brought a lot of joy into my life."

A day later, my good friend Rhesa Barksdale, a federal judge on the 5th Circuit Court of Appeals, wrote me the following note: "William, you were nothing short of *terrific* on ETV Sunday night. Great tune, great harmony, great persona, and great love. Mighty proud of you. Rhesa"

To top everything off, I heard from Bill Pinkney not long after that telecast. Bill told me he had received an honorary doctorate from the University of South Carolina. "From now on, guess you'll have to call me Dr. Pinkney," he said with that characteristic warm chuckle of his.

It always did my heart good to hear that my friends were doing well. And I was newly determined to see that Prentiss, too, should receive all the accolades and support due him.

Remembering Willie

On May 12, I traveled to Yazoo City for the inaugural episode of Remembering Willie, a daylong event of talks, testimonials, and other laudatory comments by the friends and admirers of noted journalist and one of my favorite authors, Willie Morris. I was most moved by Unita Blackwell, the first female black mayor in Mississippi, serving the town of Myersville in the Mississippi Delta.

Hearing Mayor Blackwell's words, along with many others, I was reminded of how powerfully Willie Morris had influenced my life. It was far more than the intriguing fact that, although we were not related, our names were almost identical. He was an acclaimed journalist. Brilliant editor and author. Humorist. And native son of Mississippi. So much of what I admired in a great writer.

It was fitting that this would be a day filled with warmth and wistfulness, concluding with a visit to the cemetery where Willie is buried. We gathered around his gravesite for a bit of additional testimony and a performance by the Yazoo Angelic Gospel Singers. These four women provided a deeply felt, raw, and inspirational rendition of "Swing Low, Sweet Chariot," "Amazing Grace," and several other songs. The graveside service ended appropriately with the playing of "Taps." Willie always had a great reverence for "Taps," as he would play his bugle at the burial of soldiers making their last trip home from the Korean War.

Hearing this poignant sound, my mind wandered once again to another scene, played out long ago on a humid day in Jackson. The Southern heat had set in, and as today—beside Willie's grave—not a leaf was stirring. Along with others, I was standing in line inside a fast-food restaurant, prepared to order lunch.

Having just read Willie's novel, *Yazoo*—the story of a Southern town caught up in the tension of racial conflict—I found myself standing behind a distinguished-looking gentleman of color. When he turned slightly to acknowledge my presence, I recognized him as a civil rights leader in our area. Our gazes met . . . locked . . . deepened. Something happened in that silent exchange. Two men of different skin tones and ethnic backgrounds felt a deep connection.

Still standing by Willie's grave, I was startled from my reverie by the crowd dispersing to reconvene at the Old Saxton's Hardware on South Main Street for a performance by the Ben Shaw Band, featuring the legendary Red Tops lead singer Rufus McKay. Ben asked me to do "Daddy's Home," with Rufus giving me the rat-a-tat back-up. It was over all too soon, but the memory lingered.

All the way up and back from Yazoo City, I was listening to the song "Zing! Went the Strings of My Heart" by The Coasters. Never far from my thoughts was Prentiss Barnes and the benefit I hoped to orchestrate for him the following spring.

Willie Morris's grave had reminded me of many things. Most importantly, that Prentiss, with his age and physical limitations, might not be far from *his* eternal resting place. There was no time to waste.

Grace to Forgive

Meanwhile, I made it a point to encourage Prentiss every chance I got. Another occasion presented itself not long after our appearance on ETV. I was called by the producer to bring Prentiss for a taped interview with Gene Edwards, to be aired on his program, *Conversations*. Gene was the television anchor for WAPT, the ABC affiliate in Jackson, and, in my opinion, the best interviewer in the business.

Prentiss and I were both relaxed throughout the entire program, and Gene was able to draw out even more of Prentiss's fascinating story. We concluded when Gene asked us to sing "Sincerely," for which—except for the few minutes of practice before going on the set—we were unprepared. But we did it.

Watching the program with Camille when it aired on Friday night, I was reminded of something Gene had done previously for ETV. He had interviewed James Meredith, the central figure in the integration of Ole Miss. James, who happened to be a classmate of mine, was the first African-American to apply to and be accepted by the University of Mississippi. Although riots broke out during the admission process and he endured harassment during his college days from some, James miraculously maintained love, respect, and appreciation for the university.

I was so taken by the interview in which this man held no resentment, I had decided to call James, who was now living in Jackson. Anyone who can forgive like that has won my heart.

When he didn't answer, I left a message: "James, I saw you on TV tonight, and I want to thank you for all you have done. I was a classmate of yours at Ole Miss. And though I did not do anything to harm you, I did not do anything to help you either. I need to ask your forgiveness."

He returned my call the next day. We talked for almost an hour. Before we hung up, I invited him and his wife and daughter to come to our home. "My wife. Camille. and I would also like to take you to dinner." He happily agreed. During that evening, I was able to express again how sorry I was for the difficulties he had experienced during those chaotic times.

"James," I said before we parted, "you helped your people gain their freedom, but you also helped me gain mine. I did not realize that I, too, was a prisoner. Your courageous stand taught us so much about a society where all people are created to enjoy equal opportunity."

Not long afterward, as a means of fundraising for the University of Mississippi Alumni House, people were given the opportunity to make donations at a given level. Bricks would be inscribed with names of donors as a memorial. As one leaves the Grove and proceeds toward the entrance to the Alumni Office, these bricks are prominently displayed in the walkway.

Of course, Camille and I wanted to participate and purchased bricks for our family and one for James Meredith, right next to ours.

Before it is all over and my time on earth is up, I thought, *I can help James, Prentiss, and maybe a few more.*

~ 17 ~

WE GO TOGETHER

September 11, 2001—another day that will live in infamy. I was in Chicago for an insurance meeting when I received the tragic news that the twin towers of the World Trade Center had been attacked—with great loss of life. There was also an attempt on the Pentagon, which was only partially successful, thank God. For a time, the country was thrust into the most patriotic and spiritual mood I have seen during my adult lifetime.

Unfortunately, the unity in the country did not last long. With that horrific event, the truth was starkly evident. None of the approximately 3,000 people who lost their lives that day knew that, before 10:00 a.m., they would not be at their desks conducting routine business, but on the other side of eternity. Just another telling reminder of the passage of time. My work was cut out for me—it was imperative that I move ahead with serious preparations for Prentiss Barnes's fundraiser.

Remembered Forever

It had been my vision to establish a fund with the Community Foundation of Greater Jackson to benefit Prentiss and others like him. As is usually the case, however, it took months before the vision began to take shape. I called the initial meeting with Linda Montgomery, president of the Community Foundation, and Chris Walters, a brilliant young associate from my office.

The three of us met at the Mayflower Café in downtown Jackson. Chris, then a student at Millsaps College, worked closely with me on many projects, both in and out of the office. As a result, he had developed a personal interest in Prentiss and was eager to be a part of the latest endeavor.

After checking out a few options, we ultimately settled on the Country Club of Jackson with the event to take place on Friday, April 26, 2002. Of the names suggested for this event, it seemed that "This Magic Moment" was an apt metaphor for the euphoric feelings of so many of us from an earlier generation. When recalling the music of the 1950s to mid-1960s, we were reminded of those days of rock, romance, and roses.

As we thought about the entertainment for the occasion, it was obvious that Bill Pinkney and The Original Drifters should be invited to perform. Of course, he agreed. I also called Rufus McKay, who marked the date on his calendar.

The next obstacle was convincing John Carroll Doyle, the artist we commissioned to paint the *This Magic Moment* image to give us permission to use his work as our logo. I was thinking specifically of the invitations, but my initial efforts fell on deaf ears. John Carroll had obviously had some bad experiences in the past with people who did a poor job of reproducing his images.

I decided to try once more. This time, I spoke with a lady in his gallery who seemed willing to help. When I explained the situation about Prentiss and what we were trying to do, she appeared sympathetic. The following week, John Carroll himself called, granting our request, with one stipulation. He wanted the invitations to be printed in Charleston at a local printer, where he could approve the final product. We were thrilled because the painting displayed so accurately what we felt, and we wanted the invitation to be of superior quality—a real attention-getter. (You will recognize it as the cover of this book.) All of this would cost plenty.

Money, Honey

As we began putting together a budget, Chris checked out the prices of food items at the country club and the cost of printing the invitations. The quotes we received were quite reasonable. With these in place, I began to ask various people in town if they would be willing to assist with this project. Almost without fail, their reply was positive.

As for the planning "committee," however, we kept to a minimum the number of people involved. Multiple people trying to control could cause confusion. I knew what we wanted to do, and I felt we needed only four or five people—Chris, Lelia Manning, Linda Montgomery, Camille, and myself. The work of telephoning and contacting supporters could be done later. I was aware, however, that we would need a publicity chairman and perhaps an advertising agency to guide the process of getting the word out.

I happened to mention this to Donna Ritchey, VP of GodwinGroup advertising in Jackson, who picked up on it immediately. Godwin is a prominent agency, locally and beyond. Donna said that our project was something of great interest to her, and she would like to play a part. We scheduled a meeting for the following week to discuss strategies, among them a press conference a few weeks preceding the event.

We approached the three major television network affiliates in Jackson, asking them to send reporters, along with a writer from the *Clarion-Ledger*. Jimmye Sweat, editor of the *Northside Sun* (a local weekly paper featuring social, charitable, educational, and human interest stories), was technically my publicity chairperson, but it was not quite time for her to step in. With all of this in place, we chose March 1, 2002, as the date of the press conference.

It soon became apparent that we needed a presentation booklet that would describe the foundation's purpose and goal. Chris came up with the perfect idea—downloading John Carroll Doyle's image of the painting from their website for the cover of our booklet. For this, we would also need John Carroll's permission. Once again, he agreed.

Having given a lot of thought to the different categories of participation, we decided on this list of titles for sponsorship:

- Stagger Lee/Mustang Sally $100

- Danny Boy/Angel Baby $350

- Big Bopper/Little Darling $750

- Duke/Duchess of Earl $1,000

- Book of Love $2,500

- Sincerely $5,000

- Earth Angel $10,000

I felt that people could identify with many of these songs, and to be a "Duke of Earl" or a "Book of Love" might fuel their desire to reach higher levels. Contained in the promo booklet were newspaper articles featuring interviews with the singers. Finally, I drafted a letter, stating the genesis of this project and our goals:

Dear Prospective Donor:

Permit me to share with you a vision that came to me of a need in the greater Jackson community. Living among us are singers and musicians who created wonderful music—particularly the music of the 1950s and early 1960s—for which they have never received credit nor the proper royalties. I became acutely aware of this situation through my personal friendship with a Mr. Prentiss Barnes, the original virtuoso bass singer with the world-famous Moonglows group. Although Prentiss has been more fortunate than many of his contemporaries, he still struggles to make ends meet, while millions of people continue to enjoy his music.

I have therefore established, under the auspices of the Foundation of Greater Jackson, the This Magic Moment Preservation Trust, a 501(c)(3) nonprofit organization in which we will endeavor to build an endowment that can be used for years to help people like Prentiss. He is our first year honoree, but there will be many others to come.

We invite you to attend our inaugural event, scheduled for Friday, April 26, 2002, at the Country Club of Jackson. . . .

As you peruse this brochure, you will see the first article that was published in the *Clarion Ledger* before I knew Prentiss. Notice the picture of this forlorn man, taken at that time. Then compare that with photos in subsequent articles, once he realized that someone cares about him. The pictures tell the story. Many of us paid perhaps $4 for an album of yesteryear or $15 for a CD in more recent times, but what people like Prentiss have given us is priceless. Let's do something to show him that we care. I will give you a call within the next few weeks to discuss your contribution.

Sincerely,

William H. Morris, Jr.

Chairman, This Magic Moment Preservation Trust

Living Legends

To pull off an event of this magnitude, we would need an honorary chairman—someone with charisma, prestige, and brand-name recognition, who could help to attract a crowd to our benefit. A legendary star like Morgan Freeman would be perfect. The people of the state of Mississippi are very proud of this distinguished actor. The fact that he chose to move back to Mississippi when he could afford to live in luxury anywhere in the world has earned our appreciation and admiration.

I immediately set out to write Bill Luckett, Morgan Freeman's close friend and business associate. After putting together the publicity booklet, I shipped it off to Bill, along with a couple of *True Love* Drifters CDs. I figured he would be the one most likely to get it into Morgan's hands.

I followed up with a phone call to Bill in a few days, but I got his recording and left a message. In a subsequent conversation, he explained, "Your request was only one of thirty Mr. Freeman receives each month! But your material definitely got his attention!" He paused. "By the way, I am sure he will want to know if your club is integrated."

"Of course, it is," I replied. "A number of very fine African-American families are members of the Country Club of Jackson."

"I'll be sure to tell Morgan," he promised.

★　★　★

Not having secured sufficient funding—the only money in the pot was $1,000 I had contributed and a smaller sum Chris, my student employee, had generously volunteered—I was feeling apprehensive. We needed far more than that, and we were going to need it soon.

I decided to make my first call on the highly regarded Mr. Stuart C. Irby. Mr. Irby and his entire family were outstanding philanthropists in the Jackson community. When I called and spoke with his wife, Debbie, she said that he had not been well. When I explained my mission, however, she agreed that she and her husband would meet with me the following afternoon at his office.

When I arrived, Mr. Irby, now in his eighties and looking fragile, was sitting behind his desk. He listened as I outlined our plan and handed him one of our brochures. With impaired vision, he required a magnifying glass to read.

After a few minutes, he leaned back in his chair. "I think I would like to participate . . . at this level," he said, pointing to one of the larger figures. It was the category entitled "Sincerely."

"Oh, yes, you like that song a lot," Debbie told her husband, smiling. "And I would like to be a 'Sincerely.'"

Mr. Irby nodded. "That is what I want to do." With that, he called in his assistant and asked her to write me a check for $5,000, made payable to

Community Foundation of Greater Jackson, for This Magic Moment. No longer just a desire on my part to do something for a friend who was in dire straits, this venture now held the promise of success.

★　★　★

The icing on the cake soon followed. I received word from Bill Luckett that Morgan Freeman had agreed to be our honorary chairman, though he could not assure us that he would be able to attend. (As a matter of fact, on the night of the event, he was in Brazil, filming a movie.) Nevertheless, he was completely on board with what we were trying to accomplish and was pleased to lend his name to the occasion.

Shortly afterward, I visited with Dave Kelley at BellSouth, who was in charge of reviewing proposals for charitable giving in the entire state of Mississippi. When Dave saw the presentation booklet Chris and I had prepared, he was impressed. "Bill, I need to tell you that this is the best inaugural proposal I have ever seen."

What a confirmation of our vision! "Thank you, Dave. But Chris Walters did most of the work."

★　★　★

That night, I was sitting at the Mayflower Café, having worked at the office until about seven o'clock on a dreary, drizzly night. Camille was at a meeting, so I was dining alone. In the background, I could barely hear the McGuire Sisters singing "Sincerely," their cover of The Moonglows' famous song. Other patrons seemed oblivious. It occurred to me that this music, played the world over, is so often heard only in the background, with people giving no thought to the journey endured by the artists who brought it to us.

Slowly, things were coming together. But it was taking everything we had—creatively, financially, emotionally, and spiritually. It was certainly not a one-man show. Now many of us were working together . . . as it should be. This baby was getting some legs.

~ 18 ~

CRAZY!

Four hours! With the pressure mounting, four hours of sleep was often about all I could clock during those long days and nights. Hardly enough. Not when one is running a busy insurance firm and staging a huge event like Prentiss's benefit, with a multitude of details to be worked out. My plate was full, and I was becoming frazzled, wondering if all the pieces of this puzzle would fit. Along with sleep deprivation and the craziness of our schedule came an uncommon jolt of fear.

Front-page news in the Monday morning paper was no help. Apparently, a fundraiser to benefit cancer research was scheduled for the same weekend as our event! As soon as I reached the office, I decided to meet with Chris and Lelia to figure out whether we should change the date of our function. When I called them into my office, I felt led to pray. With the realization that this thing was bigger than me, I was feeling somewhat helpless. As I began to thank God for all He was doing, fear left me, replaced with jubilation and a sense of expectancy.

Soon after that special moment, Chris and I had a long planning session with two pro bono volunteers from GodwinGroup—VickiHarper-Blake and Hazel Cole. At this time, we worked out some of our strategies, including our upcoming press conference now scheduled to be held at Walker's Drive-In, that intimate gourmet restaurant nestled in the historic Fondren district of the city.

In this session, we also discussed our forthcoming website, where people could obtain more information online. In addition, within the next few days, we would have our official signed letters back from Morgan Freeman (see Appendix). We were on a roll.

As the last week of February wore on, the pledges of major donors began to pour in. By midweek, we received $6,000 more, which put us ahead of all of our fixed costs—even before the press conference on Friday. We were especially pleased to receive permission from John Carroll Doyle to use his bio and image on our website.

Chip Reynolds and Arnie Hederman were busy working to get the site up and running. Featured were articles about Prentiss Barnes, including the one by Peggy Elam of the *Clarion-Ledger*, which told about his disastrous, attempted trip to Los Angeles, eventually leading to our meeting. Also included was the piece published just before Prentiss's induction into the Rock & Roll Hall of Fame. As to the entertainment, we then added an article about Bill Pinkney and The Original Drifters when they recorded in Jackson, as well as some information about Rufus McKay and The Red Tops. The site was set up so people could log on and print off their own invitation and choose at which level they wished to participate as donors, with a link to donate online.

With all of the moving parts of the benefit now proceeding on schedule, I had another major issue: Prentiss now weighed only 136 pounds—down thirty pounds—a drastic change for a man of his height, a little over six feet. I also learned that Bill Pinkney had a cyst on his spine that would require surgery. So, I found myself concerned about the physical state of those two dear friends—one of them the main attraction of the benefit, which was just a few weeks away.

Press Conference Spinoff

With Lelia and Camille calling many of our friends, we were able to gather a credible group at the press conference by 2:30 p.m. on a cold and rainy Friday. We had borrowed a couple of easels from one of our local art galleries to display my *This Magic Moment* painting by John Carroll Doyle, as well as a large reproduction of the letter signed by Morgan Freeman, announcing the trust.[4] Former mayor of Jackson Kane Ditto (now chairman of the Foundation) and Linda Montgomery were there, as well as Dolphus Weary of Mission Mississippi. To my delight, all three major television stations (ABC, CBS, NBC) showed up. The *Clarion-Ledger* also sent a photographer and journalist, Gary Pettus.

As the press conference got underway and the cameras were rolling, Prentiss came and stood beside me. After a couple of lines, I went off script. Didn't need it. What I wanted to say was already emblazoned on my heart. The audience was responsive, and our spirits were high.

On the evening news, our press conference was highlighted by all three networks. Saturday morning, an exceptionally well written article by Gary Pettus appeared in the *Clarion-Ledger,* entitled "Music Makers to Get Money." We could only hope Gary's title was prophetic!

That afternoon, I received a call from New York City. It was Steve Gosset of CBS News, who interviewed me. At the conclusion, I asked Mr. Gosset what he intended to do with the information I had given him.

"I'm planning to send it out over the network in case newspapers or stations want to pick it up."

Not long afterward, I received a letter from an old classmate, Bill Witt, who was now living in Cleveland, Ohio. Bill had heard of our event in the wee hours of the morning over a New York radio station! Only a few hours later, I got a call from a freelance writer by the name of Mario Roselli. Mario wrote for the *Atlanta Journal-Constitution* and the *New York Times.* And with a story this good, he told me, he was interested in writing a major article.

Later in the week, a Mr. Roger Galloway from Los Angeles called. Roger was with Westwood One Metro and specialized in oldies programs and worked with various television networks, including PBS; interestingly, he also knew Morgan Freeman and had interviewed him. Toward the end of our conversation, he asked if I knew Harvey Robbins, who wished to establish a doo wop museum in Boston and was hosting a big show in late March.

I didn't know him, but Roger gave me his number. It wouldn't hurt to keep this name among my contacts.

No time like the present, I thought when I hung up after an hour-long conversation with Roger. Right away, I gave Harvey Robbins a call and, among other things, asked if he knew Harvey Fuqua of The Moonglows.

"I just spoke with him!" exclaimed Harvey Robbins. "They are being inducted into the Doo-Wopp Hall of Fame here in Boston on the twenty-ninth. But Harvey told me Prentiss and Pete couldn't make it."

"Hmm, interesting," I murmured, thinking I could understand why Harvey Fuqua would have a problem with Pete due to his drinking issue. But Prentiss? "Prentiss hasn't heard anything about that induction. And I'm in touch with him on a regular basis." I paused, then asked, "Is there a monetary honorarium, by any chance?"

"Yes, for those who perform that night," Harvey Robbins replied. "Hey, I'd like very much for Prentiss to come. I'll pay his way and put him up in a hotel. And I'll put in a call to Harvey Fuqua to seal the deal."

In the midst of our ongoing publicity campaign, an old misunderstanding cast a shadow over the proceedings—the question about the authorship of some of the songs sung by The Moonglows. Prentiss always claimed to have been a co-writer on several of those songs, including "Sincerely," for which he was never given credit . . . or paid. Now, it appeared an event was scheduled in Boston to which he had originally not been invited to sing with his old group. *How odd,* I thought.

I thanked Harvey Robbins, hung up, then called Harvey Fuqua myself. He was fine with Prentiss attending the induction in Boston. When I told him about the "This Magic Moment" benefit for Prentiss in April, he expressed an interest in possibly coming. Maybe he would. Miracles do happen.

Serendipity-Doo-Dah

After I got off the phone with Harvey Fuqua, I was still troubled. Although I had not raised the issue of the songs with him, I knew that Morgan Freeman's letter mentioned that fact. I certainly did not want Harvey to be offended, to think that we were blaming him in any way for Prentiss's current financial crisis. The whole dilemma weighed heavily on my heart.

The next day, in church, a strong feeling came over me that I was to contact Harvey Fuqua again. I called him as soon as I got home.

"Harvey, a thought occurred to me in church."

When he asked what I meant by that, I continued, "God loves you more than you can possibly imagine. I love you, too, and so does Prentiss." It seemed to take him aback. "I also want to personally thank you for what you have given in the entire history of Rock 'n' Roll. I know that I have told you this before, but I believe you are the best arranger of slow love ballads of any of the groups of the 1950s, and there were some outstanding ones."

Those "soft words," spoken sincerely, obviously smoothed the waters, and his tone in reply let me know that all was well. I only hoped this was not wishful thinking on my part.

I called Prentiss to tell him how excited I was that he was being inducted into the Doo-Wopp Hall of Fame in Boston. Prentiss wanted me to go with him, but with "This Magic Moment," there was no way I could add one more thing to my calendar. I was concerned about his weight loss and lack of strength, but this invitation seemed to revive him, and he assured me that he was up to making the trip.

With Chris Walters's help, we were able to arrange a satisfactory flight for Prentiss, and the plans were underway. We made it a point to tell the airline about Prentiss's honor. Later, I learned that, en route to Boston, he was upgraded to first class. He was to go up on Thursday and returning on Saturday, with the induction ceremony on Friday night.

Prentiss and I did not talk again until the following Sunday afternoon. When we did, he was giddy with excitement. "Brother Morris, I couldn't have had a better time. It reminded me of back when we were singin' together in the 1950s. Reggie Gordon of The Magnificents took the lead . . . you know, Bobby Lester's old part." Prentiss paused. "Sure do miss Bobby." (Of course, Bobby had died twenty years earlier.)

"Brother Morris, it was the best we'd done since the old days. Reggie sounded *exactly* like Bobby. Pete actually showed up, too, and he did okay. But he'd been drinkin' some. 'Course, he tried to control everything."

From the sound of things, Pete's bitterness toward Harvey was on full display, and he was generally disruptive. Harvey, however, was another story, so I learned.

"Brother Morris," Prentiss went on. "I can't begin to tell you how different Harvey was. Not like I've ever seen him before . . . so nice . . . so attentive. He did everything I needed him to do. Helped me get dressed. . . you know how I can't manage all those hooks and buttons on the tuxedo. Wouldn't let me do anything for myself. Paid for my meals. Took care of everything. I just felt so special. We laughed and teased each other the whole time!"

They had performed six or seven of their songs, which was astounding since Prentiss had not practiced most of those numbers in many years. Harvey had even mentioned to Prentiss the possibility of going on the road, maybe even getting a tour bus and collaborating with other groups like The Drifters. Truly remarkable!

★   ★   ★

Shortly after arriving at my office on Monday morning, I received a call from Harvey. He was laughing and carrying on and telling me how much he had enjoyed the weekend.

"Bill," he said, "I don't think I've had this good a time since back in the 1950s. And, Bill, you can count on me for that benefit you're throwin' for Prentiss. I'll even do a few numbers if you want me to."

I could hardly believe what I was hearing! Somehow the light had come on for Harvey. And Prentiss was thrilled to receive $1,100 for his part in singing that weekend in Boston.

"Shoot!" he exclaimed. "I'd crawl to Boston for that kind of money!"

He was finally going to buy some groceries—food he could really enjoy cooking, like shrimp and other seafood. *Good!* I thought. *Maybe he can finally put on a little weight!*

Big Problems/Small Miracles

Even with all that was turning around in our favor, I could see that This Magic Moment was getting to Camille, who was feeling more and more nervous about the event. The ticket sales were not quite what they needed to be, or so it seemed. A few of the people we had counted on attending suddenly had other plans or unavoidable conflicts. I continued to hope that their circumstances would change, that hearts would be reached. But most of all, I prayed for peace for Camille.

By Monday, April 15, 2002, Camille and I were mentally exhausted from planning for the event, and I was sensing that Chris and Lelia were feeling the pressure too. I had become further concerned when two good friends of mine—a couple of years younger than I—said off-handedly that it "just wasn't their thing," but that they would send in some money anyway. My pride may have been getting to me.

Still, there was at least one good thing that was coming out of this pressure cooker. During this anxious time, Camille and I had been drawn into a much deeper spiritual relationship together. Not a day went by that we were not praying in the morning before I left for work and in the evening before we went to bed.

It was quickly becoming one of the most intense weeks I had ever experienced. Camille, Chris, Lelia, and I were emotionally and physically drained. Heavy on my mind was my business. I could only hope that it would stay strong and that we would get through this.

About that time, Camille was involved in a multi-car collision. A vehicle, headed in the wrong direction on a frontage road, distracted her for a moment. As she turned to look, she hit the car in front of her, which rear-ended another car. I felt guilty for all the pressure I had put on her.

A number of other things, however, were also going awry. Maxine Porter informed us that Bill's keyboard player could not play any of the songs on our playlist, except "Danny Boy." We needed a miracle!

★   ★   ★

Just when it seemed that our well-laid plans were going awry, suddenly there was a shift and everything began to come together. Harvey was definitely planning to attend, along with Reggie Gordon of The Magnificents and his wife, as well as Will Sanders, Pete's manager, from New York City. What we had been told about the keyboard player turned out to be just the opposite. Bennie Hill told me he could play any song he heard. He had also recorded with Harvey Fuqua in the past. Amazing!

By now, many others were showing their support by following through on their commitment to contribute, even though unable to attend. I was still praying every day with Camille; also, with Chris and Lelia at the office. The photographers, Cissy Scanlon and Karla Whitwer, agreed to help us out—again, pro bono. And to top it off, a major insurance case came through!

Late Wednesday afternoon, Laura McPherson, a reporter from WJTV, the CBS affiliate in Jackson, called to ask if she could interview Prentiss and me in my office the next morning. The coverage she gave us was phenomenal—a long spot on the five o'clock and six o'clock news and on one of the morning newscasts on Friday. In addition, Jimmye Sweat, my dear friend and editor at the *Northside Sun*, ran a color photo on the front page of the paper with a rather long caption explaining the upcoming event once again.

Craziness

The next evening, I planned to take Bill, Harvey, Prentiss, and Rufus to dinner. However, when I reached Bill on his cell phone, I learned that he was still in Sumter. He explained that he had to go to the doctor and wouldn't be coming until the following day. Could it be possible that my special friend Bill Pinkney would not be coming at all—and just didn't want to tell me? I tried to put these negative thoughts out of my mind, but I was well aware of what could happen. He wasn't getting any younger, and, like Prentiss, his health was compromised.

Somewhat subdued by Bill Pinkney's message, I picked up Harvey and Rufus at the Cabot Lodge on County Line Road, where the singers and band were staying. Prentiss and Will Sanders, Pete's manager, met me at my house. I took the four of them to the Char Restaurant in Jackson for a fine dinner.

During dinner, one of the stories Harvey told us was about the time he had brought Tammi Terrell into the business and had her come to Detroit to work with Marvin Gaye to produce their famous album "Ain't No Mountain High Enough." This album happens to be one of my favorites. I then told Harvey about my book and explained that all of these very special moments would be recorded. His beaming face told me he was pleased to hear that.

★   ★   ★

Money was now pouring in, and by Friday morning, everything was moving at supersonic speed. I decided to sleep in a little. When I saw myself on the television screen, it was obvious how truly exhausted I was; I had never seen such dark circles under my eyes. The stress on Camille, who was in charge of decorations, was also beginning to show.

On the way in to the office, I called the Cabot Lodge to find out if the band had arrived. It was 10:00 a.m., and they had been scheduled to arrive by eight, but they were still nowhere in sight. In addition, Bill had notified us that he would definitely be coming, after all, but I had no idea what time he would be getting in. He had not given us his flight information, giving further cause for concern.

I did not dare share any of these fears with anyone. Outwardly, I managed a positive demeanor, while inwardly, my thoughts were churning. Negative thinking was not like me, but exhaustion provided a fertile field.

When I got to my office, I managed to track down Paul Shields, the bus driver for the band, on his cell phone. He was about thirty miles out of Jackson. A half-hour later, I confirmed that he was in town . . . and he had picked up Bill at the airport!

Only then could I begin to breathe a sigh of relief. We could focus our concern on the statue we had ordered for Prentiss. It did not arrive until noon of that day and would not be ready to be picked up until mid-afternoon. It was truly magnificent, and I wanted to photograph it.

Meanwhile, our next-door neighbor, Lydy Caldwell, a most thoughtful and gracious woman and the mother of Pulitzer Prize winner Beth Henley, ordered a huge supply of sandwiches, cookies, and other knick-knacks from Broad Street Bakery, a local delicatessen. The band and singers would be well-fed, at least through rehearsal.

I was still worried about the music, since the keyboard player had not worked with any of us. When I arrived at the Cabot, I found Bill Pinkney and the rest of the guys standing out front. I got a big bear hug from Bill and was thrilled to see Rufus and the others. We all enjoyed fellowship and much laughter together. By now, Bill Pinkney was feeling tired and wanted to go back to the hotel to take a nap; Harvey was eager to rent a car. Things were hopping.

Rufus, the rhythm section of The Original Drifters, and I drove over to the country club to rehearse, but the microphones hadn't been set up yet. Everything had to be done without amplification, which meant the risk of straining our voices. Rufus worked with the keyboard player first. When it was my turn, we tried "Daddy's Home" in the key of E flat instead of F, my normal key. He suggested we try it in F to see how it would sound.

As I began to sing, he nodded in approval. "Oh, yeah, that's where you need to be."

It was nearly 4:15 before I took Rufus back to the Cabot. I was due to pick up Rufus, Harvey, Bill Pinkney, and Prentiss at 5:15 so we could be at the country club by 5:30, but it didn't exactly work that way. I had to go to the house to shave, grab a quick shower, and get dressed in my tuxedo so as to get back to the Cabot to pick up the guys. I had also scheduled a photo session prior to the event.

My mind was whirling as I raced to reach our destination. But my heart was full. Surely no man has ever been more blessed to have such friends—both black and white. Tonight would be the culmination of a dream—to honor one of the outstanding members of a vocal group—one who had too often been overlooked. Now to be sure everything unfolded as planned.

~ 19 ~

THIS MAGIC MOMENT

Bill, where are you? The guests are already arriving!" Camille's voice was pitched an octave higher than usual—a true indicator of her rising stress level. I couldn't have my wife in panic mode before the event was even underway.

"On our way, darlin'. Just had to wait on Rufus." I tried to maintain an air of calm, although my pulse was racing, too, in my eagerness to get Rufus there somewhat on time. Finally, we left the Cabot at about 5:45—fifteen minutes behind schedule. It took us at least ten minutes to get down County Line Road on our way to the country club, and we hadn't had the photo session yet.

The photographers were out front with Camille when we arrived. She was trying to be as kind and cordial as possible, but she was definitely displaying a little impatience since the cocktail party had already started—minus the host and some of the guests of honor! In spite of our tardy arrival, we stopped to take photographs in the lobby area of the club. We couldn't miss the late-spring natural lighting bathing the area around the entranceway.

Immediately afterward, Camille hustled us into the reception area. The dining room adjacent to the Natchez Room looked magnificent. She and several other ladies, including Cleta Ellington, Lelia Manning, Anne Young, and Monty Chotard, had been working their magic since mid-afternoon.

The place was transformed! They had found some imitation 45 rpm plastic records depicting sounds of the 1950s, and fun sunglasses by Al Underwood of Shady Deal Glasses to place on each of the tables. The glasses turned out to be a major hit!

Camille had been so busy that day that she had taken her eveningwear with her to the country club so that she could change at the last minute. She looked fabulous, with not a hair out of place. Perfection—a reflection of the entire venue! She had outdone herself!

Moments that Will Last Forever

I couldn't reach Harvey, so we had gone on without him. I had left a message in his room with instructions on how to get there. When we walked into the main area of the event, Bill Pinkney's back was hurting so badly he had to limp over and sit down. He hadn't been able to have the cyst on his spine removed; his doctor had said his heart was too weak to withstand surgery. As people approached to speak to him, he tried to stand to exchange pleasantries, but there was a noticeable grimace on his face.

By now a good crowd was on hand. Chris was looking dapper in his tuxedo and Lelia, lovely in her cocktail dress. Mike Manning, Lelia's husband, was helping out, doing a masterful job assisting with whatever needed to be done. I was delighted to see ministers Ruth and John Urban. Neddie Winters, the minister at Prentiss's church, and his wife also arrived. I was overjoyed with the turnout.

Interesting that many of the major donors in attendance were new to me—evidence that this event had spread far beyond what I could have done personally. Before I knew it, it was 6:45, and we had not even started dinner. We encouraged the crowd to move into the dining area, where we virtually filled the room.

Neddie Winters and Ruth Urban blessed the food, and I then led the dinner guests in singing the doxology—"Praise God from Whom All Blessings Flow"—before enjoying our fabulous meal. Glancing around, I was delighted to see many people from all over the country. As we were served dessert, I realized that the time had been slipping away and it was only twenty minutes until the big crowd would be arriving at eight.

Bill Pinkney had left our table and disappeared into the back with the band. I stood to tell a little about him, then introduced Will Sanders of New York City and Reggie Gordon and his wife of Chicago.

Now for the introduction of the two founding members of The Moonglows—Harvey Fuqua and the man of the hour, Prentiss Barnes. At this, the crowd rose in unison to give him a standing ovation. All the weeks and months of planning for this event would culminate in the next few hours.

This Magic Moment!

With the time approaching eight o'clock, I announced that dinner was concluded and the main event was about to begin. Toni, a gifted female singer, opened for The Original Drifters with one of my favorite songs as she belted out "At Last," made famous by Etta James. The crowd poured into the main ballroom. More than 350 people filled the large dance floor and beyond, the band on the stage behind.

I looked around, delighted to see so many friends. From the expressions on their faces, it was obvious we had struck a chord. After Toni, Rufus was next up, performing Jackie Wilson's "Lonely Teardrops," followed by his signature "Danny Boy." Tears glistened in the eyes of many as he was singing his song, and our minds were flooded with precious memories of our teenage and college years.

The Moonglows were called onstage. Harvey, Prentiss, and Reggie did a knockout rendition of "Sincerely," with Reggie sounding much like the legendary Bobby Lester. The harmony was beautiful, and the adoring fans were caught up in the magic of the moment.

Then Harvey said: "We're going to get a little help from our friend Bill Morris on this next song."

Performing with them, I did my part as we presented "The Ten Commandments of Love." The crowd entered into the mood of the moment, roaring their approval.

It was now time for me to do the lead on "Daddy's Home." Harvey, Prentiss, and Reggie were to the left of me; Rufus to my right. "Harvey, you're not leaving the stage yet," I said. "I helped you out on your song, and now I need some help on mine."

We had never rehearsed any of this together—not even in the car. But as the number progressed, I could feel the energy building and my voice swelling with power. Another small miracle! Actually, with the fatigue caused by our exhausting schedule leading up to this evening and a cold I had developed over the last several days, I shouldn't have been able to sing at all! But as my voice began to soar, I could see Harvey lighting up. Must have been doing something right.

I could hear the close harmony behind my vocals. With such good back-up, I was able to put much more into my part since I could take short breaths while the others carried the harmony. Feeling their support, I gave it everything I had. As I backed off a little on the higher notes, the guys came through in such a way that I'm sure the audience didn't even notice.

Looking to my right, I touched Rufus on the shoulder. Then, reaching to my left, I touched Prentiss, Reggie, and Harvey, all while the song was in full swing. At the conclusion, I was able to execute the classic "doo weee-uh-uh-oooh" that Shep and The Limelights used to do. We received a stirring ovation as we left the stage, and Harvey said to me, "Man, we've got to record that! I really want to. Can you get me a tape of this?"

I told him I would try and prayed that the video would turn out well. To have Harvey, a man of great stature in the music industry, say such a thing, sent me over the top!

It was then time for the world-famous Drifters to perform. They started with "There Goes My Baby," Bill's resonant bass sounding as strong as ever. Unfortunately, he was feeling so badly that he was only able to do about half of the song before he had to sit down to finish. All the while, he was singing—never missed a beat.

People were having a blast! As I walked through the audience, I couldn't go two feet before someone was tugging at my arm, hugging me, and telling me what a marvelous time they were having. It was a phenomenal experience for all of us! But it was only just beginning.

Heart and Soul

At a climactic moment, I stepped onstage again to present Prentiss with the trophy and a letter from the director of the community foundation. The letter explained that we would be assisting with some of his financial needs. As I presented the trophy to Prentiss, I also acknowledged Chris Walters who was on the stage with us. Chris had given his heart and soul to this event and to Prentiss personally. I was very thankful for what he, Lelia Manning, and Camille had accomplished. What a feeling to see Prentiss standing there in his formal tails—as proud as a man can be.

The Drifters kicked off the second set with one great song after another. People still wanted to dance, and dance they did! Then Rufus, having changed into his white tux, with red cummerbund and tie, followed with several songs, finishing with "Danny Boy" for the second time that evening. I turned and looked at my good friend, Wallace McMillan. Unabashed, tears were streaming down his face, as emotions throughout the room ran high.

It was already after 11:00 p.m., and the party was still in full swing. Very few people had left. Actually, most of the crowd stayed until midnight.

It was at this late hour that one of my favorite songs, originally by Sam Cooke—"You Send Me"—charged the atmosphere. Vernon Young, the tenor, led the group. Adrenaline pumping, I bounded out onto the dance floor with my wife. Holding Camille close in my arms, we danced to this moving tune. After that, it was father-daughter time.

Spotting my two daughters standing on the periphery of the dance floor, I gave Camille a kiss and walked over to claim daughter Camille for the next dance. I enjoyed our turn around the floor. Then daughter Kathryn, followed by several of our lady friends. As the popular song of a different era goes, "I could have danced all night."

It was thrilling to see an abundance of friends from as far away as New York, Chicago, Houston, New Orleans, Atlanta, as well as *North and South Carolina* and throughout the state of Mississippi. As the evening came to a close, everyone was telling me that we really needed to do this again. "Don't change a thing!" they said.

I made the rounds, giving hugs and expressing gratitude for those who had performed and those who had come to support us. Then it was time to say goodbye to Bill Pinkney, Prentiss, Rufus, Harvey, and the others, and to express my love for them. Other than marriages and births, I must say that in all of my life, this was by far the most affirming thing that had ever happened.

To say that the crowd was ecstatic that night would be a gross understatement. More than once, I heard, "This may be the best party I've ever been to!" and "Please do it again!" As we were clearing up afterward, the club assistant general manager, Larry Marquez, approached me and confirmed the sentiment of the crowd: "This was, without a doubt, the best party ever held here at the club."

It was well after midnight when the last guest left . . . reluctantly. It seemed that no one was ready to leave the rarified atmosphere. When Camille, Chris, Lelia, and I packed up the remnants of the decorations and closed the door behind us, there was not a trace of the enchanted era we had recreated, if only for a few magical moments.

~ 20 ~

SHOUT!

Music is the currency of my soul, and I love to spend it lavishly. The song inside of me is never silent, just bursting to be heard. That is why I have grabbed every opportunity to be with other music-makers of my era. And that is also why on September 16, only a few months after Prentiss Barnes's extravaganza, I got up a little before four o'clock for a 6:30 a.m. flight, en route to yet another awards event—this time the annual Vocal Group Hall of Fame ceremony in Sharon, Pennsylvania.

While on the plane, I read the new *Goldmine* magazine. The cover had caught my eye with photos of the various groups of Drifters. I devoured the article, telling of the artists I had long admired. Before I left home, I had searched the internet for the biographies of those listed on the Vocal Group Hall of Fame website and printed them to read on the plane. I couldn't wait to reconnect with those in the industry I could now call my friends.

When the plane landed in Cleveland, I met others who were traveling to Pennsylvania, and rode with Carl Gardner of The Coasters and his wife, Veta; Renee White and Sonia Wilson of The Chantels, famous for their hit "Maybe." On the road, I had a great time singing with Jim Freeman of The Five Satins and his wife, Cheryl. Jim spoke of his high regard for Prentiss and asked me to relay God's blessings to him.

Jim also told me he had waited for a year after he was married to tell Cheryl that he had been a member of The Five Satins. He did not want her to fall in love with him just because he was a famous singer. One night, when he and Cheryl were dining out, he heard "In the Still of the Night" over the restaurant's speaker system and exclaimed, "They're playing our song!" That's when he told Cheryl about his former vocation, and she loved him all the more.

When we arrived in Sharon, we went directly to the hall of fame, the tall building housing the museum where Prentiss had received an award the year before. In the main ballroom on the top floor, the groups were assembling to await the beginning of the program. There was an air of festivity as inductees and guests mingled, catching up with each other since the last time they had been together.

I chatted with Mary Wilson of The Supremes, one of the emcees of the event, who reminded me that she was from Greenville, Mississippi. I then saw Charlie Thomas of The Drifters and my old friend, Bill Pinkney, who was always pleased to see me. I was alarmed at Bill's gaunt appearance, however. From his usual stocky build, he had lost a noticeable amount of weight. When I greeted him with our customary hug, I could feel the bones in his back. He was on several medications, and I couldn't help wondering if something was seriously wrong. I acquired several copies of Bill's newly released autobiography. It was an honor that he had included an entire chapter about our friendship.

"Boss Man"

Charlie Thomas, a member of the second set of Drifters, came by the table where I was seated with Bill Pinkney. Spotting Bill, Charlie called out, "Hey there, Boss Man." From this greeting, it was obvious he held Bill in high esteem. If there was ever any bad blood between them, there certainly wasn't now. "Don't forget. If you ever need me to cover for you on the road or at some gig, I'm there for you."

The next morning, I had breakfast with Bill Pinkney and one of The Midnighters. We joined Charlie Thomas and others. It is amazing how bonded all of these singers had become and how much they cherished each other, even though they might have been competitive in the music field at one time. The entire room was filled with famous people who had given us the music we cherish.

Bill Pinkney bought my breakfast, apparently taking great delight in doing so. When I thanked him, tears welled up in his eyes. "Bill," he said, "I cannot tell you how much I appreciate you being here."

"Yes sir, 'Boss Man,'" I said with a little chuckle, recalling what Charlie Thomas had called our friend.

Concert at Cafaro

Of special importance was a concert to be held at Cafaro Field, a sports arena where athletic events were usually showcased. This evening would be an exception in every way. At center field, they had erected a stage where many of the musicians who had been inducted into the hall of fame would perform for the public. Rehearsals were conducted throughout the day as groups and individual performers ran through their acts. From my observation, it promised to be a stellar show!

At dinner, I struck up a conversation with Fred Johnson, the bass singer with The Marcels, who did an amazing rendition of "Blue Moon." Fred remembered me from an earlier year when I was in Pennsylvania with Prentiss. He was truly a kindred spirit, and we exchanged CDs and shared some deeply personal experiences.

When we finally wound down, Fred had a faraway look in his eyes. "Remember, Bill? You once gave me a tape of your 'Daddy's Home,' which I love. I pulled it out to listen one day and was reminded of the great times we've had."

The concert began with the "The Star-Spangled Banner," sung by The Wee Jams. The Dixie Hummingbirds with Ira Tucker were the first to perform, always unique with their classic sound. The Harptones were next with their wonderful treatment of "Life Is but a Dream." Johnny Mason and The Clovers followed with "Devil or Angel" and "Love Potion No. 9." The Chantels did their signature number "Maybe" with Arlene Smith on the lead; then, Carl Gardner of The Coasters, with "Charlie Brown" and "Yakety Yak."

Next came Bill Pinkney with "Money Honey" and his *Home Alone* version of "White Christmas," leaving the audience applauding wildly. Charlie Thomas then stepped out on the stage with two of his guys to join Bill's Drifters for one of the most magnificent performances I have ever seen! While Bill sat in a chair onstage, Charlie launched into "Under the Boardwalk," followed by the energetic number, "Shout"! Linked to the stage was a boardwalk about twenty yards long. Charlie, wearing a neon orange suit and matching shoes, used the entire stage for his dynamic performance. By the time he and his group had concluded, the ecstatic crowd was on their feet, clapping and cheering. That night, they really "knocked it out of the park!" I must have shot at least three rolls of film for The Drifters' segment alone.

★   ★   ★

After breakfast the next morning with Raoul Cita and Willie Winfield of The Harptones, I met with Bill's intellectual property attorney. At that time, he was helping Bill build his case regarding the impostor groups that had plagued him for so long.

By late morning, we headed down to the Vocal Group Hall of Fame headquarters and museum where they were holding a hearing with four state senators and others from the attorney general's office. Various people testified to the major problems in the music industry and the magnitude of the theft that many of the groups—The Drifters, The Coasters, The Platters, and others—had endured. The executive director of Friends Against Musical Exploitation of Artists (FAME) continued with a taped interview. One of the most moving testimonies, however, was given by Paul "Billy" Wolfe, director of the Truth in Music committee out of Lewisburg, Pennsylvania. He spoke with enormous passion of the injustice done when the original groups had

Bill Pinkney (The Original Drifters—Left) with Charlie Thomas (2nd set of Drifters) assisting him to a chair on the stage—Cafaro Field, Vocal Group Hall of Fame

Charlie Thomas performing to a wild crowd

Freddie Johnson (Bass singer of the Marcels- "Blue Moon") with Bill shortly after they had a contest to see who could sing the lowest bass on that number—he said I won but I think he did

Arlene Smith and the Chantels singing "Maybe." Vocal Group Hall of Fame Cafaro Field

Rufus McKay at the Millsaps College Art and Lecture Series

Pookie Hudson (Lead singer of the Spaniels) and his wife at the Doo Wop Hall of Fame in Boston

Prentiss Barnes and Chris Walters at the Jackson International Airport just before leaving for Boston—Doo Wop Hall of Fame

Harvey Fuqua directing the rehearsal at Boston Symphony Hall for the Doo Wop Hall of Fame 2005

Harvey Robbins at the Doo Wop Hall of Fame venue—Boston Symphony Hall

Bill and The Moonglows just before going on stage at Boston Symphony Hall

The Grand Finale—The Spaniels, The Moonglows, The Jive Five, and The Peanuts singing "Goodnight Sweetheart, Goodnight." On stage for their last public appearance/Boston Symphony Hall/Doo-Wap Hall of Fame Induction Ceremony 2005

Andy Anderson and the Original Rolling Stones/Dawn Breakers Vicksburg, MS for the Mississippi Musicians Hall of Fame Induction

Pine Top Perkins Vicksburg, MS—The Mississippi Musicians Hall of Fame Induction

Jim Weatherly—Ole Miss star quarterback and the writer of many great songs for Gladys Knight and the Pips—"Midnight Train to Georgia" and "Neither of Us Wants to Be the Last to Say Goodbye"

their names and style stolen by others. As a result, so many had lost major revenue and suffered emotional trauma.

Following the testimonies, Bill went downstairs to a private room where he gave a deposition to his attorney. Since the attorney seemed truly sympathetic to the plight of these musicians, I later briefed him on Prentiss Barnes. He took some notes, and I felt I would probably be talking with him again regarding Prentiss. Since the families of these groups would be impacted long after these singers were gone, it was imperative that something be done about this travesty. No doubt, the issue would continue to play out over the years.

★   ★   ★

While at the Hall of Fame, I gave a CD to a young lady behind the desk. She was studying music from a very different perspective from anything I had heard.

"I'm studying the effect of music on human body rhythms," she explained. "Your CD has really had a major effect on me, and I thank you."

I was gratified to hear that, of course, as one of the significant purposes of my attending this event—and others like it—was to bless all those with whom I came in contact, even perfect strangers.

To my delight, not a single person I met failed to respond to that simple gesture—Willie Winfield, Johnny Mason, Freddy Johnson, Ronnie McPhatter, Harold Jackson, Jimmy Beaumont and Nick Pociask of The Skyliners, Renee White of The Chantels, and of course, most of all, Bill Pinkney.

★   ★   ★

We woke up Friday morning to a heavy rain. Upon checking out, I learned that Bill had paid for my hotel room. I was deeply moved by this gesture. On the return trip to Cleveland, I was riding with Bill and Maxine, trucking up the highway in his Cadillac, with Maxine at the wheel. I was sure this would be an emotional goodbye. I couldn't help thinking that it could well be the last time I would ever see him.

As I boarded the plane, I began to reflect on Bill Pinkney and the faraway look on his face as he sat in the wheelchair at the Delta Air Lines terminal. I had said goodbye then, with a lump in my throat. I was thinking how privileged I had been to share some of the significant moments in Bill's life—moments that have translated into important milestones in my own.

White Christmas

About ten days before Christmas, our church sent a check from the discretionary fund as a gift for Prentiss. A few days later, I received a phone call from him.

"Brother Morris," came that soulful voice I loved. "This was 'bout the nicest Christmas I ever had. Not the amount on the check . . . but jus' knowing y'all really care about me."

On Christmas Day, while Camille and the girls were clearing away the clutter from our own festive celebration, I called Bill Pinkney. He was with two of his daughters and his son Terry. In the background, I could hear laughter and the childish voices of some of his many grandchildren.

We exchanged greetings, then he swung into, "I'm dreamin' of a White Christmas, just like the ones I used to know. . ." His voice sounded stronger than when we had last spoken.

Bill told me that he was much better and that his doctors were satisfied with the weight he had gained. "Bill, I am thrilled to hear that!" I said. After further banter, I told him to give my love to the rest of the family, and we would talk again soon.

I then called Prentiss at his brother Houston's home in Chatawa, a tiny community just outside Magnolia, Mississippi. He and Houston were both asleep, having succumbed to the inertia that follows a hearty Christmas dinner. When he was roused enough to come to the phone, Prentiss and I laughed and gave thanks for our fun times together. We spoke of making more happy memories in the year ahead. New horizons.

These calls to two dear friends made my wonderful Christmas even more memorable. But I was now extremely concerned about Rufus, for I had received a voice message from him and had been unable to reach him when I returned the call.

Hello, Is That You?

As I was running errands with my daughter Camille the next day, I decided to check my voicemail again. Rufus had left me another message in which he sounded even worse. However, he had left his sister's telephone number this time. When I finally reached Elizabeth, she told me that Rufus was very ill and in the hospital.

Elizabeth explained that Rufus had left Nevada on a snowy night in near-blizzard conditions. With the bad weather, it had taken him a week to reach Mississippi, and he had almost died en route, due to complications from his diabetes and the bitter cold. When he finally arrived in Vicksburg, he was immediately hospitalized.

"Feel free to call him," she encouraged me and gave me the number for his hospital room.

"Hel-lo," came a very weak voice on the other end of the line when I dialed the number.

"Hello, is that you?" I sang. "Well, baby, this is you know who. . ." On the flip side of his hit song, "Swanee River Rock," was this song I had memorized and had sung to him before.

He laughed, his spirits seemed to lift, and he told me how happy he was to hear from me. He soon recovered from that bout, and over the next few years, our friendship deepened. Now that he was living in Vickburg, we could see each other more often.

Once again, the Father had planted in my life another musical icon—one who had meant so much to me in earlier years. It was now my joy to reach out and give back to him as I had attempted to do for Prentiss Barnes and Bill Pinkney. The best of times—and, for some of my friends, difficult times—were yet to come for the four of us.

~ 21 ~

PEOPLE, GET READY

With so many of my dear friends struggling with their health, it seemed we were constantly being made aware of our mortality. Bill Pinkney had one medical problem after another. Prentiss was dealing with his diabetes. Rufus had been sick ever since returning to Vicksburg from Carson City, but Bill concerned me most of all. When I received a call from Harry Turner, our mutual friend, my first reaction was to wonder if Harry might be calling to tell me that Bill was gone. I felt a twinge in my stomach as I picked up the receiver. But the news was quite the opposite. Bill was doing well, having been in and out of the hospital. Thank God for another reprieve!

Not long after, I received a call from Jeremiah Robinson at New Life Church of God in Christ in Clinton, Mississippi. Jeremiah, a man I had known casually through Mission Mississippi—the racial reconciliation group—asked me to sing at his church on Sunday, April 4 for their seventh anniversary. I told him to give me a day or two to think about it.

That very night, three songs were on my heart. *You have always wanted to do "People Get Ready,"* came that now familiar Voice. *Here is your opportunity.*

I called Jeremiah back the next day and asked if they had any musical accompaniment. "We have some drums," he told me.

No doubt I would be better off to do this number without the drums, but I agreed to sing in his church. Still, I was a little hesitant. "People Get

Ready" is not an easy song to sing. There are certain parts that require a real stretch of the vocal cords.

On the late Sunday afternoon that I was to participate in the service, I felt a special Presence and gladly entered into the congregational worship and praise before beginning my part. No sooner had I reached the stage and was well into my first song than a woman, apparently moved by the performance, jumped up and began clearing boxes from in front of an old, "clangy" upright piano. Although the instrument was completely out of tune, she was not deterred! She began playing with gusto. This unexpected "accompaniment" threw me completely off key. Finally able to regain my composure, I finished with the whole congregation joining in on "People Get Ready."

Even after the song, the melody could be heard echoing throughout the sanctuary as others continued to sing softly. After a while, I sang "Jesus Loves Me" for the children, finishing with the doxology, "Praise God from Whom All Blessings Flow."

★   ★   ★

About a month later, I received a call from Fred Cash of The Impressions. Interestingly, this was the primary group who made "People Get Ready" famous. The Righteous Brothers also recorded a fabulous version. Fred and I had a great conversation, and we discussed my singing their song in Jeremiah Robinson's church. We then played with the idea of possibly recording a Christmas CD or a gospel CD with their group. For whatever reason, the idea did not progress beyond the speculation stage. But their wonderful song had made an "impression" on me and on countless others who needed to hear that timely message.

In the "Key" of Faith

On a Sunday in May, Camille and I met Chris Walters at the Progressive Morning Star Baptist Church where Prentiss was now a member. We went just to hear Prentiss sing and to support him, fully expecting to be observers more than participants. Moved by the powerful service, I could not restrain myself from being very much a part of it.

Prentiss sang the lead on a beautiful song with the choir backing him. His voice was rich and deep and full of love; I had never heard him sound better. No wonder his fellow church members adored him.

Unfortunately, Prentiss had enjoyed the service so much that he had neglected to eat. After a very full day, he went back to church on Sunday night for several hours. "Brother Morris, I was havin' such a good time, I didn't want it to end!" he confessed to me when he landed in the hospital two days later.

Prentiss had been transported by ambulance to the emergency room. The paramedics had not been able to get him to respond when they arrived, and they had to break into his apartment. He had only enough strength to dial the phone for help. His blood sugar had dropped dangerously low, and he almost died that night. As a result, he remained in the hospital for a few days, being monitored and tested for various ailments.

While he was there, Chris and Leila dropped by to see him. I followed shortly after, alerting the nurses to Prentiss's notoriety in the music business. After that, the staff began to take an increased interest in him and redoubled their efforts on his behalf. By Friday, he had stabilized sufficiently to be dismissed.

Chris began working on getting Prentiss a monitor to wear around his neck. In the event of another emergency, he could simply click a button and receive rapid assistance. As it was, he had been too weak to come to the door when the paramedics arrived.

A few weeks later, when Prentiss notified Chris about a lab bill he could not pay, Chris did some research. He had picked up on something that Jim Brewer, head of the Mississippi Music Hall of Fame, had mentioned about the MusiCares organization in Nashville. So Chris put together a packet of information and applied for $5,000 of medical assistance annually. It was approved—a great boon when Prentiss needed it most.

★   ★   ★

Rufus McKay was also still struggling with his health. Obviously, no longer able to work, he was in financial straits and owed the hospital over $28,000. My heart went out to him. But I suspected that the hospital would simply write it off.

At times like this, good care is vital. But so is the prayer of faith. And I never ceased believing that our good and loving Father would spare our friends for another season. I had promised Prentiss that I would come back "soon" to do an encore with him, and I intended to keep my promise. Just hoped that he would be well enough to keep his.

Get Ready

Not long after that conversation with Rufus, I called Bill Pinkney to check on him. He recognized my voice right away. (Probably not that many of his friends *sing* their greeting to him.) It was a great relief to hear in Bill's voice a vibrancy and strength I had not heard in quite a while. "Bill, you sound so good!"

"Well, I'll be honest with you—I was so tired and weak, I wanted to go on and be with the Lord. Bill, when I confessed that to Him, He restored my health. I feel wonderful! I feel so good that I'm going to be performing tomorrow night and Saturday in Myrtle Beach, South Carolina, and then going to Washington, D.C., to be in Ben E. King's celebrity golf tournament. It's kinda like a miracle!"

In our conversation, Bill Pinkney's contagious enthusiasm lifted my own spirits. "The truth is, Bill," I said, "last year when you invited me to Pennsylvania for the Vocal Group Hall of Fame as your guest, and I said goodbye to you at the airport, I wondered if I would ever see you again. It was all I could do to keep from breaking down right there in front of everyone. But when I got on the plane, I took my seat, turned my face toward the window, and let the tears fall."

People, Get on Board

The summer passed in a flurry of activity between my business, my family, and attempting to keep up with my singer friends. But it was November before Prentiss and I could get together to sing for his church as we had been planning for some time. Since that Sunday would be the third anniversary of the church on Robinson Road, we expected a good turnout and put in quite a bit of rehearsal time to prepare. Unfortunately, the rehearsals did not go well for me, especially the final one before our performance. The movement from intro to the lead on "People Get Ready" did not flow, and I felt that my voice was flat.

When it was time for our number that Sunday, the song went far better than I had anticipated. With Prentiss's encouragement, I was able to hit notes I had not been able to reach previously. When we finished, we invited the congregation to join us in singing the chorus one more time.

The service continued, not ending until one o'clock—four hours in all, far longer than Camille and I were accustomed to. Still, the experience was one I would always value. When I talked with Prentiss later in the afternoon, after we had returned home, he told me that many had come up to him after the service to tell him how much they had enjoyed the music.

"Brother Morris, if there was any doubt in any of their minds as to whether you could sing, they knew it after you finished!"

★   ★   ★

In early December, Chris and I each sent Prentiss a cash Christmas gift and card. The very next day, I received this voicemail from him. It appears here—verbatim:

> Hello, Brother Morris, this is Prentiss, and I tell you, man,
> I don't know what to say. I'll be honest about it, I just don't.
> I could say a thousand things, and still wouldn't be enough.
> And I just love you, I really love you, and God bless you! I

just hope you and Chris will come back to church, and it would be a blessin' for *you*. You would be workin' by me. And I really love you. And I am praying for all of you, your whole family, and I just really know you are going to have a good Christmas. God bless you! All I can say is I love you. I love you. Really, God bless you. I love you from my heart for all of your kindness. Okay. Goodbye.

On Thursday, December 9—two days later—Chris stepped into my office with the news that Prentiss had been taken to Baptist Hospital. It was not his diabetes this time. Apparently, he had picked up some type of food poisoning from eating shrimp. Once again, Prentiss Barnes was facing a health crisis.

According to Chris, Prentiss was also becoming very forgetful. He had lost his glasses and his wallet somewhere, but thanks to the group in Nashville, the glasses would be replaced at no cost to him.

What was most gratifying to me was the fact that younger godly men— like Chris Walters from my office—were getting on board with the idea of extending a helping hand to those who had once contributed much, but were now aging and vulnerable.

~ 22 ~

HELLO, IS THAT YOU?

In the fall of 2004, Rebecca Long, president of the Millsaps College Arts and Lecture Series, asked if I would be willing to introduce Rufus McKay at one of the events the following year. He was scheduled to perform with the Ben Shaw Band at the Ford Academic Conference Recital Hall the following February. I told her that I would be honored.

After the turn of the year, on a cold weekend in January, I called Rufus. His sister Elizabeth answered. "He's been very, very sick and in the hospital for a while. But he's expected to be discharged tomorrow."

Rufus and I talked the next night when he was home again. I encouraged Rufus to be of good cheer and assured him that I would keep in touch.

The first week of February, with the date for Rufus's appearance at Millsaps nearing, I called him at his sister's home. Again, she answered, saying that he was in bed, too ill to get up. But when I spoke with Rufus, he said he was feeling better and hoped to be able to keep his commitment. Time would tell.

Red Tops' Rufus Returns

Fortunately, Rufus made it to rehearsal in the Ford complex the night before the event. For a man who had been hospitalized only a few days before, he sounded surprisingly good. He was still very weak, however, and I found him a chair so he could sit down during this rehearsal time.

The Center for the Study of Southern Culture at the University of Mississippi contacted me about releasing an enhanced version of the Red Tops' CD. Just in case this Millsaps event turned out to be a good performance, we could possibly use some of these tracks to improve the old CD. I made arrangements with a sound engineer, Donald Thomas, to record the show.

★   ★   ★

Camille and I arrived at Ford Hall Academic Complex at a quarter to seven, some forty-five minutes before the event was due to begin. When we reached the staging area, we found Rufus already dressed in his typical white tuxedo, red cummerbund, and bow tie. Seeing his easy smile spiked my confidence that the evening's performance might prove to be successful, after all. Still, I was concerned. He had been quite weak at the rehearsal the night before and had barely made it through four songs.

Strolling over so as not to attract attention from the band and other onlookers, I looked Rufus in the eye, placed my hands on his shoulders, and leaned in to whisper a prayer in his ear. "May the Almighty God give you strength and anoint your voice to sing for Him tonight."

Meanwhile, as we milled about, Chris Walters and Camille had found our seats down front on the aisle. Rebecca Long launched the program and then introduced me. I stepped up to present Rufus. It went well—beyond my expectations—and when Rufus stood, the crowd broke out in a roar of shouts and whistles.

Thus inspired, he kicked off his set in fine style with one of The Drifters' numbers, "Save the Last Dance for Me." He followed that song with his classic recorded songs, "Swanee River Rock" and "Hello, Is That You?"

When at last Rufus swung into his iconic "Danny Boy," an atmosphere evoking poignant memories of youthful proms and parties settled over the audience, and many couples got up and danced to the music in the aisles.

With tears welling in many an eye, I silently gave thanks that, once more, this 78-year-old was able to pour out these melodies long past the point of near exhaustion. In fact, Rufus was enjoying it so much, he sang until the band literally ran out of songs for him.

As the evening came to a close, it was obvious that Rufus's energy was now totally spent and, although fans clamored for his autograph, I knew he needed to get something to eat before he collapsed. With apologies to the crowd, I rushed him to the dressing room where he quickly downed a tuna sandwich.

Camille and I sat with Rufus while he ate. The band members were busy loading their gear into their vehicles for the return trip to Vicksburg. We reminisced about the evening, and Rufus continued to marvel at the crowd response. "Just didn't know folks cared that much," he said, shaking his head in disbelief. "Thought they'd forgotten all about me."

Afterward, with a little food under his belt, Rufus felt energized enough to walk downstairs where Ben Shaw was waiting for him. As we handed over this treasure to the band leader, Camille and I departed for home, satisfied that it had been a grand evening indeed.

Reprieve for Prentiss

With insufficient funds an ongoing problem for these aging singers, we were surprised to receive a letter from Suzan Evans of the Rock & Roll Hall of Fame Foundation in New York City. I knew that financial assistance was generally limited to a lifetime maximum of $5,000 for any artist. But apparently the foundation was willing, at our request, to make an exception for Prentiss. In fact, they planned to cover his rent for an entire year.

We were grateful, but my wheels were turning. If we would have to reapply for funds for the following year, it would be wise to consider alternative donors . . . in case his situation was not renewed.

As if to confirm that approach, later that same week, I received a call from Dr. Faser Triplett, offering to do "something nice" for Rufus McKay. The "something nice" was a check for $1,000! I was profoundly moved as, I had been worrying about his financial condition too.

When it's Time to Say Goodbye

The month after these serendipitous events, I was relaxing a little over the condition of my friends when I received an email from Maxine Porter: "I am deeply saddened to report that one of our long-time Original Drifters family members, vocalist Vernon Young, passed away this evening at 8:46 p.m. in Georgetown, Grand Cayman, in the Caribbean while on tour with our group. I will provide more information as it becomes available."

Before joining Bill Pinkney and The Drifters, Vernon had sung with Archie Bell and The Drells out of Houston, Texas. I liked Vernon very much. He was an outstanding tenor and soared on the high notes when they were singing a medley of songs. Nor would I forget the great memories we made during the recording of Bill's first gospel CD in Jackson—telling hunting stories and horsing around. Vernon was always chuckling about something, and that sound would linger in our hearts and memories.

~ 23 ~

LET'S DOO WOP

The weeks and months were accelerating at an alarming rate with various events and activities. My daughters, now in their late twenties, were practically grown—sort of. My insurance firm was continuing to prosper—with a lot of hard work on the part of my associates and myself. But my passion for music and the arts—particularly the genre of rock 'n' roll called "doo-wop"—reached its zenith with the Doo-Wopp Hall of Fame Awards Show held in Boston in March 2005.

As on so many other occasions, I made my travel plans with Delta Air Lines, departing Jackson International en route to Boston by way of Atlanta. Waiting for me at Gate 19 were Chris Walters and Prentiss Barnes. Seeing Prentiss, who was looking a bit fragile, I felt a catch in my throat. Could this be our last trip together?

Following a flight from Jackson, we were now in the huge Atlanta airport, with its endless corridors and multiple concourses. Prentiss was lagging behind on our way to the departure gate. The connection was tight, so we had to hurry. The next thing Chris and I knew, Prentiss had flagged down a motorized cart, only to find that he was no more than fifteen feet from our destination. Poor Prentiss was more than a little embarrassed when he realized what he had done, but being a good sport, he managed to laugh at himself.

Once aboard the plane, he slept most of the way, as his age and physical limitations were becoming more evident.

At Boston's Logan Airport, we were picked up by a driver who took us to the Marriott Residence Inn in Westford, Massachusetts, about thirty miles outside of the city.

As soon as we walked into the lobby, I bumped into several of The Spaniels, including Opal Courtney, Willie C. Jackson, Don Porter, and Charles Colquitt. It was exciting to see them. Eugene Pitt and others from The Jive Five were also on hand. I recognized Eugene immediately, having met him at Bill Pinkney's seventy-fifth birthday celebration in Columbia, South Carolina. What a singer! And he was one of so many others who would be performing. For this aficionado of the genre, it was Christmas, New Year's, and the Fourth of July all rolled into one!

Zing! Went the Strings of My Heart

Rehearsal started at 7:30 p.m. Not wanting to miss a moment, I was there early. First up were The Spaniels, sounding great on "Zing! Went the Strings of My Heart" and "Goodnight, Sweetheart, Goodnight." Next were Eugene Pitt and The Jive Five, whose medley "Never" and "My True Story" was a knockout! Now on an emotional high, I could not resist singing along with the different groups.

Spotting someone sitting on a couch in an adjoining room, I popped in to see who it was. It was none other than the outstanding lead singer of The Spaniels, Pookie Hudson. I loved the uniqueness of his voice. He had been very ill with cancer, and I let him know I had been praying for him.

And, of course, there were The Moonglows. It was the old gang who had shown up for this event. The original members were there, absent Bobby Lester who had died twenty-five years earlier—Pete, Prentiss, Harvey, plus Reggie Gordon of The Magnificents. I would again be performing with them on "The Ten Commandments of Love." In rehearsal, Pete showed some signs of wear and tear, but the numbers sounded pretty good by the time we were through.

★   ★   ★

The next morning, when we gathered for breakfast, adrenaline was pumping and we were eager to get on with the show. After we ate, The Spaniels and The Moonglows, plus a few band members and Harvey Robbins, founder of the Doo-Wopp Hall of Fame, boarded the bus for the trip into Boston. The Jive Five would travel in their own van.

On the bus, I became a little nervous when I heard Harvey Robbins announce that the VIP reception at Boston Symphony Hall would include singers only, not band members or other parties. I wasn't worried for myself since I was singing with The Moonglows, but we couldn't leave Chris Walters out of the festivities.

At the first opportunity, I called Harvey Robbins aside. "Harvey, I would like for my associate, Chris Walters, to be able to go to the reception." He graciously agreed.

I could now relax and enjoy the ride as we listened to The Spaniels' anniversary CD. Enthralled with their rendition of "Zing" and other songs, we sang all the way to Boston.

★   ★   ★

Boston Symphony Hall is one of the grand venues in America for such functions. Historically prestigious, it is the hall where Arthur Fiedler and the Boston Pops have performed countless concerts.

We were escorted to our various dressing rooms—next door to the Jive Five and around the corner from The Spaniels—where we would later change into our tuxedos. One thing was weighing on me, however. Will Sanders assumed he would be doing the repeat part in "The Ten Commandments of Love," since he had done it before, as had I. The guys kept kidding about our having a face-off and letting the two of us audition for the part.

Harvey decided to take a vote of the members of The Moonglows. When someone asked about the outcome, he said, "Bill will be doing the part."

Shortly after that exchange, when someone else asked the same question, Pete seemed to be proud to confirm the decision. "Bill is going to be doing it."

That did not sit well with Will. Not only had the rest of The Moonglows voted for me, but to make matters worse, so had his client, Pete, whom he managed. I had to feel a little sorry for Will, who appeared to be rather woebegone.

At the VIP reception, tables had been set up for all of the singers. It was exciting to see how much the local donors loved getting to meet the participants in the awards show. I mingled with the honorees, taking photographs and getting autographs.

When the reception concluded, we rushed off to our dressing rooms, where, once again, I assisted Prentiss with his tuxedo. Nothing new here. This had become our regular routine.

But I *was* surprised when Pete asked me to help *him*. "Bill, would you get my bow tie, too?" he asked.

I obliged, then stepped back to get the full effect. "Pete, you're looking mighty sharp."

Pete only smiled, apparently feeling pretty proud of himself. In that moment, I knew I had finally been totally accepted into the group by the last holdout.

The Thrill of It All

The excitement was building. In addition to his many other duties, Harvey Robbins, decked out entirely in bright red—suit, shirt, tie, and patent leather shoes—emceed the show and introduced the first act, Little Joe and The Thrillers out of New York City. Little Joe had made the song "Peanuts" famous. I was amazed at his vocal range—from high falsetto to deep bass. In fact, when I heard him rehearsing during the mic check, I thought there was another singer onstage. But it was only Little Joe Cook. At the time, he was in his eighties, but he helped the group put on an epic performance. Following that act, Harvey Robbins presented Little Joe Cook with his Lifetime Achievement Award in the Doo-Wopp Hall of Fame.

The Moonglows then entered stage right, leading with "Seesaw," transitioning into one of their signature songs, "Sincerely." On the last few notes,

I walked out to my mic, a few feet from Prentiss, Reggie, and Pete. Harvey was walking around with the portable mic, singing lead. When he saw me, he paused to introduce me to the audience: "And here is . . . Bill Morris from Jackson, Mississippi!" With that, we moved into "The Ten Commandments of Love," their third and final number.

It was a magic moment, eclipsing almost any other with the exception of my wedding day and the birth of our daughters—and the night we honored Prentiss. I could hardly believe that I was on that world-famous stage, singing with guys who had become true friends and brothers. Guys who had formed one of the most revered vocal groups in the history of Rock 'n' Roll . . . and here we were—performing together at the Doo-Wopp Hall of Fame!

When I did the first repeat in a deep bass voice, "Thou shall never love another," I heard a woman on the first or second row give a kind of gasp.

Encouraged by this receptivity, memories flooded my mind—flashbacks to the days when I had first heard The Moonglows. I was thanking God and somehow simultaneously managing to keep up with my part in the song. It was a surreal moment—almost as if I were in another time and place on that stage with those world-class singers. Looking to my left at The Moonglows and then to the gilded balconies overflowing with adoring fans, I was in a state of ecstasy—another magic moment.

We took our bows to a long standing ovation.

Goodnight, Sweetheart

After heading backstage, I returned to my seat in the audience next to Chris, about five rows back, to watch Eugene Pitt and The Jive Five. Gene was now one of my absolute favorite singers. The group did not have many numbers to hit the big-time charts, but they sang doo-wop harmony the way I like it. That night—perhaps because I was feeling especially sentimental— they sounded better than I had ever heard them. The audience responded as I had expected—with loud and prolonged applause.

In reflecting over this period of my life, a thought occurred to me later that while these groups sang of youth and love and beauty, many singers who followed them would rant of violence and drugs and illicit sex. Yet the rappers and heavy metal groups would grow extraordinarily wealthy. One would have to ask the question: Why not Prentiss and others like him?

The second half of the evening started off with a performance by Dion and The Belmonts, as well as The Tune Weavers, standing in for Little Anthony and The Imperials, who were absent. This can happen with older groups when one of them becomes ill or has a family emergency. We missed getting to be with Little Anthony but were thankful Dion was able to fill in.

The Spaniels were last, but far from least, doing several of their famous numbers to wind up the show. Their final number was their signature song, "Goodnight, Sweetheart, Goodnight" which brought all the groups back on-stage for a grand finale. I found myself singing beside Carl Rainge, Charles Colquitt, and Willie C. Jackson of The Spaniels. Pure bliss!

By eight o'clock, we had wrapped up the performance part of the weekend, and, as the crowd poured out of the building for the ride back to Westford, in my mind, I was still on that stage!

Everything's Gonna Be Alright

The next morning after breakfast, getting Prentiss through the airport check-in process was always something of a challenge because of his prosthesis. All of that metal would set off the alarms, and, of course, the authorities would then have to conduct a search, running the wand over his body to detect the source of the metal. Frustrating, but once again, we made it through—on time.

On the flight back, I kept looking over at Prentiss, thinking of the move he would be making to Magnolia, Mississippi, in just a week. I felt my throat closing up on me. He seemed tired and a bit sad. I felt the same, yet I knew this move was in his best interest. He could no longer live alone, so it would be good for him to live near family.

Arriving in Jackson, we picked up our luggage at baggage claim and waited for Chris to bring the car. With the prospect of Prentiss moving away, I was feeling down and must have let it show, for it was he who boosted my spirits when he said, "It's okay, Brother Morris. It's okay. Everything's gonna be alright." Nevertheless, I knew it would be difficult to see Prentiss go.

★   ★   ★

Each night for the next week, after getting home from work, I called Prentiss to touch base. I was already missing him. As the day for his departure neared, it dawned on me that I was still holding onto something he had asked me to keep for him—his statue from his induction into the Rock & Roll Hall of Fame.

"Prentiss, before you leave for Magnolia, I need to return your award trophy. I have been keeping it safe for you, you know."

I wasn't prepared for what came next.

"No, Brother Morris, the way I look at it, that statue really belongs to you too. If it weren't for you, I wouldn't be here."

This time, the lump in my throat prevented any further comment. Prentiss was always so deeply appreciative of everything done for him. For my part, I was humbled, thankful for what *he* had done for *me*. Today, that statue, representing a great depth of emotion and years of profound friendship, stands proudly in my home.

~ 24 ~

SINCERELY

The savage Hurricane Katrina that was spawned in the Gulf of Mexico, slammed into the shores of Mississippi, and later flooded the Big Easy in August 2005 was not the only storm that season. News of the passing of two more Rock 'n' Rollers—Gary Rogers, Bobby Lester's nephew who headed up another group of Moonglows, and Will Sanders, Pete's manager, barely made a ripple in the music world. Yet, one note at a time, the song of a generation of musical pioneers was slipping away, and the music would never again sound as sweet.

Will was dead just three weeks after his cancer was diagnosed. We would have contacted Pete, but I didn't know how to get in touch with him.

Prentiss had barely relocated to Magnolia, Mississippi, when along came that hurricane. His apartment was the only one in the entire complex that suffered any real damage, although all of the apartments lost power. What a nightmare that must have been for Prentiss!

"Brother Morris, when the lights went out, I didn't even know where I was," he confided when I finally got through to him via the apartment manager. "Couldn't reach my brother Houston, 'cause they lost their power, too, and they had no telephone service. Didn't get it back for a month!" There was a long sigh on the other end of the line. "Brother Morris . . . sure do miss you and Chris. Wish we could get together again."

Before we signed off, I mentioned the doo-wop event we had both enjoyed so much with The Moonglows. "We really ought to do that again sometime, Prentiss," I said, hoping to encourage him.

At that remark, Prentiss perked up. "You know, on 'The Ten Commandments of Love,' you sounded jus' like you'd been rehearsin' with us for weeks!"

So the old Prentiss was still there. Weaker, maybe, but still tuned in to his friends and the magic world he had helped to create.

Tearing Down Walls

Around the first of December, I left a message on Harvey Fuqua's phone, bringing him up to date on Prentiss's condition. Much like the stock market in a volatile phase, he was up one week and down the next.

Harvey returned the call on a Saturday morning while Camille and I were decorating our Christmas tree. His call was a welcome diversion. We talked for a good while about Prentiss, and I gave Harvey the numbers where he could be reached . . . if he were lucky!

Then Harvey said, "When Carolyne and I get back from a cruise we've planned, why don't you and I drive down to see him?"

It was a fabulous idea! The ride to McComb would be an opportunity for Harvey and me to become even better acquainted. Before we hung up, I said, "Harvey, I doubt that you will ever know, in your lifetime, the significance your music has had on breaking down the barriers between our races. Your music has brought love and healing into a situation that needed it very badly. I will be eternally grateful for that as well as for the music itself. You had a major impact at Motown."

Harvey couldn't speak for a moment. It was clear that, with this conversation, our relationship had taken on a new depth.

Still Waters

Prentiss was now back in the hospital—at the McComb Regional Medical Center. Heading down to see him, I put in a call to Bill Pinkney and filled him in.

"Tell Prentiss that his big brother, Bill Pinkney, says he loves him and that everything will be alright," Bill said, adding, "Pray for him like you did for me, Bill. You've prayed for me three times in different places, and just look at me! I'm healed now!"

His comment did my heart good, but I hastened to correct him. "You do realize, don't you, that that was not me, but the Lord?"

"Oh, Bill, I know that! But you were the one who did the prayin'."

★ ★ ★

When Chris and I reached the McComb Regional Medical Center, we took the elevator to the fifth floor. At the nurses' station, we introduced ourselves. One of the nurses then pointed the way to Prentiss's room. Just outside, we noticed that someone had taken the trouble to wrap the door with red ribbon like a giant Christmas gift.

We tried to let him know we were there but got no discernible response. After a few more attempts, we gave up and told the nurse we would get some lunch and return.

An hour or so later, we tapped on the door, then walked in. Prentiss was lying there, looking small and shrunken with his snow-white hair framing his dark face.

We again tried communicating with him, but neither Chris nor I could understand anything he said in reply. His few words were so low and unintelligible, we weren't sure he even knew who we were.

When I asked, "Well, Prentiss, can you still sing?" he smiled, but didn't open his eyes.

We left soon after, wondering. . . If he survived, it would take a miracle.

★ ★ ★

On December 13, only a few days after our trip to see Prentiss, Chris burst into my office. "Prentiss is on the line!" he announced.

"What?!"

"Yeah, Prentiss wants to talk with you."

When I picked up the phone, that voice was as clear and strong as if nothing had ever happened. I asked him if he remembered our visit, and he seemed surprised that we had been there. Nevertheless, he was alive! A miracle, indeed!

No Coincidence

While dining in downtown Jackson at a family-owned Greek restaurant known as the Elite Restaurant, in walked an old friend of mine. Guy Hovis had been a classmate at Ole Miss. At this time, he was the chief of staff for Senator Trent Lott. Earlier, Guy's career path had taken an interesting turn when he moved to Hollywood and landed a spot on the *The Lawrence Welk Show*. It was Guy & Ralna, the singing duo who had captured the hearts of Americans every Saturday evening for many years.

Over lunch, we shared our stories. Whereas singing had once been Guy's vocation, my foray into the musical world had always been a passionate avocation. But one thing we could agree on:

"From the sound of it, I believe each of us is exactly where we were meant to be," I said. "There have been too many miraculous turns in the road."

He nodded. "Exactly. For one thing, what happened to you in Washington, D.C., with The Moonglows twenty-six years ago had to be a miracle. Professional singers don't normally invite a total stranger into their act to do the lead on a song!"

From that experience, I told Guy how that evening led to the friendship with Prentiss Barnes and the others. As a singer, he was fascinated with the story. Eventually we wrapped up our conversation, concluding that our meeting on this day was no coincidence, but an opportunity to share life.

★   ★   ★

Chris Walters had come to love Prentiss almost as much as I. As business ramped up, Chris began to take over more of the responsibility for keeping tabs on Prentiss and making sure he had what he needed. As a result, Prentiss formed a deep attachment to Chris and began calling him from time to time, leaving voice messages:

> Hello, Chris. This is Prentiss. I'm home. Guess I called you at the wrong time. But anyway, I'm home. I'm feelin' kind of like a stranger around here, so I'm gonna have to do a lot of catching up. I love you. Tell all the rest of y'all that I said hello. Tell Brother Morris hello. I'll be gone this afternoon. I have to run and have some tests done. I'll get back with you later. Thank you very much. 'Bye 'bye.

Meanwhile, Chris took it upon himself to contact the Rock and Rock Hall of Fame Foundation regarding the extension of Prentiss's financial aid. He promptly received an affirmative response, with a check enclosed.

The Call

September 24, 2006. Early Sunday morning, as Camille and I were having breakfast, she told me that she had awakened in the night and was impressed to pray for Prentiss. I made a mental note to call him, but with the next two weekends spent in Oxford at football games, seeing old friends, I never got around to it. I should have viewed Camille's dream as a sort of premonition.

Almost exactly a week later, while still in Oxford on an early Sunday morning, I was roused from a deep sleep with a call on my cell phone from Cloteal Barnes, Houston's wife. "We lost Prentiss this morning," she said.

Maybe I was in denial, but I could only blurt out, "You *lost* him! What do you mean?"

"He died this morning. He was in a single-car accident yesterday evening. They don't know whether he had a heart attack or what caused the accident, but he ran off the road and the car flipped over. He was severely injured . . . and he died this morning,"

The thing I had dreaded most had come to pass. I knew Prentiss's time in this world couldn't be too much longer as his health had been failing on several fronts. But he had always rebounded. This time, though, our more than twenty-six-year journey together had come to an end. My detailed journals, chronicling our many magic moments, would serve me well to recall our friendship and the love of the music we shared.

After the shock of the moment, my next thought was to call Chris, Bill Pinkney, and Harvey Fuqua. I was able to reach Harvey and Bill, who were equally saddened by the news. Harvey was scheduled to undergo medical tests in Palm Desert, California, in the coming week, so it was doubtful he would be able to get back in time for the funeral.

"Bill, I knew when you called me this early in the day that something must be going on with Prentiss," Bill Pinkney said. "You know, Bill, the Lord giveth and the Lord taketh away. We all got to go at some point."

He went on to explain that he had engagements Friday, Saturday, and Sunday so it would be impossible for him to be at the funeral.

"Bill, I will say something on your behalf," I assured him.

I then spoke with Chris, who had heard about the accident through Prentiss's landlord. After that call, I spoke with various members of Prentiss's family, including Amile Barnes, Prentiss's nephew, and his wife, Bernice. They were sorrowful, of course, yet rejoicing in the fact that Prentiss would no longer have to suffer—whether pain, illness, poverty, or loneliness.

★   ★   ★

The next morning, when I got to the office, I composed an e-mail to the many friends and associates who knew of my friendship with Prentiss:

> It is with great sadness that I tell you my dear friend and great singer companion, Prentiss Barnes of The Moonglows, died this Sunday morning, October 1st, following a single-car accident on Saturday. He was driving himself to choir practice at his hometown church in Magnolia, Mississippi. Funeral

arrangements are incomplete at this time, but the service will be held on Saturday October 7th, at Rose Hill Baptist Church in Magnolia. . . .

There is pain in my heart right now—a void that will surely never be filled. I can, however, give thanks for the gift of friendship with one of my heroes.

I will sign off with one of the songs he helped to create.
Sincerely . . . oh, yes, sincerely,
Bill Morris

As I continued to grieve the loss of my good friend, I was remembering the question posed by the Father when He asked, *Would you have wanted Me to leave Prentiss here until he could no longer care for himself?* With that memory, God comforted me—as He always does.

Getting to Know You

In the next few hours and days, I received condolences in the form of emails from people both near and far, including many of Prentiss's fellow singers and associates: Carl Gardner of The Coasters and his wife, Vera, Jimmy Merchant of Frankie Lymon and The Teenagers, and Maxine Porter of Stars Unlimited in Las Vegas. They all knew how much I loved Prentiss.

Harvey called to tell me that he was going to be able to make it to the funeral, after all. He would be coming in on Friday, and we would drive to Magnolia together the next day. I also called Reggie Gordon of The Magnificents in Chicago and left a message. Jim Brewer, president of Mississippi Musicians Hall of Fame, responded with the offer of a contribution toward Prentiss's gravestone. It was clear to me that this news had touched a chord in many hearts.

★ ★ ★

Harvey flew in from Las Vegas on Friday. When I met him at the airport, I stuck out my hand to shake his, but he objected. "Huh-uh. I want a hug." And it was a bear hug indeed! Harvey was a huge man—about 6'4," 260 or

270 pounds. Judging from size alone, he could have easily been a professional football player.

Even under these sad circumstances, it was great to see Harvey, and we reminisced about Prentiss all the way to the Hilton, where he would be staying over the weekend. The music was on both of our minds, and we talked about who had hit "that note" . . . who was doing backup on a particular song . . . which instruments were used . . . the intricacies of the sound known as "blow harmony," and, of course, the contribution Prentiss had made to the success of The Moonglows.

At the hotel, I waited for Harvey while he checked into his room and unpacked. I had invited him to stay with us in our home, but he'd declined. "Haven't been sleepin' well. Don't want to bother you folks. And besides ... I might rest better here."

We then headed home to pick up Camille for dinner. When she insisted he come in for a bit, he agreed. Looking around our den, he loved our art, especially the painting of the singers we had commissioned John Carroll Doyle to paint—*This Magic Moment.*

Shortly afterward, the three of us drove to the Mayflower Café, where Camille and I spend many of our Friday evenings enjoying the outstanding seafood and catching up with friends. I was pleased to introduce Harvey to them. When dinner was served, he raved about the fine piece of grouper he had ordered. While we were dining, many came by to snap photographs, for they knew of Harvey's fame.

After dinner, I dropped Camille off at the house en route to taking Harvey back to the Hilton. Before the evening was over, we shared many more memories. Tomorrow would be bittersweet as we laid our friend to rest.

Remembering Prentiss

The next day—the morning of the funeral—I rose earlier than usual. As I had been asked by the family to deliver a eulogy, I had spent much of the night pondering what I would say about Prentiss. Jotting down a few notes, I then dressed and drove over to pick up Harvey, who was immaculately attired as always. We then hurried to meet Chris.

On the way down to Magnolia, Harvey filled in the blanks on the history of The Moonglows, including the misunderstanding between himself, Bobby Lester, Prentiss, and Pete. The group parted ways in the late 1950s for various reasons. There was much dissension. After the split, there was the struggle to find work again.

"You know, Bill, it was because of you that I reconnected with Prentiss at all. We had been separated for twenty or twenty-five years. But it was your friendship with Prentiss that closed the gap between the two of us."

For a moment, I did not respond as I reflected back on the message I had received in church for Harvey a few years ago. It seemed vital that day that I contact him immediately and relay that message from God—that Harvey was deeply loved by His Creator. Oh, no, it wasn't I who had brought the two men together! It was the Father's love. I was just the instrument He had chosen to use for a greater purpose.

When we pulled up to the Rose Hill Missionary Baptist Church, quite a number of cars were already in the parking lot. It seemed that virtually everyone we met had the last name of "Barnes." Prentiss had seventeen brothers and sisters, of whom twelve were already deceased. That left only five living siblings—Houston, Bertha, Sam, J. Lee, and Jethrow . . . and all of their progeny.

As directed, Harvey, Chris, and I gathered with the family at the front of the church for the processional. Each of us was given a bulletin with a picture of Prentiss on the front, along with the words: "A Service of Memory Celebrating the Life of Our Beloved Mr. Prentiss Barnes, Saturday, October 7th, 2006, 12 o'clock p.m., Rose Hill Missionary Baptist Church, Magnolia, Mississippi."

Quickly leafing through, I found several photos of Prentiss, including some of Chris and me with him. Under "Expressions" was my name, along with Brother Harvey Fuqua and Brother Pete Graves. As far as I knew, though, no one had yet heard from Pete.

Thirty minutes into the service, it was time for me to speak. It was difficult. Prentiss was so dear to me. But I made it through sufficiently.

In concluding, it seemed appropriate to sing the song Prentiss and I had sung earlier that year at his church in Jackson—"People Get Ready." On the final note, I added, "When Prentiss left home to travel the short distance to this church for choir practice that evening, he had no idea that before the sun rose, he would be singing with the angels in heaven. There is not a doubt in my mind that Prentiss *was* ready. And he would want us to be ready too. We never know what breath will be our last on earth . . . and our first breath of celestial air.

"I would be even more heartbroken in losing Prentiss if I were not assured that one day I will be joining him in singing a glorious new song that has never been heard on earth. The Lord was merciful in sparing our friend any more suffering . . . and taking him Home while he was on his way to rehearse for the heavenly choir!"

~ 25 ~

MISTY BLUE

As we made our way back to Jackson, Harvey and I continued to discuss the history of The Moonglows while Chris listened in from the back seat. Digging a little deeper, I dared to mention the lengthy resentment that Prentiss and Pete had held toward him.

"All I know, Harvey, is that Prentiss—a long time ago—let go of anything he had against you." I glanced over at Harvey, who was sitting beside me in stony silence. "What I mean is . . . he forgave you."

We drove for a while, discussing less sensitive topics. I could tell, though, that Harvey was deep in thought, and I decided to broach the subject again.

"Last time we talked, Pete was still upset," I went on. "He felt he helped to write some of the songs for which he never got credit." I waited for some response from Harvey. He was obviously still processing this information.

"And, Harvey," I said, "I think Prentiss felt like he helped write 'Sincerely.'"

"He did?" Harvey finally replied. "Hmmm." Then again, silence.

I was hoping Harvey would not be irritated with me or Prentiss. But what I was about to say was too important to keep to myself. "Harvey, if there is any question in your mind about that, I would ask for God's forgiveness."

Nothing more was said, and before long, we dropped Chris off. Prior to returning to the Hilton, Harvey and I headed to Great Scott, the fine men's clothing store located in the same building as my office. As a man who appreciated nice clothes, Harvey wanted to check it out. After looking over the selections, he purchased a new shirt from Wright Scott, the owner's son. Purchase in hand, Harvey and I drove on to the hotel, where I left him to get some rest. I would pick him up at seven for dinner at Walker's.

★ ★ ★

Since Camille was still tired at dinnertime, it was just Harvey and I at Walker's. This restaurant was known for its fine dining, with an outstanding chef, and the conversation was stimulating.

Over dessert, I said, "Harvey, you know I love singing so much that sometimes in my soul, I wish I had been a singer."

He looked puzzled. "What do you mean? You *are* a singer."

I was stunned. According to what Prentiss had once told me, Harvey did not normally hand out compliments. Actually, I have since come to the conclusion that many people could sing if only they would just release the music inside of them and let it flow. That is what happened to me, for I never had a lesson—except for a few impromptu "sessions" with Prentiss when preparing for some event.

After the good meal and fellowship, we headed back to the Hilton. I told Harvey I would pick him up for church in the morning. But before he left to go back into the hotel, we listened to the sounds of The Moonglows on the car stereo for the next hour or so. I noticed that Harvey was listening to each song on my double CD as if he had never heard it before. He seemed to be analyzing every little detail.

I laughed a little. "I'm so familiar with this music, I can tell when you come in, then Bobby, then Pete, and Prentiss. I know you don't care much for the song 'Starlight,' but the reason I like it so much is because of the exceptional contrast between the high notes and the low notes. And you guys did that number so well. Your arrangement is fantastic, Harvey!"

Al Bell—President of Stax Records—Pioneer Awards 2008—Philadelphia, PA

Bill with The Whispers—R&B Ceremony—Kimmel Center in Philadelphia—R&B Foundation Awards 2008

Earl "Speedo" Carroll (The Cadillacs) Kimmel Center in Philadelphia—R&B Foundation Awards 2008

Dionne Warwick performing at the Kimmel Center R&B Pioneer Awards Ceremony—Philadelphia

Baby Washington, Maxine Brown, Bonnie Raitt, and Mable John—R&B Pioneer Awards Philadelphia

GC Cameron (The Spinners/The Temptations) singing "It's So Hard to Say Goodbye to Yesterday"—recognizing those lost in 2007-2008—Philadelphia—R&B Foundation at the Kimmel Center

Backstage GC Cameron and Bill at The Pioneer Awards—The Kimmel Center Philadelphia 2008

Backstage—Gary US Bonds with Bill Withers who had just received a Pioneer Award at The Kimmel Center in Philadelphia 2008

Brenda Holloway, Bill, and Kim Weston—Rhythm and Blues Foundation at The Kimmel Center in Philadelphia

Bill speaking to the Mississippi Senate posthumously recognizing Prentiss Barnes 2007

Bill and Bill Pinkney—the last time Bill saw Bill Pinkney was at his home in Sumter, SC—two months before he passed away—July 4, 2007

WILLIE (BILL) PINKNEY PARK

DEDICATED OCTOBER 28, 1996

Willie (Bill) Pinkney was born August 15, 1925, in Dalzell, SC. He enlisted in the US Army in 1943 during World War II, receiving four Bronze Stars for heroism during the Battles of Normandy, Saint-Lo, Bastogne, and the Rhine River. After Bill's discharge from the US Army, he, along with Clyde McPhatter, and Gearhart and Andrew Thrasher, formed a singing group, THE DRIFTERS, which went on to gain national and international fame. The fact that Bill grew up during the turmoil of segregation in our nation, adds to the greatness of this man who overcame adversity to reach the pinnacles of success. To those who do not know Bill Pinkney or who will never have the opportunity to meet him, he is a kind, humble person who never met a stranger, A TRULY GREAT AMERICAN.

A bronze placard which speaks for itself—Great American, Great Singer, Dear Friend

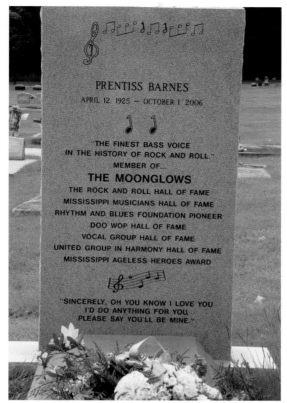

Prentiss Barnes' granite marker located outside of Magnolia, MS

Harvey Fuqua, Bill, and some of the members of Prentiss' family gathered around the gravesite

Bill delivering a eulogistic message singing Bill Pinkney's "White Christmas" in July 2007 for 3500 people in the Sumter Civic Center

About that time, Prentiss's mournful bass voice could be heard, pulling the group along, undergirding the entire number. So much was racing through my mind and heart at that moment. I shook my head. *Is this a dream? Am I really sitting here with one of the all-time greatest arrangers and contributors to doo-wop music, and experiencing all the nuances of the The Moonglows' songs?*

For all Harvey may have done or not done, as perceived by other members of the group, he truly deserved great acclaim for the magnificence of his arrangements and his voice. Without him, The Moonglows would probably have never been recognized.

Though highly controversial, Alan Freed, too, deserves some credit for their initial success. He recognized the genius of these guys and renamed them The Moonglows instead of The Crazy Sounds. Then he promoted them all over the Upper Midwest and East Coast via his radio program, live shows, and movies. Since such groups had no means of paying a fee for marketing, the promoters, such as Alan, were often given partial credit for some of the songs in remuneration for their services. This type thing later became the subject of a congressional investigation, leading to incarceration for some. Maybe the explanation for the long-time feud between some of the singer/songwriters and their agents/promoters is simply a matter of a partial solution to the ongoing problem of paying people for their part in disseminating the music to the public.

One Miracle after Another

The next morning, as pre-arranged, I picked up Harvey and took him to Holy Trinity for Sunday school and church. Delighted to meet him, the people greeted him warmly. He seemed to fit right in. After the service and lunch, on our way to the airport for his return flight, he commented on all the events of the weekend.

"You'll hear from me soon," Harvey promised as we parted.

True to his word, he called the very next day as I was dictating a letter to him. "Bill, I don't know when I have enjoyed anything as much as I did this past weekend. As sad as it was to bury Prentiss, there was a joy in doing so as well. We know that he is with the Lord." Harvey paused, then added, "One of the things I liked the most was going to your church with you."

Then he proceeded to ask about the various people who had taught the Bible lesson, arranged the music, preached, etc. "There was such happiness and peace there. It was really wonderful," he went on. "Made me happy."

"So glad you were blessed, Harvey. I have an idea that our paths will cross many times in the future. And I, for one, will be looking forward to that!"

★   ★   ★

About a week later, I received a call from Tyler, Texas. It was Bruce Barnes, Prentiss's nephew. His voice, mellow and mournful, reminded me of Prentiss, and I felt a fresh wave of grief. "Brother Morris, I've just got to tell you something," he began.

"What's that, Bruce?"

"What you said last weekend at my Uncle Prentiss's funeral went right straight into my soul, and it's stayed with me. Just can't get over it." He went on to say, "A few years ago, Uncle Prentiss showed me the newspaper article, telling all you had done to help him. I read that article over and over."

I thanked Bruce. "You understand who actually did the work, and it wasn't me. It is the Father's work. He just used me to help your uncle."

Bruce began to pour out his story. "I never knew my father. My mother, Maggie was Prentiss's youngest sister, but she died last year. . . ."

Apparently, because Bruce didn't have a hands-on father, his Uncle Prentiss and Prentiss's brothers had filled that gap.

"It was like having *seven* fathers!" he continued, again reminding me of Prentiss. "Now that Uncle Prentiss is gone, God has given me *another* uncle. It's you, Brother Morris!" My heart melted.

Mississippi Musicians Hall of Fame

At the request of Dr. Jim Brewer, head of the Mississippi Musicians Hall of Fame, I attended the annual ceremony at the conference center in

Vicksburg, Mississippi. Plans for this event, which would have seen the induction of Prentiss and others the previous year, had been disrupted when Hurricane Katrina hit the coastline. Evacuees had scurried for shelter throughout the state and beyond, many of them finding a temporary safe haven at the Vicksburg Conference Center.

I arrived at the VIP reception a little before six o'clock, at which time I met Jimmy Weatherly, the ex-star quarterback of the Ole Miss football team, turned singer/songwriter. So many of the great songs he penned were recorded by Gladys Knight, including "Midnight Train to Georgia" and "Neither One of Us." It was nice to meet Jimmy and his wife, Cynthia, along with their two children. Like so many with his talent, they reside in Nashville today.

Also on hand were Andy Anderson and The Rolling Stones and his later group, The Dawn Breakers. Of course, these were not the world-famous Rolling Stones out of England, who came later. Interestingly, Andy once said that his former agent in England was hired by that group of Rolling Stones. So . . . the question might arise: How did they come up with that name for their group? It could have been the internationally known blues singer Muddy Waters . . . who knows?

It was so good to visit with my old friends Doug and Melvin Williams, along with their mom and sisters. Once the opening reception came to a close, we all moved to the main venue for the presentations. Performing were Andy Anderson and his group of Rolling Stones, Jimmy Weatherly, who did "Midnight Train to Georgia," The Williams Brothers, as well as Ace Cannon. And then—my dear friend Rufus McKay, mesmerizing yet another audience with his iconic "Swanee River Rock," "Danny Boy," and "Hello, Is That You?" In fact, he was a little tentative about doing "Hello, Is That You?" and asked me to come up and help him, but I declined, knowing he could do it. He and the band handled that number quite well. There were many other songwriters and families recognized, including Willie Dixon, "Pinetop" Perkins, and Mississippi John Hurt.

Over the past several decades, much had transpired to change the racially charged atmosphere in the South. On Saturday night, many of the singers who had suffered rejection now expressed their appreciation for their warm reception and the recognition extended by the Mississippi Musicians Hall of Fame. They were all praising the state and saying what a wonderful place it had become.

When it was time for me to respond to Prentiss's induction from the previous year, I kept it short. I recapped the story of our friendship and how it had been my privilege to travel with him during his latter years. "God gave Prentiss to me as one of my best friends, and if you are not familiar with the music of The Moonglows, you need to tune in. They were one of the quintessential groups of slow doo-wop. Many in the field of music feel a sense of awe when hearing Prentiss's impressive bass voice. I have seen it. Gosh, I miss him!"

★ ★ ★

In mid-October, I received a call from Harvey Fuqua, saying he had been trying to get in touch with Pete but still hadn't been able to locate him. He also wanted to make sure we had the marker for Prentiss's grave executed properly and wanted to assist with that.

"One more thing," he said before signing off, "I want to tell you again what a wonderful time I had during the three days I was down there. And I'm not talking about you buying my meals and things like that. I'm just talking about the friendship we have."

"Harvey, now that Prentiss is gone, I need someone to fill that hole in my heart. I guess that's you."

"Man," he said, "I feel the same way."

Singing the Blues

Only a day after my conversation with Harvey, I got in touch with Chuck Rubin in New York. Chuck is the founder of Artists Rights Enforcement Corporation and has a passion for helping artists receive uncollected royalties. He had been able to reach Pete's family.

"I hate to be the one to break the news," Chuck began hesitantly, "but Pete is dead. He died Sunday, October 15, of cancer. I'll give you the telephone numbers of his sister, Sharon Graves, and his wife, Rusty, if you want to contact them."

I followed through right away to extend my condolences. "So heartbroken to hear of Pete's death," I said, then shared with them about Prentiss. "Isn't it ironic that they died just two weeks apart, both on a Sunday? My heart goes out to you. Now I will be getting in touch with you soon. God bless you."

After speaking with Sharon and Rusty, I put in a call to Harvey. "Harvey, you're the last one standing. Pete's gone."

"No! He can't be!"

"Yeah, he died Sunday. And the funeral is tomorrow at the Griffin-Peters Funeral Home on Seventh Avenue in New York City. He is to be buried in the Rosedale Cemetery in either Elizabeth or Linden, New Jersey—I don't know which."

Harvey, most likely thinking of the bad blood that had existed between himself and Pete, was obviously upset. "I'm going to that funeral tomorrow!" he declared. "Rusty probably won't be glad to see me, but it's not about her . . . it's about Pete."

"Harvey, it might help if you offered to do something nice, maybe through the foundation. You know, for the tombstone, or something."

We talked for a while longer, then concluded our conversation, agreeing to touch base again after Harvey attended the funeral. We still had to help settle Prentiss's estate with his heirs. The needs were ongoing.

Mistletoe Marketplace

November 2006. With Thanksgiving and Christmas less than a month away, one of my favorite social events of the year was coming up—Mistletoe Marketplace. This was an annual affair to kick off the holidays, beginning with an opening night gala and lasting four days. The event was staged at the Trade Mart, a large facility at the Mississippi State Fairgrounds, magically transformed into a sparkling wonderland. There were gifts for sale by vendors from all over the country, musical entertainment, and fine food and drink, served in one of the large central rooms.

The much-anticipated weekend attracted the gentry of Jackson and people from throughout the Southeast, all of whom dressed for the occasion in their finest. Camille and I enjoyed donning our most elegant formal wear. We entered a white tent, walked past a flowing fountain, then strolled through the various rooms and booths, decorated with garlands of green and myriads of twinkling lights. Here the enticing wares included books, art, jewelry, clothing, tasty treats, and you name it! Many of those who attended often did all their Christmas shopping on this one weekend.

For some reason, this particular year, I had a strong sense that I was supposed to be a blessing to someone I would encounter at the marketplace. Of course, there was always a host of friends in attendance. Would it be one of these? Someone who needed an encouraging word? A gesture of kindness?

As we were making our way through the Trade Mart, I recognized a familiar face. It was Dorothy Moore, the famous singer and four-time Grammy nominee, who recorded "Misty Blue." She was seated behind a table displaying some books and CDs.

I rushed over to tell her how happy I was to see her. She smiled, apparently glad to see me too. And as I frequently do when greeting a singer, I launched into a version of one of her songs, sung softly so as not to attract attention.

"You know how much I love your music," I explained, "especially 'Misty Blue.' I heard you do a twenty-minute rendition of that number at Jubilee Jam." At the time, the jam was an annual event put on by the Jackson Arts and Music Foundation. Singers, musicians, and fans would pour in from all over the nation.

She seemed pleased that I remembered, but Camille and I didn't linger. We moved on, wandering through the Trade Mart, greeting so many of our friends. It is always such a joyous time, and everyone is in a festive mood. But Dorothy was still on my mind. Inexplicably, I felt drawn to go back and talk with her.

While Camille examined some jewelry on display, I returned to Dorothy's table to find someone sitting with her—Marcia Weaver, a former Jackson City Council member. "Marcia," Dorothy said, "this is the gentleman who was singing with me."

That encouraged me to sing a bit more with them, after which Dorothy said, "Yeah, I'd really love to sing with you sometime . . . maybe at the Alamo Theatre." With that, I started into "Let It Be Me," a song made famous by two former Mississippians, Jerry Butler and Betty Everett. Dorothy joined in.

When we finished, Marcia took our picture, then left to check out some items in the mart. It was then I sensed the need to pray for Dorothy, not knowing exactly why.

Speaking in an undertone, I asked, "Dorothy, *how* are you doing?"

With that, she lowered her head and began to cry. Something was happening as huge tears dropped onto her lavender satin dress. I stood there for a moment, then leaned over to comfort her.

She began to tell me she had not been paid what she felt she was due from her contributions over the years. Even her most famous song, "Misty Blue," which had been used in an award-winning movie, had brought in little revenue for her.

Where had I heard this before? My heart ached for her.

Looking at the books on display in her booth, I picked up one entitled *Little Dorothy.*

"It's my story as a child," she explained. "I tell about growing up and going to the Mississippi Delta where my grandmother would pick cotton. I'd get so sleepy on those long, hot summer days that I would lie down on the cotton sack Grandma filled."

I bought the book and a couple of her CDs. There wasn't much more I could do at the moment. But I could support the foundation and other organizations that addressed those needs. And I could pray.

Well, I have come to find out that Marcia Weaver, her dear friend and manager, continued to pursue this and now Dorothy is receiving royalties and fees. Dorothy is at peace and very thankful for this excellent outcome.

~ 26 ~

SUDDENLY THERE'S A VALLEY

With Prentiss gone, my life was strangely void. I missed his mellow voice as he crooned a well-loved tune, that throaty chuckle when he was tickled about something, the poignancy when he rehearsed memories of those golden days. So I sought other ways to relive that bygone era. While watching a Jerry Lee Lewis special on television, I flashed back to the night I had met Jerry Lee for the first time. 1986. Hartford, Connecticut.

A lavish affair was planned in celebration of the 140th anniversary of Connecticut Mutual*, the company I had used as my primary insurance carrier since entering the business in 1966. On the last evening of the convention, which met in the Hartford Civic Center in downtown, four headliners had been invited to entertain—Chubby Checker; the second set of Drifters, featuring Charlie Thomas and Elsbeary Hobbs; and two others, Jerry Lee "The Killer" Lewis and Chuck Berry. Although the event was open to all, I was fortunate to have two front-row center seats; plus, I was one of only a few with an all-venue pass. They knew how much I loved the music.

Waiting for the show to begin, I wandered around backstage and conversed with all of the performers. Chubby Checker was first up and hadn't changed a bit. A big, husky man, he bounded onstage with an ear-splitting grin, singing, "Come on, baby, let's do the twist!"

While he was finishing, I poked my head inside one of the dressing rooms. "Where's my friend, Bill Pinkney?"

"Down South somewhere, I guess," came a deep, resonant voice.

I learned that this voice belonged to Elsbeary Hobbs and introduced myself. I now realized that I was speaking with one of the second set of Drifters. Then I met Charlie Thomas, their lead, and began talking to him about The Moonglows and my experience in singing with them. Before long, we were harmonizing there in the dressing room.

Since The Drifters were up next, I ducked back in and sat down as they took the stage, thrilling the audience with their performance of "Under the Boardwalk," "There Goes My Baby," "Up on the Roof," finishing with "This Magic Moment"—a truly spectacular medley of songs.

At intermission, I went backstage again to see if I could meet Jerry Lee Lewis. I found him in the corridor, heading for his dressing room. He was wearing white trousers and a black shirt. His pale face matched his trousers. I recalled that he had been very ill for several years and had almost died.

But onstage, there was no indication of any infirmity. Jerry Lee brought the house down! To close his segment of the show, he stood up and started banging on the ivories, producing his raucous style of music, then kicked the stool behind him all the way across the stage. I found out later that it was a producer on either *The Ed Sullivan Show* or *The Milton Berle Show* who had made that suggestion—for effect!

Another story has it that once when Jerry Lee was playing "Great Balls of Fire," the audience went wild. With that, he pulled out a can of lighter fluid, poured it all over the piano and lit it. Flames roared, but he continued playing with the band until it got too hot and stagehands had to rush out with fire extinguishers. That's showmanship in the extreme!

Jerry Lee Lewis—along with Elvis Presley, Carl Perkins, and Johnny Cash—was one of the four greats in the early days of this genre. They recorded for Sun Records and today are revered by fans the world over. There is a very popular play about these four, entitled *Million-Dollar Quartet.* The play was based on a moment when, by chance, they were in the studio together for the first—and only—time!

Chuck Berry closed the Hartford show with a masterful rendition of "Roll Over Beethoven." When I visited with Chuck, I reminded him that around 1959, he had been in Jackson for a public dance at the National Guard armory. He played so feverishly that hot Mississippi summer evening, he was completely drenched with perspiration. There was no air conditioning in the Armory, only huge fans. At intermission, we walked out together to a refreshment truck—one of those affairs that was propped up on one side from which to sell ice-cold drinks—and I bought him a Coke.

The Hartford show closed for the night, but my memories lived on, punctuated by photographs.

Friends Forever

On the morning of July 5, 2007, I was headed into a very important business meeting when I decided to check my voicemail. There was a message from the leader of These Days, a local band in Jackson: "Bill? Raphael Semmes. I am so sorry to hear about your friend Bill Pinkney. I saw on television last night that he died in Daytona Beach."

I gasped and replayed the message to be sure I had heard correctly. This devastating news had come out of the blue! It had been only a few weeks since I had visited with Bill in South Carolina. I certainly hadn't expected him to go this soon.

Stunned, I wondered how I could go on to make one of the most consequential presentations of my career. Still, I had no choice but to tell the truth and beg the indulgence of my audience. "I have just learned that one of my very best friends—Bill Pinkney of The Drifters—has died. I ask you to cut me a little slack right now, please."

The committee was exceptionally understanding, and the presentation was highly effective and successful, in spite of the news I had just heard. But I don't know how I made it through without a meltdown. Bill Pinkney . . . gone.

★ ★ ★

When I got back to the office, I was eager to learn the details of his death and told the receptionist and my assistant to put through all calls regarding Bill. I got on the computer immediately and read the news report. One account stated that Bill and The Original Drifters, along with his full band and other singers, were in Daytona Beach to perform at a Fourth of July celebration. When a stagehand went to Bill's room to let him know it was time to go on, he had "gone on," all right—to his everlasting destination. He had apparently died of a heart attack.

The show continued as planned, just as Bill would have wanted. Shortly after reading the article, I received a call from Toni, one of Bill's female vocalists, who typically fronted for him. She filled in the details for me as Bill's entourage—fifteen in all, including Toni—were riding on The Drifters' bus back up to South Carolina. They were all in shock. Bill's son, Terry, was also on the trip, and Toni said the enormity of what had happened to his father had left his son bewildered.

Toni and I shed some tears, and then, at her suggestion, I began placing calls to Bill's family. I spoke first with Eartha, his sister, who had been so kind in assisting me with directions when I was in Sumter a couple of months earlier. She encouraged me to go ahead and call Marion and Liza (Bill's sister) Pearson. We were all choked up, with tears flowing on both ends of the line.

When we hung up, I received a call from Harry Turner, the Carolina businessman who also loved Bill and his music. "Bill . . ." he began hesitantly, "have you heard?"

It took me a few seconds to mumble a reply. We spoke briefly before Harry had to hop off the line to respond to a reporter.

Before the day was over, I composed a letter to my daughters, Camille and Kathryn, who were now living in Charlotte, far away from home. They would be saddened, too, knowing the depth and breadth of our friendship:

Well, I must say goodbye to yet another very dear friend. It was but a few weeks ago when I went to visit you two in Charlotte. You may remember that I took an extra day and went down to Sumter, S.C., to visit Bill Pinkney, feeling an exceptionally strong urge to do so. Bill and I listened to some of his music and were trying to decide about putting out a new CD. . .

The last thing he did, in the driving rain, was to take me out to Dalzell, just about eight miles out of Sumter, to show me the park his family dedicated to the city. . . . There was a beautiful monument and bust of Bill Pinkney, which the state of South Carolina had erected. He was so proud of that. I still remember him waving goodbye to me as I was headed back up to Charlotte, and I thought to myself, *Will this be the last time I will see him?*

Remember how precious life is and do not assume you will always have the opportunity to spend time with someone or tell them that you love them. Everything we have is a gift from our Heavenly Father. Be thankful every day, all day, and every minute. I love you dearly.

Dad

Throughout most of the day, I sat in my office with the door shut. Grief can be very cleansing and clarifying. Mingled with my heartbreak was gratitude for the time I had been given with both Bill and Prentiss. My singer heroes from those early days were leaving me. I could no longer call them nor dream about doing another CD nor sing with them again. Oh, the memories were pulling at my broken heart! Once again, I was comforted by the message I received at Prentiss's death: *Would you have wanted Me to leave him here?*

Amazing Grace

Traveling to the funeral, I arrived in Columbia, South Carolina, a little later than anticipated due to delays in Atlanta, then picked up a rental car for the short drive to Sumter. My hotel accommodations were conveniently located near Bill's house, the funeral home, and the Sumter County Civic Center where the memorial service was to take place. On the drive over, I spoke with Harry Turner who suggested that we meet at Bill's place.

As I approached the house, I could see children—probably Bill's great-grandchildren—playing outside in the spacious front yard. Inside, the wonderful family had gathered to mourn their loss and to share memories of happier days. Sisters, brothers, nieces, nephews, and his own children greeted me like one of their own, and we wept together. Bill was the source of so much love and joy—therefore, all the bigger void now that he was gone.

Marion and Liza Pearson—Bill's brother-in-law and lovely sister—were still at their house. Harry and I drove over to visit with them for a while before returning to Bill's home place. We attempted to console Eartha, Marcel, and Debra, Bill's daughter. I was also introduced to Henry, a brother I had never met, and a sister who startled me with her resemblance to Bill—same facial features, skin tone, and mannerisms.

Since it was still relatively early, Harry suggested that we stop by the funeral home. As I walked into the viewing area, I noticed that toward the front of the room, people were kneeling and praying. Suddenly aware that Bill was in the Presence of God and His angels, I began to sing the timeless words of that world-renowned hymn "Amazing Grace."

Recognizing my voice, Maxine Porter turned around and looked up, tears rolling down her cheeks. "Why, there's Bill Morris, Bill Pinkney's dear friend! Bill loved you so much," she said.

"Yes, and I loved *him.*"

A tender moment.

★ ★ ★

Back in my hotel room, sleep did not come easily. But I managed to linger in bed a little longer the next morning, hoping to get enough rest to fortify myself for the trying day ahead.

At breakfast, I spotted Clifford Curry, who wrote the song "Just Drifting Along," especially for Bill's 40th anniversary celebration. Moved by the story of The Drifters' journey, I had asked Bill to record it on our gospel CD. After Clifford joined me, two others pulled up chairs—Joe Ross and Al Hartford. Joe had sung with Bill for about ten years, and Al was active with a group out of Melbourne, Florida, who performed The Drifters' "imitations," as they called it.

As Clifford and I headed out the door back to my room, he pointed toward a lean and dapper man across the parking lot. "There's Bobby Hendricks."

"Bobby!" I called to him.

He came over right away, sporting a pair of shades and a finely tailored outfit. The way he carried himself . . . he just *looked* like a celebrity. Bobby was one of the early members of The Original Drifters. We chatted for a while, and I realized that here was one of the few surviving members of The Drifters. I felt my pulse quicken. Bobby had sung the lead on "Drip Drop" and "Suddenly There's a Valley," a song with enormous contrast between the tenor and the bass. Like so many others, he loved Bill too.

In my room, I was going over my notes when the phone rang. It was Harry Turner, asking if he could come by to wait for a friend.

"Sure," I told him. "Come on down."

"Looks like the whole industry is turning out for this service," he said, dropping into a chair. "I've seen Ben E. King, Harvey Fuqua, several of The Orioles, and at least one member of The Heartbeats. Oh . . . saw John 'Bowzer' Bauman, too."

Harry left to join his friend shortly afterward, and I made my way over to the civic center about an hour early. Even then, the parking lot of the Center was almost full. My guess was at least a couple of thousand people were already on hand, including dignitaries from all over.

Inside, I recognized that many of the state's elected officials, including folks from the governor's office, the attorney general, legislators, and senators, were in attendance. After all, Bill was a part of the fabric of their lives. It seemed that everyone in South Carolina revered Bill Pinkney. By this time, mixed emotions were building—sadness, of course, yet a curious excitement as I wondered what the next hours might hold.

Rainbow in the Valley

As I walked into the convention hall, I scanned the crowd, seeing familiar faces and members of the press, who were interviewing some of the celebrities here to honor their deceased colleague. A television reporter from CBS interviewed me, but I struggled for words. I found my seat, reserved for me down front, near where the family would be making their entrance. Despite the circumstances under which we had all come together, the energy in the room was electric.

I turned to see Harvey Fuqua coming toward me. But a number of other singers corralled him first, and he was soon surrounded by his admirers. Meanwhile, we all continued to mill about the room for the next hour, greeting old friends and meeting new ones. Harry Turner, who was well connected in the state, introduced me to many of his friends. I also saw some of the old Drifters, including Russell Henry and Ali-Ollie Woodson, who had initially sung with Bill's Drifters and later sang lead with The Temptations. As it turned out, I was seated by Harvey and Ollie during the service. Ollie, who had one of the strongest voices in the business, was scheduled to sing a solo.

As a prelude to the service, "America the Beautiful" from our CD was playing over the PA system. All of the family, accompanied by the dignitaries, proceeded down the middle aisle of the civic center: the family, filling several rows on the left-hand side; the dignitaries, on the right. Bill's body was lying in state at the base of the stage. His casket was flanked by massive floral arrangements and two easels displaying oil paintings of him.

Throughout the vast hall, the sound of soft weeping could be heard. When I looked over at Harvey, I could see tears streaming down his face as well. By now, there must have been around 3,500 people in attendance to pay homage to this icon who had made a significant musical contribution over a period of more than fifty years. In many ways, Bill was a part of the culture of South Carolina, performing for countless special occasions—proms, school events, wedding receptions, and celebrations of national holidays.

The minister in charge took the podium to give us some highlights of the program, asking those with comments to limit them to two minutes each. Not possible! None of us could do justice to one of the greatest pioneers of Rock 'n' Roll in that amount of time.

The accolades were wonderful. Much of this was already printed in the memorial bulletin, which would be a lovely keepsake of the occasion. But I knew my eulogy would be a bit different. I would be sharing a more personal account of our friendship.

When I began my presentation, I immediately sensed an almost palpable response from the audience. After a few comments about our relationship, I acknowledged Clifford Curry as the writer of the song, " Just Drifting Along," and began to sing in the manner in which Bill would have rendered the song.

Toward the end of my comments, I went into "White Christmas." As Bill would say when he wanted his singers to join in on a song, "Fellas, can I get a little help?" Remembering Bill's classic comment, Henry and the other singers over to my left were laughing as they stepped up. By now, the entire audience began to sing along, and we ended on a crescendo.

Bill's sister later said, "You sounded so much like Bill that if I closed my eyes, I would have thought it was him up there for a moment!"

Harry Turner was next. "You can relax," he told the audience. "The one thing I am *not* going to do is sing to you!"

He then asked all the servicemen and women who had served in the Armed Forces—both active and retired—to stand. Having been an officer in the army in the mid-1960s, I proudly stood with the rest of my fellow servicemen. Bill Pinkney, of course, was a decorated World War II hero with four bronze stars, a silver star, and a presidential citation. I remember calling Bill one Memorial Day just to tell him how much I appreciated his service to our country.

Following Harry, Ollie Woodson came to the stage and just blew us away with his powerful voice. What strength! By the time the minister spoke, it was after 3:00 p.m. He delivered a fine eulogy, incorporating details of Bill's life into his message of consolation. The ceremonies finally wound down, and the recessional began. It was a solemn moment as Bill's family filed out behind his casket.

Harry rode with me to the interment. Bill was buried behind a little church on the western side of town across from Shaw Air Force Base. As the final words were spoken over him and his mortal body was laid to rest, I mourned his passing.

~ 27 ~

IT'S SO HARD TO SAY GOODBYE TO YESTERDAY

On Friday morning following Bill Pinkney's memorial service, Harvey Fuqua, Chris Walters, and I drove from Jackson to Magnolia, Mississippi, for the dedication of the tombstone for Prentiss. I was thankful that Harvey had come for this occasion.

When we arrived, approximately twenty-five family members were already present, along with the Reverend Carl Hughes, pastor of Rose Hill Missionary Baptist Church.

We gathered in the sanctuary. Reverend Hughes had asked if I would give the dedication. We began with a few moments of silence to offer thanks for the life of Prentiss Barnes. Following that was a brief ceremony in which I presented liturgical and scriptural passages.

At the conclusion, we proceeded out to Prentiss's gravesite behind the church. There stood a magnificent granite stone, approximately six feet high, three feet across, and a foot thick. The stone was beautifully embellished with musical notes and inscribed with laudatory words.

Reverend Hughes led us in prayer. Afterward, we took some photographs. We didn't linger long because of the blistering heat and humidity of that July afternoon. The family stayed long enough, however, to express their appreciation. I particularly recall Prentiss's sister Bertha and brother Houston, who, in their own fading years, carried themselves with dignity and remarkable serenity. I remembered the first time I had met Houston. Prentiss had been so proud to introduce me to his brother. When he brought Houston to my office, I knew immediately I was meeting a stellar individual, one whose integrity was visible in his kind countenance. Most of all, I could see the Presence of the Lord there.

As the family was dispersing, Prentiss's nephew, James Barnes, stepped up to speak with me. James was a strapping young man of about six-foot-three or so, with massive hands and a gentle expression on his face. Fighting back tears, he said, "Brother Morris, you do not know how much this family appreciates what you have done."

"I'm just thankful that Chris and I were able to help your family," I replied. "Prentiss did as much for us as we did for him."

Cryin' in the Chapel

The drive back was interesting. Harvey continued to unfold his personal history—the frustrations of racial discrimination, the drug culture as it had affected some of his singers in the 1960s, and the continuing conflict within the various groups. Once, when things got out of hand, Harvey stated, "That's it! I'm outta here!" With that pronouncement, he had disbanded the group and formed another set of Moonglows with Marvin Gaye, Chuck Barksdale (The Dells' bass singer), and Reese Palmer, originally with The Marquees.

As for those seasons of strained relations among the singers, I never knew exactly why. Drugs? Resentment? Professional jealousy? Dishonesty? Unfairness? Competition? Maybe all of the above. One thing was clear: While Harvey and the others had had their differences, he wanted me to be his friend. And though I was far closer to Prentiss, I tried to understand all sides and to promote reconciliation.

That night, when we arrived back in Jackson, he joined Camille and me, along with Jimmy Young, an attorney and a close friend of mine, at the Mayflower Café. A great way to nourish our deepening friendship. Harvey was the kind of guy who just looked distinguished. Therefore, people were coming by our booth to shake hands and find out about him. Then the photos began.

★ ★ ★

It wasn't long after our trip to Magnolia that Harvey called me to see how I was doing and to tell me that he missed all of us.

"I do have a little news for you. I've been diagnosed with a pre-diabetic condition."

"They're doing a lot with that disease these days," I assured him. "Just take care of yourself, and you'll be around a long time."

Harvey paused, then hurried on to tell me about his plans for taking a new show on the road. "I'm going to book some venues around the country, but I'll need auditoriums that seat at least 750," he said.

"Well, if you're in this area, I'd love to book you for my younger daughter Kathryn's wedding reception. She's getting married in December. But frankly, I know it would be expensive to bring you guys in unless you were already in the vicinity for some other gig."

"Aww, Bill, you know I wouldn't charge you anything! Your daughter's wedding, huh? December, you say? We've got some time, so let's just see what happens."

That's how we left it. But I was thinking it surely would be a delight to hear one of my boyhood heroes do a few numbers at that special time. It occurred to me then that Kathryn's wedding would be another bittersweet moment. Welcoming a new son, Chris Trotter . . . saying goodbye to a daughter. Well, maybe not "goodbye" . . . I was willing to share.

Why Do You Have to Go?

The summer months passed slowly, heavy with the humid Mississippi heat. Camille and the girls were deep into wedding planning. I had been debating with myself as to whether I should attend the Rhythm & Blues 20th

Anniversary Pioneer Awards to be held in Philadelphia in early September. When I learned that Harvey Fuqua would be attending the awards show, I decided to seize the opportunity to spend a few days with this friend.

When the time came for the event, I learned that of the two host hotels—Loews and the Doubletree—I would be staying at Loews, while Harvey would be a guest at the other, a block or so down the street. I was getting off the elevator at my hotel to head to the Doubletree when I bumped into two of the stellar singers who were there for the occasion—Jerry "Iceman" Butler and Gary "U.S." Bonds. Since both of these guys had magnetic personalities, this encounter started my engine racing.

When I reached Harvey's hotel, the lobby was filled with people from the genres of Rhythm & Blues and Doo Wop. So many were here to perform for the festivities. The singers were swarming Harvey, reaffirming to me just how much he was idolized by his peers.

After about an hour of mingling with the musicians, Harvey and I hopped into one of the limos, which took us to the Philadelphia Clef Club, a historical venue, for a discussion of the history and current affairs surrounding this part of the music industry. The structure was rather small—an auditorium-type setting that held around a hundred people. I was on the front row so I could take pictures, with Darlene Love and Baby Washington in the row immediately behind me. Harvey moved around constantly, greeting his many friends before he finally took his seat beside me.

On the small stage were five or six gentlemen, including past movers and shakers in the business. One I recognized was Kenny Gamble, who was a major force in the development of the music industry in the Philly area and throughout the nation. Another impresario was Al Bell, president of Stax Records in Memphis. Most of the evening was spent in a discussion of the development and struggles of the era. Almost everyone in the room could have shared a personal testimony of those times. This event was just a warm-up preceding the main ceremony the following evening. The suspense was building.

★　★　★

On the big day, I joined Harvey and others at the Doubletree and was hustled into one of the stretch limos out front for the ride to the Kimmel Center for the Performing Arts. There was a sense of déjà vu as photographers clicked away and TV cameras filmed footage for various television networks. Already seated in the limo were The Whispers, one of the groups to be honored. I had never met them, but when I mentioned that I was with Harvey Fuqua, who was in another limo, they lit up immediately.

As is my custom, I began singing and hit a few bars of "Sincerely." One of the guys promptly said, "Hey, man, this is the first time I've ever heard anyone who could sound like Harvey."

We arrived at the back of the center and entered via the rear door. Security was tight, but I sailed through with my VIP badge slung around my neck. Sitting down front of this magnificent auditorium were a few of the performers awaiting their turn to rehearse. Among them was my friend, Mable John, the late Little Willie John's sister, whom I had known over the years. Unfortunately, her brother had left us much earlier, as a very young man. From the time I met Mable, she had encouraged me to record. I never took her seriously enough to follow through, but I did appreciate her thoughtful suggestion. If I had ever felt the Father leading me in that direction, I would have followed!

For the next hour or so, there were mic and sound checks—all that is required for a major show. I absorbed the atmosphere, delighting in watching the professional technicians who were orchestrating this rehearsal and hearing snippets of songs that were part of my own history. Before I knew it, it was time to head back to my hotel to change for the main event.

Now all decked out, I returned to the Doubletree where I met up with members of The Five Satins, including Jim Freeman and Fred Parris and his wife and son. There was Earl "Speedo" Caroll and his group, The Cadillacs. The Cupcakes, a great female group from New Orleans, were also in the lobby. Darlene Love and so many others were strolling around, embracing one another. It is one thing to hear the music that helped to make the memories; it is another to be surrounded by these music-makers as they interact. My heart was pounding with anticipation.

Don't Want It All to End

The time was nearing to head to The Kimmel Center. As the venue was only a couple of blocks away, we walked over. But Harvey's knees were killing him, and I told him to rest one of his arms on my shoulder. Until he took me up on my offer, I didn't realize how that might feel as I steadied him. Harvey was a big man, and I soon felt his weight bearing down. Frankly, it hurt, but I was proud to help.

As we walked along, I had the thrill of chatting with Fred Parris, lead singer of The Five Satins. If I could listen to only one doo-wop song in my life, it would be this quintessential one: "In the Still of the Night." I think it is in everybody's top ten, as stated by some, including TJ Lubinsky of PBS specials as "the number-one, all-time best doo-wop song!"

When we arrived at The Kimmel Center, floodlights were sweeping the sky and cameras were rolling. Professional and amateur photographers alike were lined up on both sides of the long, blue carpet. I felt so privileged to walk in with my heroes. The feeling was indescribable.

Inside, the hospitality was marvelous, with sumptuous food and wine for all. Various singers and stars were constantly coming up to Harvey, wanting to get a photo with him. Once again, the magnitude of Harvey's presence was obvious. He was truly a star among stars.

As the cocktail party progressed with much laughter and joviality, I found myself constantly clicking my camera. Once, I strolled back over to find Harvey talking with someone I recognized. Though I had met Chuck Jackson at previous celebrations, Harvey was unaware of that and grabbed my arm to draw me in. "Bill," he said, "I want you to meet my good friend, Chuck Jackson. Chuck lost his son recently."

I could read the deep pain in the singer's eyes and spontaneously threw out my arms to give him a hug. Chuck was one of my favorites of the R&B artists of the era, recording "Any Day Now" and "I Don't Want to Cry." Both were major hits. But at the moment, he was more than a famous recording star—he was a grieving father, and I felt for him.

It seemed such a short time before we moved into the Kimmel auditorium. Harvey and I sat about three rows back from the front to enjoy the proceedings. Throughout the evening, several emcees steered the program— Dionne Warwick, Jerry Butler, Bonnie Raitt, Jerry Blavitt, and Wayne Brady. Jerry Butler would perform his fabulous hit "For Your Precious Love" later that night. Bonnie and I were also well acquainted through the various musical events we had attended through the years. She was always so warm and friendly and a marvelous entertainer in her own right.

Most of the singers being honored with a pioneer award actually took to the stage and performed. Others who had long since put aside the microphone were recognized. All were shown great appreciation. A very special part of the evening was a time of remembrance as photographs and names of those who had passed in the preceding year were shown on a large screen.

At that time, Dionne Warwick introduced G.C. Cameron, a singer friend of mine from Jackson. He was the lead with The Spinners when they recorded the song "It's a Shame." He later sang lead with The Temptations. As Dionne introduced G.C., she said, "He is going to knock your socks off!"

That was an understatement. As G.C. Cameron sang the panegyric in the poignant lyrics to the beautiful song "It's So Hard to Say Goodbye to Yesterday" and the images of the deceased singers were displayed, there was not a dry eye in the house. As the last picture rolled across the screen, a spontaneous burst of applause erupted from the audience, in tribute to those singers now departed. All the while, G.C.'s voice soared higher and higher.

Shortly after his performance, Harvey took me backstage where we chatted with various singers who had already performed or who were getting ready to go on. I shot some photos of G.C., Bill Withers, and others. After a bit, we returned to our seats and watched one stellar performance or recognition after another—Chaka Khan, Donny Hathaway, Teena Marie, Bill Withers, Sugar Pie Desanto, Cool & The Gang, The Whispers, The Funk

Brothers (the Motown band), and Al Bell of Stax Records. The feeling I was having was all too familiar. Never wanting these moments to end, my heart was on an emotional roller-coaster—the thrill of being with these singers, yet knowing that in a few hours, it would all be over. It is somewhat like the feeling we get when we are on vacation and know that, in another day, it will be done.

As we poured out of The Kimmel Center and back to our hotels, I stopped off at the Doubletree to spend a little more time with Harvey and a number of his friends. However, his knees were causing him so much pain, he had to turn in early, and I headed back to the Loews. Judging from the laughter coming from a lounge area, the party had not ended here.

Determined not to miss anything, I strolled in and found clusters of the friends I had met in the last couple of days, including members of Berry Gordy's family and various other exciting and energetic people with his entourage. The place was sizzling with the electricity of serious mutual interests and the spectacular show we had just experienced. Cherishing the moment, I entered into the fun. It was with much reluctance that I finally retired—later.

But long into the night, I reflected on all I had seen and heard. Above all, I was remembering those whose brief candle had been snuffed out. They had had their moment of fame on life's stage, had sung their songs, and were now no longer with us. Still, the melody of their lives lingered on.

★　★　★

The next morning, I could not stay in bed long. Perhaps I could see a few more of my friends before they headed off to destinations far and near. Being an annual contributor to the Rhythm & Blues Foundation, I was invited to a somewhat select breakfast hosted by the Board.

There were about twenty of us in a private room where Bonnie Raitt conducted the meeting. Bonnie is so much more than the fabulous entertainer most people recognize. She has a heart of compassion for those singers who have given us priceless music, but in their fading years, have fallen upon hard times and need help. She has worked tirelessly through this foundation, whose main function is to honor and support deserving artists.

After the breakfast meeting, Bonnie and I visited for a bit. She told me how sorry she was for the loss of Prentiss Barnes and Bill Pinkney, remembering my special friendship with them.

"By the way," I told her, "this is my wedding anniversary, and Camille—that redhead I'm married to—encouraged me to come."

Bonnie laughed. "My condolences to any man who is married to a redhead!"

Before I knew it, breakfast was over, and I was on a plane heading home to Jackson. All I had left of this remarkable event was a heart full of memories—and hundreds of photographs . . . and a story to write!

~ 28 ~

GOOD NIGHT, MY LOVE

Now it was time to focus on daughter Kathryn's wedding ceremony and reception. My main task—other than picking up the tab for the whole thing—was to line up the entertainment. It was Camille who had the greater share of the responsibility for organizing and facilitating this joyous celebration.

It was late July with the wedding date in early December. There was much to do, and Camille was in full mother-of-the-bride mode. She noticed one day that I was distracted and challenged me, saying, "What is it you're so busy about? With all we have ahead of us, what could be all that important?"

I looked up from my place in the den of our home, where I was writing to one of my lifelong friends, Wes Godwin, on the occasion of his seventieth birthday. "It's the most important thing I can do right now." Little did I know that my answer to her would be prophetic.

Wes and I had been friends since age three. We were in kindergarten. We had experienced every year of formal education together—even taking most of the same classes at Ole Miss. He was president of Sigma Chi; I, president of the Dekes. We were tight friends.

Unbelievably, after graduation, we were even stationed at the same military base—Fort Rucker, Alabama—as officers in the U.S. Army. We remained close throughout our professional careers—Wes, in Atlanta; I, in Jackson. Now, as this momentous birthday neared, I was writing one of the letters that the family would include in an album of notes and stories from his closest buddies.

On the Monday morning after that festive weekend, Wes was recalling the event with his wife, Eileen. "I think I am the luckiest guy in the world!" Only minutes after uttering that statement, he had a massive brain aneurysm and died a few hours later.

Camille and I discussed this unexpected turn of events after sixty-seven years of friendship. She reminded me of what I had said to her: " . . . the most important thing."

I grieved deeply for a while . . . still miss him. But in the weeks to come, I followed Camille's lead and threw myself into the wedding planning.

The Music Makers

Harvey and I had discussed his bringing in The Moonglows to perform for the reception. But after checking his schedule, he found that they were to be on a cruise ship for ten days prior to the wedding, would land in L.A. the morning of, and probably could not make it in time. Disappointing as this was for both of us, we agreed that it would be a stretch to try to pull it off.

My next thought was G.C. Cameron. I recalled vividly his rendition of "It's So Hard to Say Goodbye to Yesterday" at the Rhythm & Blues Ceremony in September. That song seemed so perfect for the marriage of our daughter, who had given us so many precious memories. I began talking to G.C.'s agent about booking him, but that idea didn't seem to get sufficient traction as he was heavily committed both in and out of the country. Reluctantly, I scratched G.C. off the list.

Then I began to consider the orchestra out of Nashville that had played for a charitable event in Jackson the year before. They had performed for one of Eli Manning's pet projects here in Mississippi—the Batson Children's Hospital. Eli was able to raise well over five million dollars for this deserving institution by hosting some events that attracted donors like myself. Camille and I still give to this pediatric hospital, which is now building a major addition. Who doesn't care about children struggling with life-and-death issues?

It was at one of those functions where I met Pat Patrick. Pat's orchestra boasted a wide variety in its repertoire of songs. I particularly appreciated the fact that the music was continuous. Most of his musicians were so versatile that they could play different instruments, so they would rotate when a player needed a break. In that way, there was never a pause in the music, which made for a much better party and still complied with union rules.

When I called Patrick, he fondly recalled the Manning event in Jackson and indicated that he would like to perform at Kathryn's wedding reception if he had the date open. When checking his calendar, he found that the day of the wedding was the only weekend date he had available in the entire month of December! To my delight, he agreed to accept the engagement.

One thing remained—to bring in another Mississippi singer, my good friend Dorothy Moore, to sing her standout song "Misty Blue." Because of our friendship, her manager, Marcia Weaver, felt she would be willing to do it. With that agreement finalized, my part was complete. I had only to be available to Camille, Kathryn, and Chris Trotter, our son-in-law-to-be . . . and await the wedding day—December 6, 2008.

"We're Gonna Get Married!"

Our daughter Kathryn and Chris were married at Galloway Methodist Church where my family history dates back to its founding in 1838. As Camille and I left the beautiful church wedding, we raced out to the Country Club of Jackson. Fortunately, I found a few minutes to rehearse with the band the two songs I was planning to sing. Up to this point, our only rehearsal with Pat Patrick in Nashville had been over the speaker phone in the conference room of my office in Jackson.

True to form, I was still rehearsing with Pat when someone called out, "Bill, you'd better get over to that front door. Camille is already receiving your guests!"

Before long, the entire ballroom was filled with friends enjoying the festivities. The bride and groom had arrived, and their joy was contagious. As I looked around, I spotted acquaintances from far and wide, and my own euphoria was mounting.

It seemed only a moment or two between rushing around to cut the bridal cake, do photo ops, and embrace some of the guests before we were ready for the bride and groom's first dance to the song Kathryn had chosen—The Dreamlovers' and Larry Graham's version of "When We Get Married." Pat Patrick's band and singers captured the essence of that enchanting song.

Next, it was time for me to dance with the bride to the tune "My Girl," a song made famous by The Temptations. I danced with Kathryn for a few moments, then handed her back to Chris. Finding Camille, I danced with her and then with Chris's mom, Marie, and ultimately, daughter Camille.

Shortly afterward, the band called me to the stage to perform the two songs Kathryn had requested I sing. The crowd circled the stage, and I said a few words of appreciation.

"I want to thank all of our friends for being here tonight to help Kathryn and Chris celebrate this wonderful occasion. One of the things Kathryn and I have always enjoyed together is music—especially music of a certain era—and two people who would have been with us tonight are Prentiss Barnes of The Moonglows and Bill Pinkney of The Drifters. Unfortunately, we lost them a couple years ago. Therefore, in their memory and in honor of the bridal couple, I am going to take a shot at doing two of their more famous songs."

I led off with "Sincerely," one of The Moonglows' top hits. It was a genuine thrill to sing this song as Kathryn and Chris danced. I ended with The Drifters' "White Christmas," backed by Pat's vocalists.

Now it was time for me to introduce our special guest artist—Dorothy Moore. As I presented her, I told the crowd, "Dorothy is a multi-Grammy nominee and is world-famous for 'Misty Blue,' which she will perform for Kathryn and Chris right now."

There was a rousing round of applause from the audience as Dorothy stepped onstage and took the mic. "But first," she said, "please listen to 'I

Believe in You,' a song that reflects the deep love and trust a bride and groom have for each other."

Dorothy acknowledged our friendship, then dedicated the song to Kathryn and Chris, who danced as she sang. When she started into "Misty Blue," it seemed that the entire room surged to the dance floor, and I rushed to find Camille. As I held her in my arms, moving to the music, tears were trickling down my cheeks in the emotion of that moment. It is impossible to measure the magnitude of such feelings.

I later heard from Kathryn that, on the first night of their honeymoon in Hawaii, when Chris carried her over the threshold of their hotel room, "Misty Blue" was playing over the intercom.

When Dorothy finished, I met her at the side of the stage to lead her down the steps. We posed for some photos, and I took her outside the ballroom to a private area to thank her for coming and to give her a nice check. As I had done a couple years earlier, when she was at Mistletoe Marketplace, I asked if I could pray for her.

"Of course," she said.

Knowing that she had been dealing with pain in her knees, I offered a short prayer before saying good night.

★   ★   ★

The rest of the evening was exhilarating, and it seemed only a moment before it was over. When it was time for the bride and groom to leave, I kissed Kathryn goodbye. As part of the band came outside to perform "When the Saints Go Marching In," Kathryn and Chris raced off to jump into a vintage 1950s-era red Thunderbird convertible, which they drove to a waiting limo a few blocks away.

I went back inside and finished a couple songs with the band—"Daddy's Home" and "Goodnight, My Love." The guests might have danced all night if Pat Patrick hadn't signaled. "That's all, folks!"

The event exceeded all of our expectations. From time to time, people who attended that wedding still express their delight. It remains a time we will all remember and long to recapture.

Double Trouble

One such memory resurfaced during this happy occasion. As in the case of Pat Patrick and his band, my musical journey has placed me on the same course with other singers and musicians. At times, that path has taken some bizarre turns. For example, one spring, on a weekend evening when Kathryn was a junior in high school, Camille and I were chaperoning her sub-deb dance at the Country Club of Jackson.

The band entertaining that night was none other than The Tyrone Smith Revue out of Nashville. Tyrone's band played fabulous music, most of which spanned a period from the 1960s to the date of this dance. Camille and I were thoroughly enjoying the music and even danced a few numbers ourselves.

As the evening was coming to a close and all the kids were clustered around the bandstand, the band swung into a vulgar song by a rap artist. It was hard for me to believe what I was hearing! And this was the singer whose music I had relished for nearly three hours.

I was furious, and Camille knew I was about to explode. "Wait, Bill! What are you going to do?"

"I can't listen to that vulgarity he is singing in front of my daughter and her young friends!"

"Please don't do anything rash," she cautioned.

I stalked out of the room and into the foyer. Minutes later, the song was over, signaling the end of the dance. When the saxophone player wandered out of the lounge area, I voiced my displeasure.

He shrugged. "Don't blame me. I didn't have anything to do with it. I can't stand that music. You'll have to take it up with the boss."

"Where is he?" I demanded.

Little Milton Campbell and Bill—Jackson Music Awards Jackson, MS

Tyrone Smith—The Tyrone Smith Revue—Jackson, MS

Three Record Producers—Tommy Couch (standing), Founder of Malaco Records, Bill Morris (left) Founder of Hallelujah Productions, and John Vincent Imbragulio, Founder of Ace Records— Jackson, MS

Tyrone Davis, Fred Parris (Lead singer of the Five Satins) and Screamin' Jay Hawkins—R&B Pioneer Awards NYC

Walter Williams of The O'Jays with Bill—Pioneer Awards NYC

Bill with Wolf Stephenson (Co-founder of Malaco Records) and Floyd Taylor (son of the late great Johnnie Taylor)—Jackson, MS – Jackson Music Awards

Rudolph Isley (Isley Brothers) and Bill—R&B Awards in LA

Eddie Floyd and Bill—R&B Awards in LA

Maceo Parker (formerly of the James Brown Orchestra)—1996 Pioneer Awards in LA

Duke Fakir (Four Tops) and Mary Wilson (The Supremes) at the Vocal Group Hall of Fame Ceremonies—Sharon, PA

Bill with Fred Parris (The Five Satins) R& B Pioneer Awards NYC

A very rare photo—The Five Satins—R&B Pioneer Awards NYC

Dorothy Moore singing "Misty Blue" at Bill's daughter Kathryn's wedding in Jackson, MS—Jackson Country Club—Image by Karla Pound

Bill and Deacon John and the Ivories performing at his daughter Camille's wedding reception at Antoine's restaurant in New Orleans—photo by Will Jacks Photography

Bill and Deacon John—Antoine's New Orleans—photo by Will Jacks Photography

"Tyrone is in there." He motioned toward the dressing room.

I strode in and approached Tyrone. "Man, I was really enjoying your music tonight until you did that last number. That really *hurt* me," I said, borrowing the lingo of his culture. The word *hurt* implies a profound sadness as well as disgust. "I'll bet you wouldn't play that song for your grandmother."

Suddenly all conversation in the room ceased. There was stunned silence as the band members wondered what was about to go down between this well-known singer and me.

It seemed an eternity, but in about fifteen seconds, Tyrone extended his hand to me. "Thank you so much for coming in here and telling me that."

We became friends that night. On other occasions, when Tyrone would appear in the Jackson area, he would always make an effort to come talk to me.

Sometime later, Camille and I happened to be at Ole Miss where our daughter Camille was a freshman and Kathryn, still in high school, was visiting friends. Following the football game, different bands were entertaining at the local fraternity houses up and down Fraternity Row. We ended up at one of the frat houses where The Tyrone Smith Revue was performing.

When Tyrone spotted me in the audience, he called me to the stage to do a number with him. Without thinking, I hopped up onstage and joined him in a song made famous by Kool & the Gang, "Play that Funky Music." Afterward, I rejoined wife Camille in the audience. We hung around for a little while, then made our way down Fraternity Row.

We had not gone far before we saw our daughter Kathryn making a beeline for us. "Dad! I heard you just sang with Tyrone!" We laughed together, and she seemed quite pleased with the idea.

Not so with my other daughter. I'm not sure how long it took for word to reach her, but the next morning, the phone rang early in the room of the local hotel where we were staying.

My wife answered, handed the phone to me, and with a teasing smile, said, "It's for you, *Tyrone.*"

Puzzled, I took the phone and my older daughter Camille let me have it, telling me in no uncertain terms that I had probably botched her chances to go out with a particular guy she had been wanting to see. He was a member of the frat house where I sang with Tyrone.

I felt terrible and did my best to apologize. "Honey, I'm so sorry."

About a week later, that very guy asked her to go out with him. To her great surprise, he thought it was really "cool" that her dad had been up there singing.

The next time daughter Camille and I spoke, I said, "Now that he has asked you out, you're not mad at me anymore, are you?"

There was a brief pause, a sigh, then . . . "No, but just don't do it again."

~ 29 ~

WHEN I'M WITH YOU

Time. A concept with endless connotations. In some moments, it seems that time stands still—those fleeting seconds of ecstasy and joy at a loved one's kiss, the sight of a breathtaking work of art, the sound of an unforgettable melody. Yet all those moments of time combine to form eras marked by great events that change our very culture, the warp and woof of our lives. One day, all of earthly history will cease in "the twinkling of an eye" and time, as we know it, will be no more.

I was pondering this vast subject as I was heading home from the office one spring evening. How I wished I could arrest time, capture it, prevent it from advancing so rapidly. Already, I had lived some moments with people who were now only fond memories. With that thought, I began missing my chats with Harvey Fuqua, one of the few heroes of that grand era of rock 'n' roll who was still around. I gave him a call.

"Well, hello, Bill!" Harvey's voice sounded strong, and he began to tell me that he was in the process of building a studio at his home in Las Vegas and was getting ready to release a new CD. "I'm doing it with Etta James," he went on. "And some of The Moonglows and Smokey Robinson, too. I'll overnight you a copy when it's done."

I was relieved to hear that he was well and engaged in the work he loved so much. "When are we going to get together again?" I asked.

"Well, man, as a matter of fact, there is another Rhythm & Blues Foundation awards ceremony in September. This one will be in Atlantic City. I'll let you know more when I have all the details."

"Let's do it!" I agreed.

Unfortunately, when the date for the event rolled around, my plate was more than full, and I didn't make it to Atlantic City that fall. Later, I would regret missing this opportunity to enjoy some more time with my friend.

★   ★   ★

On Monday night, May 11, 2009, I received a call from Richard Dunbar, one of the last of Bill Pinkney's Original Drifters. Prior to joining The Drifters, Richard had a group of his own called The Knight Brothers. He recorded on Decca, Mercury, and other labels before finally coming to be a part of Bill's group.

Richard, a really sweet guy, was calling to inquire about whom he should consult for help in producing and distributing the gospel CD he had put together.

I tried to be helpful, but the outlook was bleak. "Richard, the music industry today is fairly complex, and getting the distribution correct is something that few achieve, regardless of the quality of the product."

He said he had not worked in a while and that when Bill Pinkney died, much of his work died with him. I felt so badly for Richard, and yet there was really nothing I could do. There was no way I could take on the project of trying to help him launch his gospel CD. It is truly sad that so much talent yearning to be expressed will never reach the public's ears.

A Part of Our Heart

On Thursday, November 12, 2009, the first major signing for my coffee table book, *Ole Miss at Oxford: A Part of Our Heart & Soul,* was held at Lemuria Books in Jackson. The genesis of this project was a book I had just completed for the Eli Manning family. My daughters came to town for the event, along with Kathryn's husband, Chris Trotter. I was surprised—and pleased—by the size of the crowd!

The next night was a signing at Square Books in Oxford, which recently has been recognized as the number-one private bookstore in America. Let's face it: Oxford is a mecca for writers. Because of the aura and legacy of William Faulkner, they come from all over the world—writers of all genres, journalists, students, intellectuals. Some have wondered how so many famous writers could have come from one state. Willie Morris used to say, "It's in the soil." Might I add: It is in the struggle of our people, combined with the extraordinary gene pool of creative talent.

Again, I was overwhelmed by the crowd's appreciation of my first literary endeavor—although I had written two successful insurance books back in the 1980s. The line was long and lasted well past the assigned time for the event.

After the signing, we had reservations for a late dinner at one of our favorite Oxford restaurants—Waltz on the square, now McEwen's. As we had come to expect, our meal was superb. Then Camille and our daughters hung out around the lively, iconic Square, while I walked about a hundred feet down Van Buren to the restored Lyric Oxford Theatre for a performance by The Four Tops.

I was very late in arriving and missed a great deal of the show. For me, everything was behind schedule. However, I was able to catch the last half as the foursome thrilled the audience with their marvelous repertoire of songs. Duke Fakir, the last surviving member of the original Four Tops—a singer with whom I had fraternized when I was with Prentiss and Bill Pinkney in Pennsylvania—was still going strong onstage.

Melissa Swaney and her husband, Dr. Walker Swaney, were the prime movers in putting this event together. I had learned this back in the summer when I was working on my coffee table book and called Melissa for information regarding her historic home on North Lamar Street. I told her that I wanted to be sure to speak to Duke at their function.

Upon entering the Lyric, I saw Melissa and she directed me, "Just go on up to the front."

I lost no time in doing just that, taking my camera equipment with me. The Four Tops were in full swing, belting out their top hits, "I Can't Help Myself," "Reach Out, I'll Be There," and "Walk Away, Renee."

Guarding the door leading to the dressing room were two security officers. I was certain that this would be my only way of accessing the backstage area after the show to renew my acquaintance with Duke. As the evening moved along, I began to make friends with one young security guard, telling him that Duke was a friend of mine. I asked him to pass the word along. It's amazing how a professional-grade camera in your hands is the "Open, Sesame" to certain places that might be off limits otherwise.

When the show concluded with a rousing roar from the audience, I quickly made my way to the backstage area and up a winding circular staircase to the room where The Four Tops were changing out of their performance duds. There I encountered a stern-faced guard who would not let me pass.

"What's your name?" he asked in a not-too-friendly tone.

When I told him, he left and reported to the Duke.

He had news for me when he returned. "You wait here, and I'll tell you when you can go back."

Ten minutes later, I was escorted into the dressing room. Duke seemed glad to see me. He had just finished a photo op with Melissa and Walker Swaney. To my knowledge, the three of us were the only people allowed backstage out of all who attended the performance that night.

Duke and I visited for a few minutes before I got some photographs, including one of the two of us together. We chatted a bit, reminiscing about the time we had been with Prentiss Barnes and Bill Pinkney at the Vocal Group Hall of Fame in Pennsylvania. I was humming and singing some of The Four Tops songs they had just performed.

"You've still got the full range in your voice, don't you?" Duke asked.

"Well, I guess I do, if you say so."

It was a wonderful conclusion to a grand night. As we made our way out to the limousine, I bade them all farewell, looking forward to a day when I might see them again. As usual, months passed . . . and I lost track.

Last Call

It was June of the next year when I received a call from Harvey Fuqua. "Bill, Harvey here," he announced in his customary greeting. "Don't know what happens to the time," he said. "Man, just seemed like yesterday when we were at some awards ceremony together. But it's been too long, and I've been missing you."

"I've been missing you, too, brother. How are your knees?"

"Oh, had 'em operated on last December," he replied. "I'm doin' alright. . ."

But I suspected that maybe he wasn't.

"Carolyne and I are heading to Detroit for a Circles of Light meeting." I knew this was a religious organization in which she was heavily involved. Harvey was very supportive of her in this endeavor.

Little did I know that this call from him would be a prelude to an email I would receive only a couple of weeks later.

★　★　★

"Hi, Bill, I am a friend of Harvey Fuqua," wrote Sandy Fleming of Charlotte, N.C., in an email. "He has spoken highly of you and considers you a dear friend. I need to talk with you. When you have some time, would you please call me?"

It did not sound good, and I called with some trepidation. As I feared, she gave me unwelcome news. "Harvey has had a heart attack in Detroit and is in the ICU and is not expected to live. I doubt if you'll get to talk with him again."

Sandy and I quickly began exchanging emails and phone calls as his condition worsened. At one point, she mentioned that Harvey's son wanted to speak with me and gave me his cell number.

I called him immediately, and he said, "My dad loved you. Would you pray for him?"

Of course, I agreed. He held the phone to Harvey's ear. I could hear the steady and ominous beeping of the heart monitor as I prayed. Not knowing if he had any active brain waves, a thought occurred to me.

"Harvey, remember this?" And I began to sing the lyric to the song "When I'm with You"—the hit he had arranged and one that meant a great deal to both of us. I had sung it to Harvey on a number of occasions.

Earlier in the call, Harvey's son had told me they would likely have an announcement on Tuesday. He did not tell me the nature of the announcement, but I pretty much knew.

★   ★   ★

At five o'clock on Tuesday, July 6, it was announced that Harvey Fuqua had died. Now the third of my Rock & Roll Hall of Fame buddies was gone. But not his music. It would live on until time ceased.

I made a few calls here and there, exchanged some emails, and talked again with several friends who gave me the names and contact information of some of Harvey's other children. I spoke with Harvey and Carolyne's daughter, Lana, who had just moved to Las Vegas. Lana filled me in on some details of the memorial service in Detroit.

Once again, I called Harvey's son. As we continued speaking, he said, "I need to tell you something. I haven't told anyone else because I didn't want them to think I was crazy. When you were praying and singing with my dad, he jumped!"

"That's not crazy at all. I would guess that the Lord was doing something for your dad that defies understanding in the natural realm."

Because of Harvey's vast popularity, two services would be held—one in Los Angeles on Monday, August 2, where Berry Gordy would be attending; another, in Detroit a few days later. Harvey had been cremated, so the timing was only contingent upon the families' schedules. I so badly wanted to be there, but if I made it, I would have to rearrange my heavy schedule . . . and I put the thought aside for further contemplation.

Remembering Harvey

On Monday night, August 2, I was watching a PBS special hosted by Aretha Franklin. As I listened to the music and heard Aretha talking about the contributions of the singers, I felt a tugging in my heart. I turned the TV off and headed back to my bedroom.

Camille was propped up in bed, reading. When she saw me, she put her book down. "Bill, have you thought any more about going to Harvey's memorial service?"

I nodded. "Yes, I have."

"I really want to encourage you to go," she said. "You loved Harvey, and he loved you. You should be there."

"Well, if things line up tomorrow for me to go, I'm going."

On Tuesday, everything came together. I was able to get a good airline ticket, even though it was a last-minute reservation. I even spoke with some of the memorial's organizers whom I had previously been unable to reach. Sarah Morgan, my trusted assistant, arranged all of the details of my accommodations for the Detroit trip. With everything in place, my heart lifted as I realized that I was, indeed, supposed to be there. After all, the Lord willing, I could sell insurance for many years, but this would be my most important opportunity to date to pay tribute to Harvey Fuqua—my friend—the singer!

Around mid-morning the day before the memorial, I boarded the plane for my flight to Detroit. I would be staying at the Marriott, situated on a scenic waterway. Having no one to join me, I ate dinner alone in the upscale hotel restaurant, contemplating Harvey's life and the service to come.

Upon arising after a good night's rest, I headed to the Bethel A.M.E. Church on St. Antoine Street. The church was beautiful and quite modern, and a crowd had already gathered in the sanctuary.

Walking down the aisle to the front of the church to meet the family, the first person I saw was Carolyne, who was orchestrating the logistics. She invited me to sit by Terry Stewart. Terry was the president and CEO of the Rock & Roll Hall of Fame Museum in Cleveland, Ohio. He remembered me from the various times we had been together at industry events. I also learned later that we were fraternity brothers from our respective universities, both of us Dekes. Seated to my right was Harvey's oldest son, Harvey Fuqua III. On the other side of him was Harvey Fuqua IV.

To begin the service, a video presentation got things going. This video featured highlights of Harvey's life, including a photo of Harvey, Prentiss, and me. There were hymns, but the bulk of the service was spent in memorializing Harvey. It was a star-studded cast—Johnny Keyes of The Magnificents, who had come in from Chicago; Martha Reeves of The Vandellas; Bertha Barbee-McNeal and Caldin Street of The Velvelettes. And just before my tribute, a doo-wop singer named Prentiss, named for my dear friend Prentiss Barnes!

I was privileged to be one giving testimony. Beginning with my initial experience with Bobby Lester, I recounted how I had become best friends with Prentiss Barnes, a friendship that spanned over 26 years, then with Bill Pinkney, and later, with Harvey. I told about the sweet bonds we had enjoyed and how we had sung together at various venues. Finally, I shared about praying with Harvey only hours before he departed for his heavenly Home.

When I finished, I began singing "When I'm with You." Of all the Moonglows' hits, this was our favorite arrangement. As I sang, a man from the audience jumped up, moved to the aisle, and started singing with me. He had a tremendous voice and hit those high notes with gusto. It was the perfect ending to my eulogy.

A Sound Heard 'Round the World

Shortly after Harvey died, I was contacted by Larry Cotton, the radio personality and writer in New York City who wrote about R & B and vocal group harmony for the British publication *In the Basement.*

I had met Larry and his colleague, Tim Marshall, in Sharon, Pennsylvania, when I was with Prentiss at the Vocal Group Hall of Fame ceremonies. Knowing of my deep friendship with Harvey, Larry invited me to participate in a ninety-minute international radio broadcast, highlighting the enormous contributions Harvey had made to the Rock 'n' Roll genre. His unique brand began to be felt in the early fifties and was sustained throughout his long career.

The three interviews—in thirty-minute segments—featured Diane Brown, a Philadelphia radio and television personality, Henry Fambrough of The Spinners, and myself. Henry was especially close to Harvey because he had tutored the group in their formative years, leaving his stamp of artistic genius on them. The interviews, conducted by Larry Cotton and Tim Marshall, were powerful and explored the depths of our individual relationships with Harvey, allowing the three of us to tell our stories, citing ways in which this musical giant had impacted our lives and thousands upon thousands around the world.

Harvey Fuqua would never be forgotten. Every time I heard his name or any of the nostalgic songs he had arranged, my heart would beat a little faster, remembering those magic moments when I was with him.

~ 30 ~

DADDY'S HOME

Of the four singers whose friendship had so enriched my life for many years, only Rufus McKay of The Red Tops remained. After losing Prentiss, Bill, and Harvey, Rufus was especially on my heart. Like the others, his singing talent and warm personality had touched my soul. With his October birthday nearing, I dictated a letter to him and enclosed a check.

A couple of days later, Rufus called. I was busy at the office, and my assistant, Sarah, conversed with him for a few minutes, assuring him that I would be available to talk soon. When I returned the call, it was Elizabeth, Rufus's ninety-one-year-old sister, who answered. Elizabeth was a very special lady—rock-solid in her faith—and I knew how close they were. She called Rufus to the phone, and I began singing my traditional greeting to him, "Hello, is that you? Baby, this is you know who..."

It was good to hear that gentle chuckle of his. "Bill, you don't know how much this birthday check means to me," he said. "I need to go to the doctor, and I didn't have the money to go. Now I can." I was reminded again that some who have enjoyed celebrity for a season often fall into poverty at the end of their lives.

Rufus paused before hurrying on. "Aw, Bill, been real troubled . . . ever since your daughter Kathryn's wedding when you wanted me to come sing. Thought you might be a little mad at me . . . but I was sick then too."

"Oh, Rufus, I had no idea you were worried about that! Of course, I completely understood your situation. I felt only that you had made a wise decision not to come because of your health."

I knew that he had never truly recovered from the serious illness that had threatened his life when he had driven through snow and ice from Carson City, Nevada, to his home in Vicksburg several winters ago. But obviously, Rufus had also been feeling alone and forgotten by his friends. Time had passed so quickly, and with my business requiring more and more of my time and attention, along with family and church duties, I had neglected to stay as closely in touch with him as I had in the past.

"Rufus, we're good friends," I said, "and that will never change."

He seemed quite relieved. I did not know it at the time, but as I look back, I suspect some degree of dementia was creeping in. In any event, I would try to contact him more frequently to reassure him of our bond.

Then I asked for his forgiveness for something I had been carrying since my junior year of college when my roommate Ernest Thomas and I had rented the National Guard Armory on Northwest Street in Jackson to throw a dance. This event followed the Ole Miss/Tulane football game, and we had hired Rufus McKay and The Corvettes to perform that night. This was the group Rufus put together in 1960 after he split with The Red Tops to form his own band.

What I had *not* anticipated was that many other fraternity parties would be competing with our function. As a result, about thirty couples showed up instead of the hundreds we had expected. Of course, that meant we had little money to pay Rufus and his group or the security guards. This caused me to have to call my father to the rescue. He brought enough cash to pay them a partial wage. (Out of fifteen dances I threw, this was the only one that was not financially successful. It was, however, a valuable life lesson in not making assumptions or becoming over-confident!)

I had always felt badly about that and wanted to apologize to Rufus, but the time had never seemed to be right. Today was perfect for laying to rest both of our concerns. I confessed it to him.

Funny thing. Rufus didn't even remember that dance!

Before we hung up, I had one last request. "Rufus, do you recall an interview I taped with you at the time of my fortieth class reunion? It would have been back in 2000."

He wasn't sure. I reminded him that he had an album with photographs, souvenirs, and memorabilia he had collected from his days performing with The Red Tops, The Corvettes, and later when he sang with various groups, including Stanley Morgan's Ink Spots out of Las Vegas. I was hoping to assemble a complete record of his long career, fleshing out our interview with photographs and articles from his album. He did not remember the album, but I asked him to think about it, and I would be happy to pay for the privilege of copying the pages. He promised to look for it.

As luck would have it, weeks and months passed without further contact. Rufus probably forgot about the album . . . and I was distracted with other pressing matters. It would be another year before Rufus and I connected in person, though we would speak on the phone occasionally.

Not a Thousand Miles Away

Despite my busy schedule, from time to time I received nudges that I ought to check on Rufus—in person. It's not that we were very many miles apart. Vicksburg was only a short, thirty-five-mile drive from Jackson. But when I got the distinct impression that I might not have long to see Rufus, I began to make plans to visit him on his birthday.

When I called his home, his sister Elizabeth answered, informing me that she had recently had a heart attack and a mini-stroke, and that Rufus was not well, either. She called him to the phone, and he told me about some of the problems he was having, including some medical tests he was undergoing. It sounded serious.

I had seen an article in the *Vicksburg Post,* which included an image of Rufus going through his memorabilia and explaining his musical journey. When I saw the article, written by Gordon Cotton, I realized once again that I needed to make a copy of the photo album to go along with the other documentation in my files.

★   ★   ★

It was a gorgeous day when I set out for Vicksburg. Upon arriving, there was Rufus, waiting for me on the front porch. From a distance, I would not have recognized him at all. He was wearing thick glasses. His hair was grayer, and his face was gaunt. He looked like a man who had not many days ahead of him.

Although he had not located the album, we spent about two hours sitting in his front room, looking at all the pictures of himself and The Red Tops, mounted on the wall, along with various plaques inscribed with words of commendation honoring an outstanding career. Two images caught my attention—one of Rufus in his U.S. Navy uniform, the other, The Red Tops orchestra. I photographed both.

Rufus always had a wonderful sense of humor, and in his kind and gentle voice, he began telling me one of many stories he related to me over the years. In the 1940s or 1950s, when he was a young man, he loved going to the theater to see cowboy movies. This was back in the days when the South was pretty much totally segregated. One group was seated in the balcony, while the other group occupied the lower level. It's the way it was back then.

Rufus told me that he was watching a cowboy movie once in which the "bad guy" was sneaking around a corner to shoot the "good guy"—Buck Jones, in the white hat. Sitting on the same row as Rufus was a man who interjected his thoughts bodaciously as the story progressed. He must have been either inebriated or demented for he began yelling, louder and louder, "Look out, Buck! Look out, Buck!"

Just before the bad guy could shoot, this overly excited man pulled out a revolver and unloaded it on the silver screen, apparently attempting to defend Buck. Pandemonium broke out! The door to the projection booth was flung open, and the lights came on. People began jumping off the balconies and running for the exits. It did not take long for that theater to become fully integrated! My side was splitting from this delightful story, which Rufus told so well.

Shortly afterward, I took Rufus for a drive to downtown Clay Street, which runs perpendicular to Old Man River. On the last big hill as one approaches the Yazoo Diversion Canal, just before it pours into the mighty Mississippi, there are many historical buildings. One place in particular I wanted to visit with Rufus was a location where there is a Mississippi Blues Trail marker for The Red Tops, between The BB Club and the old Strand Theatre. These markers of Mississippi's deep heritage of musical talent can be seen all over the state. Most of them contain photos and other documentation of a particular musician, singer, or group. This one was entirely devoted to Rufus McKay and The Red Tops.

We took several photographs in front of the marker before I drove Rufus home. I gave him a check for his birthday and thanked him for spending the time with me. I told him if he ever found the album, I would love to come over and make a copy of it, doubting I would ever see it. I wondered if I would ever see *him* again.

A Little Help from My Friends

In mid-December, I received a call from Rufus. "Bill," he began in a subdued, almost shy voice, "I need your help . . . can you help me?"

"What is it, Rufus?"

"I ain't got any money, and I won't get my Social Security check until January third."

"Rufus, you know I'll help you! I'll see what I can do."

I wrote a check, then decided to contact Robert Johnson, a close, lifelong friend who hosts a music blog of sorts, frequented primarily by Murrah High

School alumni, as well as friends from Ole Miss, Mississippi State, and other schools. I emailed Robert to reach out to his blog list with this information about Rufus:

"Though I talk to Rufus fairly often, he has never asked me for anything," I told Robert. "Rufus was very hesitant to ask today, but he is out of money, and his Social Security check does not come in until January. He is in his eighties, he's sick, and he lives with his older sister in Vicksburg. Both are in very poor health and have almost no resources.

"Please ask your friends to consider helping Rufus with a check of any size and a card or letter expressing what he has meant to them. No gift is too small. If they cannot do that, ask them to pray for him. I will collect the gifts and deliver them.

"Frankly, I do not think he will be around much longer. He is going through tests at the VA hospital, and his condition doesn't sound very hopeful. All I know is this: here is a man who, along with The Red Tops Orchestra, blessed many of us greatly during our youth, and he needs us now. But he would never ask you for help. If you or any of your friends feel called to give to the guy who gave us 'Danny Boy,' 'Swanee River Rock,' and so many other wonderful memories, please encourage them to do so. God bless you and have a wonderful Christmas.

Sincerely,

Bill"

Robert forwarded my email, and the response was overwhelming. I had sent the communication on Friday. By Tuesday, $785 had come in. This was followed by a steady stream of cards, letters, and money. My daughter Kathryn and I drove to Vicksburg on a rainy day to deliver the packet. Rufus was overcome, nearly speechless, when I handed it to him. We couldn't stay long as I had a business meeting, but before leaving, I hugged him. "So many of us love you, Rufus, and we thank you for giving us your music."

Over the next week, I continued to talk to Rufus daily, and the money kept coming. In all, there were contributions from Maine, California,

Florida, Arizona, and seemingly everywhere in between, totaling thousands of dollars. Rufus later told me that many friends had dropped by his house, bringing more cash, cards, checks, and letters.

When I spoke with Rufus again, he said, "Bill, I just keep thanking God every day that He put it on your mind to do this, and then He put it on everybody's heart to give."

"Yes, Rufus, that's exactly what happened. This is God's work, not mine. I am just the lucky guy He asked to head this thing up!"

Hello, Is That You?

Here it was June 2012, and it had been several months since I had called Rufus. It was past time I was checking in on him. When he heard my voice, singing that familiar song, he seemed, ironically, both relieved and disturbed. "Bill, why are you so mad at me?"

"Rufus, I'm not mad at you."

"Do I need to apologize? Have I done anything wrong?"

"Of course you haven't done anything wrong! You're wonderful."

"You're not the only one, Bill," he went on. "Even my own people don't call me anymore. Feel like y'all have forgotten me."

Apparently, if Rufus didn't hear from someone in a while, he thought the worst. At his age and with nothing to do, the void was filled with fear and dark imaginings.

I did my best to reassure him that he was not forgotten, that people were busy, preoccupied with their own responsibilities. Still, it was another wake-up call to me. I would reach out to Rufus more often—even if only for a few minutes. No one must feel that they are no longer visible.

★   ★   ★

The days whizzed by. It seemed only yesterday that I had visited with Rufus and his sister Elizabeth. Yet eight months had passed, and we had not communicated often during all that time. It was a cold and cheerless day in February of the following year when I received word that Elizabeth had died.

"Now that she's gone," Rufus said mournfully, "only my daughter Carol, my sister in Connecticut, and a couple of others and me are left."

Fortunately, Carol still lived in Vicksburg, so she saw her father often. Since she worked, however, he would be lonelier than ever, and I feared for his emotional state. To lighten the moment, I reminded Rufus of the first time Elizabeth had seen me. "Do you remember what I did when your sister and I met?"

"Don't guess I do," he replied.

"Well, I could tell right away what a kind, caring person she was just from her demeanor. It is a trait that runs in your family." I paused, laughing a little. "When I realized she was sizing me up to see if I was okay, I started singing the 'doxology.' She stepped back and looked at me as if to say, *Who is this white man coming into my house and singing to me?* But I could see that she 'got it.' That was the moment we connected—years ago."

I was comforted to learn that a visiting nurse from Serenity Hospice would pop in on Rufus from time to time to check his vitals; she happened to be there at the time of this call. He wanted me to speak with her. It concerned me greatly that Rufus was with hospice, but when I spoke with the nurse, she assured me that while he was sick, she did not anticipate that death was imminent. They suspected a heart problem, causing pain to radiate from his sternum to his abdomen.

Believing her to be rather young, I suspected she had not heard of Rufus McKay, nor would she know of his stellar career. When I told her, she was surprised and pleased to have that information. It always amazes me that people who have at one time been famous can drift into oblivion in their later years.

★   ★   ★

The next time I called Rufus, he reported that he had found the photo album he had been looking for. I was eager to copy it before more time passed and Rufus either lost it again . . . or forgot that he had ever found it!

The Way You Look Tonight

By now, my other daughter, Camille—the one with the strawberry-blond hair—was living in New York City. She was engaged to be married, with her wedding set for mid-November 2012. Mother Camille and I were determined to plan an extravaganza to equal our daughter Kathryn's event. This, however, was to be a destination wedding—New Orleans—where we had enjoyed so many special trips together. Of course, this venue would provide rich choices in both menu and music for the reception. The wedding vows were to take place at the St. Charles Avenue Presbyterian Church, with the reception to follow at the famed Antoine's Restaurant in the historic French Quarter. We rented out the entire restaurant for that night.

The music selected would forever imprint the memories of this special day in Camille's very soul. Knowing that my wife would make sure every detail of the décor was perfect and in place, I focused on securing musicians who would entertain our daughter, her new husband, Jason Hellwig, and their guests in a manner that would make this an unforgettable experience for all.

The ten-piece orchestra I had arranged was none other than Deacon John & the Ivories. Deacon John was influential in the entire New Orleans music genre from the mid-1950s, having recorded and performed with many of the greats.

Since her mom and I were going to be in New Orleans the weekend before Camille's wedding, I decided to contact Deacon and see if I could go over and review some of the music from his playlist. As I pulled up to his house on Friday, November 9th around 2:00 p.m., he greeted me at the door with a big handshake.

Stepping inside, everywhere I looked were signs of his celebrated musical career. Guitars, saxophones, various other musical instruments, and music stands crowded the room. We sat down at his kitchen table and looked through his repertoire, available to be performed at the grand occasion. I was astounded at the depth and breadth of this array, and picked a number of songs I thought would be appropriate.

We laughed together and sang, finishing some three hours later.

"I don't know when I've had this much fun!" he said to me. Once again, a connection was made, the platform of music providing the way.

★ ★ ★

On Saturday, the 17th of November, all the plans had been made and the wedding was on. As I glanced into the sanctuary from the vestibule where the bride and I, along with her attendants, were waiting to enter, it appeared that most of the men in the audience were praying. Not so! They were staring down at their cell phones, keeping track of the Ole Miss/LSU football game in Baton Rouge some eighty miles up the highway, where the game was in overtime! Meanwhile, I walked my beautiful daughter down the aisle to meet her groom, Jason, at the altar and to hear their tender vows exchanged. Although it was a monumental occasion, the ceremony seemed to be only a few moments before we were on our way to the reception.

The awaiting buses and limos were filled to capacity. Due to the heavy traffic in the city, we had arranged for a police escort to the restaurant. With sirens blaring and blue lights flashing, we entered the exciting French Quarter. Exiting the vehicles, we proceeded through Antoine's front door, opening into the main dining room. Front and center was a table displaying the bride's and groom's cakes. We were then hustled into the larger room—warm and inviting, with the salmon-colored walls filled with historical photographs—and were greeted with more evidence of my wife's fine work. The table decorations were gorgeous!

Deacon John and his legendary orchestra were already in full swing, and when daughter Camille and Jason appeared, she was radiant. I was exceptionally proud of them as they danced to Sam Cooke's famous "You Send Me." Then Camille and I, followed by Jason and his mom, took the floor to "The Way You Look Tonight," followed by Satchmo Armstrong's "What a Wonderful World."

I sang at least eleven songs with Deacon and his orchestra. One of my favorites was from *Ray Charles Live at Newport*—a five-minute rendition of "I've Got a Woman." In tribute to Bill Pinkney and The Drifters, I did the lead on the song "White Christmas"—the one he had made famous in the movie *Home Alone.*

We had several hours of fun, but before we knew it, the festivities wound down as the bride and groom were ready to make their departure. In grand old New Orleans tradition, we formed what is called "the second line," where diminutive umbrellas come out and the band plays "When the Saints Go Marching In." Everyone takes a large napkin and raises it over their heads; they dance and march around the room before escorting the bridal couple to the waiting getaway car.

As Camille and Jason pulled off into the distance, I could not help having a deep sense of euphoria and gratitude for yet another mountaintop experience. I wrapped my arms around my amazing wife and pulled her close. It was a moment I will never forget.

And for this flash in time, at least, all sadness and anxiety over the fate of beloved friends were held at bay.

Teardrops in My Eyes

In the next year, I witnessed my friend Rufus's condition deteriorate. As with many people who suffer with the insidious onset of dementia, he would seemingly improve for brief periods before lapsing into a more confused state. Much like some stock market graphs, this one was trending downward. With dementia, there are ups and downs, but the complete descent is inevitable. Eventually, the patient must have around-the-clock care and begins to lose awareness of even his closest kin. Several of us noticed that while Rufus had keen recall of events that occurred forty or fifty years ago, he would forget that we had talked within the week. He would call, complaining that he had not heard from me in a long time.

I felt a growing sense of urgency about producing some type of documentary in which we would film a discussion with Rufus and go through the photo albums and other memorabilia he had found. I was determined to get it done while Rufus could still communicate.

On Saturday, August 10, 2013, Chris Walters and I drove to Vicksburg and stopped for a quick lunch of bacon, lettuce, and tomato sandwiches at the fabulous Tomato Place, a rustic and funky shack on that historic Highway 61 South. When we finished, we ordered "one to go" and headed for Rufus's house.

When we arrived, he was happy to see us and thoroughly enjoyed the sandwich while we set up the video recording equipment. Before long, Rufus and I were seated side by side in his cozy living room, ready to look over his photos and other items, which would take us back to his past together. Chris stood behind us with the video camera to record each page. Two and a half hours later, we completed our task.

But before we left that day, Rufus had a request. "Bill . . . when that time comes"—he shuffled his feet a little and cleared his throat—"I'd like for you to have a part in my memorial service."

★　★　★

The months went by, and on Father's Day 2014, I was taking a nap when Carol called again. "Mr. Morris, this is Rufus's daughter. He's with me right now. I brought him to my house from the nursing home to spend Father's Day with us. He loves you so much. Would you sing that song to him?"

As I sang, I could hear Rufus chuckling in the background. When I tried to engage him in conversation, however, there was only silence. In spite of this, I was very glad she had called, and I hope I had brightened his day a little.

★   ★   ★

A month later, I received a text that simply stated: "Daddy's gone."

As soon as I arrived at my office, Carol called to confirm the sad news. "Mr. Morris, Daddy passed last night. He's gone."

"No, Carol, he isn't 'gone.' Your daddy's Home . . . in Heaven with God. Let's praise Him right now that your daddy will never again be in pain. No more tears. No more suffering."

We talked for a while longer and then prayed together. Carol asked me to have a part in the funeral service, as Rufus had requested.

Strangely enough, on the Saturday night before Rufus's death, Camille and I had been having dinner at the house when she asked, "When Rufus's time comes, will you sing at his funeral?"

"Yes, that's what he wants. I plan to do 'Hello, Is That You?'"

"What about 'Danny Boy'? That's the one he made so famous."

"Well, he was so good at it that, no one else could even come close. But maybe I will try . . . in his memory."

We ended on that note, not knowing that within hours, my friend would be on the other side, no doubt singing as he had never sung before. I could only imagine Rufus's reunion with those three who had preceded him. Prentiss would be running on two strong legs to greet him, eager to embrace him with two good arms; Bill Pinkney, no longer crippled by age and infirmity, only a step behind. And Harvey, inspired by the music of the spheres, would be helping Gabriel orchestrate some majestic piece for the celestial choir. Ah . . . that incomparable, sublime Magic Moment.

Elegy for Four Friends

When we laid Rufus McKay to rest in the Vicksburg soil—

    once stained with the blood of brothers from North and South,

      black and white—

        my journey with four singing friends was also laid to rest. . .

        until we meet again and join that heavenly choir.

Their memories linger to this day, memories of joyous times together—

    traveling . . .

      laughing . . .

        weeping . . .

          harmonizing—a harmony in song and spirit.

They were my heroes.

    They were my inspiration.

    They were my friends.

      My own band of brothers.

While their bodies now lie beneath the sod of ancient battlefields

    and sacred churchyards,

      their music lives on to bless and beautify.

For it is the language of music that soothes the soul,

    lifts the fallen and the downtrodden,

      illuminates the darkness,

      and gives wings to the lonely heart.

And now these memories, this music I give to you, my dear readers.

    As you experience your own magic moments,

      May you find joy beyond anything you could create or contrive.

      May you encounter the Music-Maker Himself.

          —William (Bill) Morris

Appendix

THIS MAGIC MOMENT PRESERVATION TRUST

William H. Morris, Jr.
Chairman

Morgan Freeman
Honorary Chairman

March 1, 2002

We are thrilled to announce the formation of the *This Magic Moment Preservation Trust*, under the auspices of the Community Foundation of Greater Jackson, a 501(c)(3) non-profit organization. The establishment of this fund is in response to a need that has been expressed within our own Jackson community.

There are many of the singers and musicians in our region who have given us wonderful music over the years, particularly those of the 1950's and early 1960's. These people were never given credit for many of the songs that they wrote, nor did they receive proper royalties for their music recorded which is still sold today. A perfect example of this situation is our first year's honoree, Mr. Prentiss Barnes of Jackson, MS. He is the original virtuoso bass singer with the world-renowned "Moonglows" group. Prentiss helped write many songs that became famous and he was given no credit for them. He has been more fortunate than most to have received some meager reward, and yet he still struggles to make ends meet while millions of people continue to enjoy his music. In the year 2000 Prentiss was inducted as a member into the Rock and Roll Hall of Fame and the Vocal Group Hall of Fame. He also is a Mississippi Ageless Heroes Award recipient and a Rhythm and Blues Foundation "Pioneer". Prentiss is 77 years old, disabled, and barely able to pay his bills on his monthly Social Security check. He is just one that we refer to, but there are unfortunately many others.

Please help us give assistance to these singers and musicians who have given us the priceless gift of a lifetime of music by becoming a member of the *This Magic Moment Preservation Trust* and attending our inaugural event on April 26 at the Country Club of Jackson. This year's entertainment will be provided by *Bill Pinkney and the Original Drifters*, along with *Rufus McKay of the Red Tops* (performing "Danny Boy"). We anticipate this becoming an annual event and we seek to have many more famous entertainers participate year after year. Becoming a charter member insures your ticket priority for the following year's event.

Tickets to this year's gala are limited, so please respond as soon as possible. Various levels of participation are indicated on the enclosed response card. Fine hors d'oeuvres, dancing, and entertainment will be provided. Please make your check payable to The Community Foundation of Greater Jackson with an indication that the funds are intended for the *This Magic Moment Preservation Trust*.

Thank you for your support and interest in a most worthy cause!

William H. Morris, Jr.

Morgan Freeman

188 EAST CAPITOL STREET, SUITE 1075
JACKSON, MS 39201-2189
601-948-0030/ FAX 601-948-0041

*A PROUD MEMBER FUND OF THE COMMUNITY FOUNDATION OF GREATER JACKSON

Endnotes

[1]CD Liner Notes: Born of a prayer in a motel room in Vicksburg, Mississippi, in August 1994 with Prentiss Barnes, the original bass singer of The Moonglows; Bill Pinkney, the only surviving member of The Original Drifters, and yours truly; this powerful musical production found its start. It was Bill's sixty-ninth birthday and what started out to be merely a taped interview proved to be spiritually anointed.

Bill Pinkney learned to sing many hymns when he had no shoes to wear and no shirt on his back while picking cotton in the hot fields of South Carolina with his mother. Recently, the governor of this state presented Bill with the Palmetto Award, its highest honor. Dalzell, South Carolina, his birthplace, is now designated as the site for a memorial park, which will include a statue in Bill's likeness. A highway has also been named in his honor, and he is now a member of the Rock & Roll Hall of Fame, a first inductee into the Vocal Group Hall of Fame, and a pioneer award winner of The Rhythm & Blues Foundation.

Bill took what was a hard existence and turned it for God's glory in his life. No wonder millions have come to have such affectionate regard for him. As he sings in his song, "Just Driftin' Along," he speaks of the many blessings he had enjoyed while traveling through this great country, singing to legions of friends. People of all races have come to love and embrace this man and his music.

There have been numerous members of The Drifters, and various groups have used the name. But Bill's group—the only one authorized to use "The Original Drifters"—is composed of Richard Dunbar, baritone; Vernon

Young, second tenor, and Gregory Johnson, first tenor. Other stellar stars have joined this endeavor.

Our producers, five-time Grammy nominees, Doug and Melvin Williams of the world-famous Williams Brothers gospel group, make this music technically proficient and spiritually uplifting. In the notable hymn, "Amazing Grace," Doug Williams, with Bill Pinkney and the expressive voice of Richard Dunbar, along with sixteen select members of the Mississippi Chorus, combine to give a wonderful rendition of this celebrated standard. Melvin Williams' voice and his wonderful hands-on production capabilities permeate this CD. You hear the mellow Sam Cooke-type vocalizations of Vernon Young, followed by the dynamic sounds of guest artist Paul Porter of The Christianaires, belting out Paul's song, "That's Why I Love Him So." Bill Pinkney's godson, Ali-Ollie Woodson, previously one of the lead singers of The Temptations, does the lead, as guest artist, on "True Love." Ollie did this out of love for Bill, who gave him his start with The Original Drifters back in the 1970s.

As you listen to "America the Beautiful," you will hear Bill Pinkney once again singing with sincerity that will just zing the strings of your heart. Bill, a true patriot, is a highly decorated war hero. He was in four major battles during World War II, including the Normandy Invasion and the Battle of Bastogne. For this service, he received four bronze stars and a presidential citation from Harry S. Truman.

We finish with Irvin Berlin's beloved "White Christmas," which Bill Pinkney and the late Clyde McPhatter made famous with their own unique arrangement. Their version of this song has been used in several movie productions, including *Home Alone*. Since it is such a fan favorite of The Original Drifters, we thought it only appropriate to present it with the beautiful voice of Gregory Johnson joining Bill's.

To God be the glory,
Sincerely,

William "Bill" Morris
President, Hallelujah Productions

[2]Willie Morris. *North Toward Home.* (Boston: Houghton Mifflin Publishing Company, 1967), 3.

[3]My love of photography is a significant part of this journey with my singer friends. In the 1980s, I began photographing scenes at Ole Miss and Oxford and the surrounding area. In April of 2009, I did what I had promised Archie and Olivia Manning I would do for them—produce a compilation of photographs of their son Eli's days at Ole Miss. Only ten copies were printed, most of them going to their family or mine. When I showed a copy to Joe Hickman, the general manager of Lemuria Bookstore of Jackson, he encouraged me to publish a similar book for the general public. "It would sell for years," he assured me. Taking him at his word, I assembled a coffee table version, covering over twenty years at Ole Miss and Oxford. The photography reveals the essence of this storied place nestled in the hills of North Mississippi where the famed writer William Faulkner lies in his final resting place.